The Role of Affect in Consumer Behavior

Emerging Theories and Applications

Edited by

Robert A. Peterson
University of Texas at Austin

Wayne D. Hoyer
University of Texas at Austin

William R. Wilson
Rice University

Lexington Books
D.C. Heath and Company/Lexington, Massachusetts/Toronto

Library of Congress Cataloging-in-Publication Data

The Role of affect in consumer behavior.

  Papers from a symposium held Sept. 21–22, 1984, at the University of Texas at Austin and
sponsored by the College of Business Administration and the IC² Institute of the University of
Texas at Austin.
  Bibliography: p.
  Includes index.
  1. Consumers—Congresses. 2. Affect (Psychology)—Congresses. I. Peterson, Robert A.
II. Hoyer, Wayne D. III. Wilson, William R. (William Raft), 1947–   . IV. University
of Texas at Austin. College of Business Administration. V. IC² Institute.
HF5415.3.R65   1986   658.8′342   85–46042
ISBN 0–669–12874–0 (alk. paper)

Published simultaneously in Canada
Printed in the United States of America
International Standard Book Number: 0–669–12874–0
Library of Congress Catalog Card Number: 85–46042

The paper used in this publication meets the minimum requirements of American National
Standard for Information Sciences—Permanence of Paper for Printed Library Materials, ANSI
Z39.48–1984.
♾™

The last numbers on the right below indicate the number and date of printing.

10 9 8 7 6 5 4 3 2 1

95 94 93 92 91 90 89 88 87 86

To Our Families

Contents

Preface

On September 21–22, 1984, the University of Texas at Austin sponsored a symposium with the admittedly ambitious goal of bringing together both academics and practitioners interested in the role of affect in consumer behavior. Organized around five formal paper presentations and one free-for-all, the symposium also offered numerous opportunities for informal exchanges and discussions on the topic, including a Texas-style barbecue on a ranch outside Austin. Approximately seventy-five individuals—from both academe and industry and from all regions of the United States—attended the symposium.

Two interrelated considerations motivated the symposium. One was the manner in which affect has been defined. The following definitions illustrate various ways affect has been defined:

Affects are sets of muscle, vascular, and glandular responses located in the face and also widely distributed throughout the body. (Tomkins 1970)

Affect is a sensation of pleasure, impleasure, or both, plus the ideas, both conscious and unconscious, associated with that sensation. (Brenner 1974)

Affect is a major personality subsystem with self-generating motivational properties. (Tomkins and Izard 1965)

This brief compendium of affect definitions is not claimed to be exhaustive; however, it probably constitutes a representative sampling of the definitions of affect currently in use. Moreover, as revealed by these definitions, there is little consistency or unanimity as to what affect is; affect is simply not well defined. Hence, one of the goals of the symposium was to attempt the development of a common definition of affect.

However, symposium participants agreed that, although a single, common definition of affect might facilitate communication among researchers investigating this phenomenon, it might actually stifle creative research. Consequently, the participants agreed that it may be more important for researchers to explicitly divulge their personal definition of affect when writing or presenting results involving affective constructs rather than attempting to force a definitional constraint on them. Given the current status of research on affect, especially as it relates to consumer behavior, it may be better to approach the phenomenon from a variety of perspectives rather than spending time trying to agree on a specific definition.

Neglect constituted the second reason for the symposium. Traditional models posited to explain and/or predict consumer behavior have either implicitly or explicitly assumed that consumer decision making is largely a result of cognitive processes. Furthermore, these models have assumed that if there is any affect present in the consumer decision-making process, it occurs as a result of or ancillary to cognitive processing. However, researchers in disciplines such as social cognition, social psychology, or cognitive psychology have recently begun to realize that affective responses may possibly develop independently of cognitive processing. Indeed, in certain instances, they may actually precede cognitive processing. Consequently, to more fully understand consumer behavior, the role of affect must be examined and incorporated into current (cognitive) models.

Consumer behavior researchers have begun to acknowledge the importance of affect in consumer decision making in areas such as responses to advertising stimuli and low-involvement decision making. However, in spite of this awareness, theories and applications relating to the role of affect in a consumer behavior context still remain at elementary levels.

Thus, the second purpose of the symposium was to address the concept of affect in depth so it can be more fully incorporated into consumer behavior theory. Toward this goal, five distinguished researchers were asked to prepare original papers on the role of affect in consumer behavior. These papers were to serve as the basis of a broad-ranging discussion of affect and stimulate thought on a particular approach to its study. Those individuals were requested to emphasize theory and applications, not merely the results of empirical research. They were also asked to suggest future research directions in the area and to be provocative, imaginative, and speculative.

Professor Robert Zajonc of the University of Michigan was asked to prepare a paper on the role of affect in preference formation. Professor Zajonc, unquestionably one of the leading researchers in the area of affect, is a recent winner of the American Psychological Association Distinguished Researcher Award. Professor Morris Holbrook (Columbia University), recently described as exemplifying the conceptual humanist approach to consumer behavior, was asked to address the role of affect in motivating and directing hedonic consumption. Rajeev Batra, also a professor at Columbia University, was asked to examine the role of affective responses in mediating the acceptance of advertising from a conceptual perspective. John T. Cacioppo (University of Iowa), an expert in the area of unobtrusive and psychophysiological measurement of affect, was asked to reflect on and propose new approaches to affect measurement. Finally, Dr. Rebecca Holman (Young & Rubicam) represented the practitioner's perspective. She was requested to address the role of emotion in advertising.

The result of these requests is this book. The first five chapters reflect the papers these individuals presented at the symposium. In addition, a sixth chapter has been added that not only summarizes certain aspects of the symposium but also attempts to stimulate further research on the role of affect in consumer behavior by presenting the results of two experiments and suggesting possible study avenues. The experiments not only illustrate research directions for investigating the role of affect in (consumer) decision making but also illustrate several difficulties faced when attempting to empirically investigate affect.

Given the nature of the phenomenon addressed as well as the backgrounds of the authors (marketing academics, psychologists, an advertising practitioner), this volume should be required reading for all those interested in researching or capitalizing on the role of affect in consumer behavior.

The symposium was cosponsored by the IC² Institute and the College of Business Administration at the University of Texas and held at the RGK Foundation Building. Consequently, appreciation is expressed to Dr. George Kozmetsky, director of the IC² Institute, and Dr. William H. Cunningham, then Dean of the College of Business Administration (now president of the University of Texas at Austin). No preface is complete without a statement of appreciation to those who made the symposium and this book possible through their tireless efforts. Although numerous individuals deserve such thanks, two are singled out: Linda Teague and Bobby Duncan. Thank you all.

1
Basic Mechanisms of Preference Formation

Robert B. Zajonc
University of Michigan

By demonstrating how preferences are formed and how they can be modified, psychologists can make a unique contribution to the understanding of consumer behavior. The bulk of the work in social psychology—the study of attitudes—has been concerned with just this issue. Historically, the field of attitude research has been dominated by a variety of approaches, such as stimulus–response, Gestalt, psychoanalytic, semantic, and the like (McGuire 1985).

However, over the last several decades the primary emphasis in attitude research has been cognitive (Eagly and Himmelfarb 1978). Researchers have emphasized the analyses of preferences—their origins and their modification—by focusing on cognitive aspects of preferences and choices. A frequently employed paradigm in consumer behavior research has been (1) to specify the attributes of objects and products; (2) to find the values of these attributes (that is, how much the individual likes these attributes); and (3) to write equations for how these component attribute values combine to produce an overall preference (Abelson and Levi 1985).

This approach, dominated by cognitive concepts, makes three basic assumptions. The first is that overall preference is some function of component preferences. The second is that preferences remain stable during the process of decision making—that one can depend on preferences remaining constant. (Otherwise, equations for decision making could not be written in the traditional ways.) Finally, there is an assumption that if one knows preferences one can predict choice.

These assumptions are not always tenable. There are critical questions for each of them. Let us examine briefly the first assumption that component preferences are constant across objects. Price is an important component of choice. It *is* indeed important when one is buying a car, but it *is not* important when one is buying a candy bar. Perhaps, then, component preferences are not constant across objects but are constant within certain price ranges. Although this may be generally true, there are conditions under which price is readily overcome by other considerations, for example, brand loyalty. Brand loyalty can easily dominate price in certain instances.

If the influence of price on choice (price being a general attribute of objects) can vary from object to object or from consumer to consumer, then the assumption that component preferences can lead to the writing of an equation for overall preference is questionable. The problem is accentuated because there are many component attributes of objects that are not as general as price. If weights for preferences are not constant across objects or individuals, this approach leaves something to be desired. Simply imagine a chemistry in which atomic weights of elements vary from compound to compound, depending on the compound they enter. This would not result in a very useful set of principles.

The second assumption, that preferences within a choice structure remain constant over the decision process, is also not unequivocally true. This phenomenon is very common and can be easily illustrated. A consumer is shopping for a house and is considering three equally attractive alternatives, A, B, and C. If the real estate agent says, "I have an offer on House B," suddenly the preference for that house has changed. Somehow this house has become more attractive than A or C. There are a number of well-known theories—for example, dissonance (Festinger 1957), reactance (Brehm and Brehm 1981), or attribution (Kelley 1973)—to explain this sudden change. This phenomenon, of course, creates difficulty with theories of choice and decision making that depend on preferences remaining stable during the course of the decision process.

The third assumption, namely, that one can predict individual behavioral choice by looking at preferences, relies on the construct of rationality. It assumes people look at their alternatives, consider their balance sheet of pros and cons, and on the basis of this balance sheet make their decision. This assumption is also not always true, and there are a lot of instances and a significant amount of psychological research indicating that one cannot depend on it. Research in social psychology and cognitive dissonance continually shows that a rational choice may be easily dominated by other considerations. If, for example, one is somehow cajoled into investing a great deal of effort on behalf of a political candidate and then discovers this candidate does not really deserve to be elected, the person still votes for this candidate, presumably because he or she wants to justify the effort invested previously (Aronson 1966). There are many phenomena studied in social psychology in which a rational choice is dominated by a host of nonrational considerations (Nisbett and Ross 1980).

Phoebe Ellsworth once wrote me about a decision process in which she was engaged. She was at Yale University at that time and had received a very attractive offer from Stanford University. Being at Yale, she of course followed the Irving Janis (1982) procedure for decision making in which one takes a large sheet of paper and on the left side lists all the positive points and on the right side all the negative points. All of the points are then weighed very carefully. At the end of this process, the decision maker should know exactly what to do. Phoebe wrote me that she and her husband tried to follow the procedure. They looked at the sheet for a long time and finally Phoebe exclaimed, "Oh hell, this is just not working. I have to get some more pluses on the right side or else I will make the wrong decision." In other words, there was an underlying prior predisposition that preempted what would be, in normative terms, a rational choice.

Other considerations also question the stability and wisdom of choices. Take, for instance, the sort of work Kahneman and Tversky (1984) have been doing on choices, an example being predispositions of people toward risk. In one sense people are averse to risk. They buy insurance. They behave as if they did not like risk. They invest money in pension plans. If you ask somebody what he or she would rather have, a certainty of obtaining $1,000 or a fifty–fifty chance of getting $2,500, most people would prefer the $1,000 for sure than taking a fifty–fifty gamble on $2,500. This preference should be constant under transformation, such as multiplication. So if we multiply the bets by ten, people would still prefer $10,000 for sure than to gamble on $25,000. But the preference changes when we multiply it by minus one. When given a choice of a sure $1,000 loss or a fifty–fifty gamble for $2,500, they prefer a fifty–fifty gamble on losing $2,500. In the case of positive gambles, there is a preference for certainty. In the case of negative gambles, there is a preference for risk.

Preferences and Exposure Effects

Preferences arise in a large number of ways and are not simple phenomena. Some preferences have biological origins. Certainly many preferences are hard-wired. Infants prefer sugar to quinine without prior experience with either, and there are many other such preferences that one need not learn, acquire, or form on the basis of extensive consumer behavior procedures. However, preferences can also be established in other ways. They can be acquired by learning, conditioning, generalization, imitation, social influence, and diverse other processes. Research must eventually answer the question about the basic elements of preference formation and modification.

Little is known about the basic processes that may be implicated in preference formation and change. In our work in the mid-1960s, we stumbled onto something that seems at times trivial and fairly obvious. This was something that looked like a minimal condition for forming preferences— the repeated exposure of a stimulus, in fact, the *mere* repeated exposure, that is, the exposure of a stimulus not accompanied by any contingency. There is no reinforcement; there is no requirement that an individual perform any responses; the stimulus need not be accompanied by any other conditioned stimuli; and there need not be any special means of drawing the individual's attention to it. Mere repeated exposure—making the stimulus accessible to the individual over and over again—can enhance that person's attitude toward the stimulus and make him or her like the stimulus slightly better (Zajonc 1968). This seemed at first to be a fairly trivial finding. However, it turned out to be not so trivial after all because the explanation one could supply for this phenomenon was quite complex, defying our theoretical and empirical effort for a considerable period of time. Many people have worked on this problem in our laboratory: Bill Wilson, Margaret Matlin, Hazel Markus, Dick Moreland, and others.

I first came across this phenomenon quite by accident. I usually have a book or two in the bathroom. One of those books was a rather strange one. It was *The Teacher's Workbook of 30,000 Words* (Thorndike and Lorge 1944), which lists 30,000 words with associated usage frequencies. The book was written during the depression of the 1930s. At that time Thorndike and Lorge were charged with the task of finding employment for unemployed journalists, novelists, poets, and writers. Creative as Thorndike and Lorge were, they sat the unemployed down in front of a large sample of English words from such sources as the *Bible, Popular Mechanics,* etc., and had them count the occurrence of words in these sources. As a result of this effort of the Works Progress Administration, there now exists a collection of 30,000 words whose frequency of occurrence in English is known exactly. It turned out that during my encounter with this book (the reasons for finding it in the bathroom remain unclear), I became aware that the book contains a wealth of cultural information—information about our values, our culture, what we want, and what we need.

Consider the following sample of words with their frequencies found in the Thorndike–Lorge count. The word *love* occurs 5,129 times in a sample of four and a half million. *Life* occurs 4,804 times; *mother* is a little less (3,993); *father,* less still (3,235). Then comes *money* (3,089). This finding is significant because if there is a relationship between frequency with which words occur in language and their value, certain interpretations about our culture follow. For example, one would not sell one's mother for money, but beauty (frequency = 776) is not worth as much as money, and truth (frequency = 698) rates certainly far below money. Happiness (frequency = 761) comes between beauty and truth; health (frequency = 591) is worth less; freedom (frequency = 256) is insignificant; wisdom (frequency = 139) is practically worthless; fame (frequency = 107) can be thrown away; and equality (frequency = 30) is a very minor value according to the Thorndike–Lorge count.

If one looks at the frequency with which these common words occur in our language, the following conjecture is inescapable: words that occur with high frequency are positive. This observation prompted us to look more systematically at the variety of phenomena that are associated with exposure. We started by looking at various classes of stimuli, beginning with words.

Figure 1–1 contains a graph derived from data collected by Anderson (1968). In his research on impression formation, Anderson collected favorability values for 555 trait adjectives from students at the University of California at Los Angeles. He asked, for each trait adjective, how well a person would be liked if he or she were characterized by that trait. I took the frequency of occurrence of these adjectives and plotted them on a log scale against likability ratings. These adjectives included *honest, sincere, intelligent, mad, dishonest, creepy,* and so on. When the favorability ratings of these adjectives are plotted against frequency, there is a systematic progres-

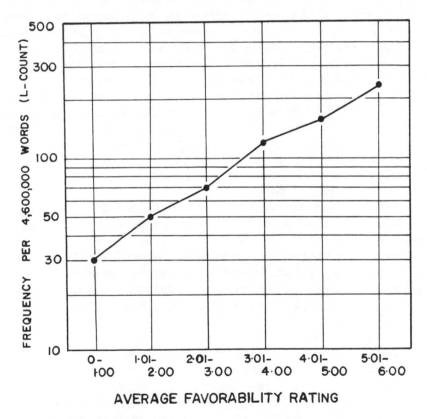

Source: Data from Anderson, 1968.

Figure 1–1. Average Frequencies of 555 Adjectives Rated for Favorability

sion. Higher frequencies are associated with adjectives rated as positive, such as *honest* and *kind*. Lower frequencies are associated with negative adjectives, such as *stupid* and *mean*.

These are just correlational observations. We also have done a few experimental studies in which we showed Chinese ideographs or Turkish-looking words with which subjects were unfamiliar. Some items were shown frequently, others infrequently. The frequencies used were 0, 1, 2, 5, 10, and 25, and after the exposures subjects were asked to rate how much they liked these stimuli or whether they thought the words' meanings were positive or negative. This exposure effect is a very robust phenomenon and has been replicated several times for different subjects, stimuli, and conditions of exposure (Harrison 1977).

Exposure effects occur not just for humans and not just for words, but for almost any kind of encounter. One of the most interesting exposure studies was done with rats. Some ingenious experimenters at Wittenberg College in Ohio exposed rats to a twelve-hour-per-day diet of music by either Mozart or Schoenberg (Cross, Halcomb, and Matter 1967). The rats lived with the music for two months and afterward were given a test of musical preference. They were placed in a cage in which the floor was hinged in the middle and suspended over microswitches. If the rat were on one side of this floor, Channel I of a tape recorder would be activated and Mozart would be heard. If the rat crossed to the other side, the microswitches would activate Channel II, and the rat would hear Schoenberg. The tests were performed over a period of fifteen days. A control group also was given this test without prior musical experience.

The results of this experiment (presented in figure 1–2) show the number of minutes the rats listened to Mozart and Schoenberg. For the group exposed to Mozart, there was a considerable preference for Mozart over Schoenberg. The group exposed to Schoenberg preferred Schoenberg to Mozart. The control group elicited a slight preference for Mozart over Schoenberg, which is consistent with the pattern of difference between those two conditions. The Mozart preference is much stronger than the preference for Schoenberg. This may mean that rats are similar to people, or vice versa.

People have preferences for almost anything, and these preferences can be explained by frequency of exposure. If one asks people how much they like *any* object at all, they will be able to give consistent ratings. Consider the numbers *one* to *twenty*. Digits do occur with systematic frequencies in language and in mathematical tables. In mathematical tables, *one* occurs much more frequently than *two*, *two* more often than *three*, and so on. The same is true of their occurrence in the Thorndike–Lorge count. In figure 1–3, preferences for numbers one through twenty are ordered according to the frequency with which they occur, again, on a logarithmic scale. Numbers such as *one*, *two*, and *three* are very highly preferred numbers, but larger

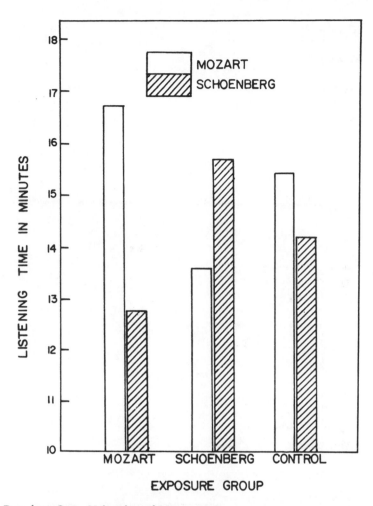

Source: Data from Cross, Halcomb, and Matter, 1967.

Figure 1–2. Musical Preferences of Rats Following Exposure to Mozart and Schoenberg

numbers are less well preferred. There are other numbers that are pre-ferred—round numbers, for example, such as *five* or *twenty*. Odd numbers are preferred less than even numbers and prime numbers, except for one, two, three, and five, are not very well-liked numbers at all. People can reveal preferences for all kinds of objects and generally produce an orderly and reliable rating.

The phenomenon occurs in a variety of situations with diverse stimuli and is quite reliable. As such, however, this is just the beginning for research,

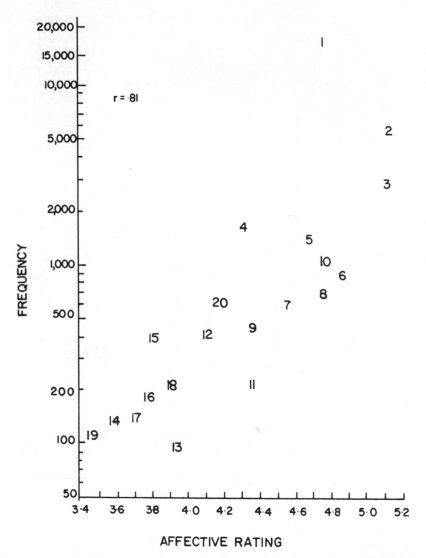

Figure 1–3. Preferences for Numbers and Their Frequency of Occurrence

because we need to know why it happens. Why is it that repeated stimulus exposure results in increased preference? How is it produced? We have been working on this problem for many years without understanding the phenomenon in any concrete fashion. Only very recently a glimmer of hope appeared that will perhaps allow us to understand some elements of this process better.

The first big research disappointment came when we tried to approach the problem from a cognitive perspective. The cognitive point of view of the familiarity effect was first introduced at the turn of the century when Titchener (1910) posited a theory about why familiar objects are attractive. He invoked the phenomenon of recognition-pleasure—the great joy, the glow of warmth, the feeling of being one with the object when it is recognized as familiar. Titchener gave the example of listening to familiar music, music that one has heard before. The experience, the consciousness of recognizing something that one has heard before, gives a sort of unity with the object and makes one feel good. It is this process of recognition that explains why familiar objects are liked better than unfamiliar objects, according to the cognitive view.

In her studies, Matlin (1971) tried to verify that Titchener was right. Titchener turned out to be wrong. Matlin presented stimuli a different number of times. These were Turkish words, Chinese ideographs, and various other stimuli. After the exposure series, she gave subjects two tests. In a recognition test, she asked subjects if they had previously seen an object. She also asked them how much they liked the object. Table 1–1 contains Matlin's data. What was more important, the *objective* familiarity of the object or the *subjective* familiarity of the object? Do people like things they think are familiar or do they like things that in fact *are* familiar, independently of what they think? The marginals for the subjectively old and subjectively new objects are 4.55 and 4.05. There is a difference of .5 in favor of subjectively old objects such that people *who think* an object is familiar like that object better. However, independently of what they think of the objects as familiar/unfamiliar, *objective familiarity* has a strong effect such that old objects are preferred to new objects, the marginal means being 4.47 to 4.01.

This experiment had some limitations because judgments of familiarity and judgments of likability were collected simultaneously, and it was not until Wilson (1979) ran his dichotic listening procedure experiment that we

Table 1–1
Average Stimulus Affect Ratings As a Function of Objective Familiarity (Old–New) and Subjective Familiarity (Old–New)

Objective Familiarity	Subjective Familiarity		Row Mean	Difference
	Old	New		
Old	4.90	4.20	4.47	
				.46
New	4.20	3.90	4.01	
Column mean	4.55	4.05		
Difference		.50		

Source: Data from Matlin, 1971.

obtained some indication of what was going on. The subject was induced to listen to a tape of a story about a horse in one ear while a series of tone sequences was simultaneously broadcast into the subject's other ear. The subject's task was to follow the story of the horse without paying any attention to the tones coming to the other ear. Under these circumstances, subjects had great difficulty in recognizing the tones again when they were presented in a recognition memory test. One group in this experiment was given the task of identifying whether tones were *old* or *new,* whereas another group was asked for their preferences—how they liked these tones. Wilson's results are displayed in table 1–2.

The subjective feeling of familiarity for the tonal stimuli was, of course, random. Subjects could not distinguish between the stimuli because the dichotic listening procedure was devised especially to prevent them from achieving any recognition or familiarity with them. *Subjective* familiarity did not produce any differences in favor of old stimuli. However, the *objective* history of the subjects' experience with the stimuli was very significant. Subjects liked the old stimuli better, the ones to which they were previously exposed. We have here, therefore, an effect of objective history of the subjects' experience with the stimulus, independently of what the subjects thought was or was not familiar.

Wilson and I then carried out an experiment with visual stimuli, using random polygons presented to the subject at an exposure so impoverished that there was no possibility of any recognition at all (Kunst-Wilson and Zajonc 1980). In fact, there was virtually no possibility of detection. These stimuli were presented at an exposure frequency of one millisecond and no subject had the slightest idea of whether the stimulus was or was not presented. The stimuli were presented five times each. Afterward, they were compared with stimuli never shown, both for recognition and for liking. Figure 1–4 contains the results of this experiment. Of course, if something is shown for only one millisecond, it is nearly impossible to retain any trace

Table 1–2
Average Stimulus Affect Ratings As a Function of Objective Familiarity (Old–New) and Subjective Familiarity (Old–New)

| *Objective Familiarity* | *Subjective Familiarity* | | *Row Mean* | *Difference* |
	Old	*New*		
Old	4.20	4.03	4.12	
				.82
New	3.75	3.07	3.30	
Column mean	4.02	3.52		
Difference		.50		

Source: Data from Wilson, Experiment I, 1975.

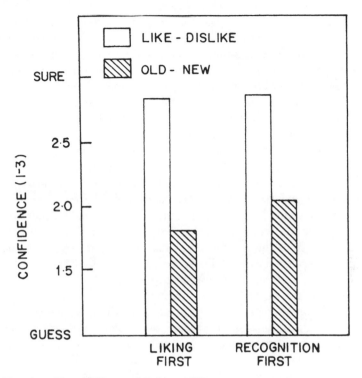

Source: Data from Kunst-Wilson and Zajonc, 1980.

Figure 1–4. Confidence in Liking and Recognition Judgments

of the event and recognition judgments hover around 50 percent, which is the chance level. The recognition procedure consisted of showing two stimuli simultaneously, side by side, and the subjects' instructions were to choose which of the two was *old* and which was *new*. This procedure avoids response bias. However, liking judgments show a different pattern. Subjects liked the old stimuli better. Thus, although discrimination was not possible at the level of cognitive judgment, there was significant discrimination of stimuli on the basis of preference, with the objectively old stimuli being favored over the objectively new stimuli. This is evidence against the recognition theory of the exposure effect (Seamon, Brody, and Kauff 1983a, 1983b).

Waynbaum's Theory

If the feelings of subjective recognition cannot explain the exposure effect, how can we explain it otherwise? The possible answer comes from a totally different and unexpected source. It comes from a theory of emotional expression written by a French physician (Waynbaum 1907). This theory is based on the action of the vascular system but is relatively unknown. It is amazing because it is completely ignored in the literature on emotion. It is not to be found in the citation index, and not a single volume on emotions—French, American, or English—cites this theory. Yet it is brilliant. More importantly, it introduces notions of emotional expression that have some promise of explaining the elusive phenomenon of exposure effect.

Waynbaum essentially proposed that we have been misguided in the study of emotional expression by the very word *expression,* that the word suggests a causal explanation in which the internal state necessarily precedes the facial gesture and that the primary purpose of the facial gesture is to communicate one's own internal state to other animals. In this manner, one's intentions become known to others, and one's internal states can be communicated throughout the community; thus, they have survival value. This is the basic assumption, based on Darwin's classic work on emotions (1872), that dominates all theories of emotional expression.

But questions can be raised about Darwin's classic theory of expression. Why is it that human beings—who, of all animals, have a very powerful means of communicating their emotions, namely, language—developed such fantastic musculature of the face, mainly to broadcast their internal state to others? We have very efficient ways of telling other people "I am mad," "I am angry," "I am hungry," "I like you," "I am disgusted," or "I am surprised." Why should we also have a mechanism in the face? It is an interesting paradox that animals other than humans do not have as rich a repertory of emotional expression as humans, for they do not have language to communicate their internal states among each other.

Second, some expressions are not unique. Hence, they can become a serious source of ambiguity. For example, Darwin associated the baring of canine teeth with rage and threat. But canines are also displayed in a grin, and there is little difference between the display of teeth in a grin and in rage.

Waynbaum believed that emotional expression has a completely different function. He started with a number of propositions, which he used as building blocks for his theory. First is the fact that the face has very few moving parts although it has eighty muscles. What is the purpose of these muscles? Why do we need eighty muscles if there are only a few bones to move? The *mechanics* of the face do not require this fantastic configuration of muscles.

Waynbaum also observed that all emotional gestures have a vascular connection. There is something about blood circulation that is connected to all emotional expression. For example, in laughing or sobbing the diaphragm becomes quite active to allow oxygen to fill the lungs and to be distributed among the blood cells. Weeping is also a vascular process in which tears are supplied by the lachrymal gland; the lachrymal gland is in turn supplied by the lachrymal artery, which is a branch of the internal artery that supplies the brain. All emotional expressions have some important vascular connection.

During an emotional incident there is a mobilization of energy associated with a disturbance of blood circulation. Blood is deployed to various parts of the body to support the motor response that follows the arousal of emotion: to flee, to strike, to laugh, to investigate. But most important is the supply of blood to the brain. The supply of blood to the head comes from the main artery. When it enters the neck, this artery splits into two branches. One branch supplies blood to the brain and is called the internal artery. The other branch, the external artery, supplies the face and skull.

This is a very interesting arrangement because the supply of blood to the brain requires great stability. Sudden changes—sudden drops or rises in blood flow—cause the organism to suffer shock or fall into a coma. This important fact was taken by Waynbaum as a key to the explanation of emotional expression. Waynbaum assumed that muscular actions of the face may serve as tourniquets or ligatures pressing against the bony structure of the face, and that they may thus alter the facial blood flow. If the facial blood flow is altered, it can allow more or less blood to the brain because the facial and cerebral blood come from one source, according to Waynbaum. So, the facial expression acts as a safety valve or control mechanism that can regulate the supply of blood to the brain.

Waynbaum thought that a surge of blood to the brain is positive since getting more oxygen is *good*. So laughing is good. The cells fill with oxygen, the veinous blood is converted faster into arterial blood, and in the case of hyperemia one feels good. In contrast, when the flow of blood to the brain is restricted, the result is subjectively negative. When a person is angry, a lot of blood flows into the surface of the skull. Anger, therefore, is felt negatively. Blushing is unpleasant also because it deprives the brain of blood. Waynbaum goes on through these emotional phenomena one by one, trying to point out the vascular consequences of emotional expression. This is the first theory, the only theory other than that of Lange and James (1922), to specify the process by which the subjective state arises from emotional expression. Waynbaum insists that the expression of emotion may cause an emotional subjective state, without denying the converse possibility. One is happy because one smiles. One is sad and uncomfortable because blood is redirected from the brain to the face, where it should not be.

Of course, Waynbaum's theory has many problems. Eighty years ago not much was known about the circulatory system. We did not know about the physiology of the vascular system and about the brain. For example, Waynbaum's thinking that there is such a close dependence between the internal and external blood flow is wrong. There are independent neural controls, vasol dilators and vasol constrictors, that can regulate blood flow independently of facial musculature (Zajonc 1985).

But it is entirely possible that a subjective state can be changed through a change in brain blood temperature. The temperature in the brain produces 20 percent of body heat in a resting adult organism and much more in an infant. The metabolic processes of the brain are so active that a tremendous amount of heat is produced and the brain requires cooling. Control of cerebral blood flow, therefore, is also the control of blood temperature. If it is the case that cerebral blood flow can affect the temperature of the brain, it is possible that these changes in temperature can influence the release and synthesis of neurotransmitters associated with subjective states such as depression, excitation, or rage. Neurotransmitters have been isolated that control a variety of subjective states such as depression, euphoria, or analgesia. If one assumes that making certain motions of the face produces a change of blood flow in the brain, one can change the temperature in various regions of the brain that affect different configurations of neurotransmitters. In addition, if it is possible to affect some critical neurotransmitters, it is also possible to produce differences in subjective states.

For example, in anger there is a tremendous amount of heat in the forehead. In anger, the corrugator and the frontalis muscles (the muscles above the eyebrows) press against the veins of the forehead, which partially drain the blood from the brain. This veinous blood is, of course, of higher temperature than the blood in the brain. Hence, it is the hotter brain blood that is arrested. It cannot leave the brain at the same rate that would be possible if the person did not make a frowning gesture at the same time. Thus, the increased temperature of the forehead caused by alteration of blood circulation is a feature of the anger expression. It is not an accident that people are called *hotheads* or that one says "I am boiling mad" or "I am really steamed." These are not accidental metaphors. There is some truth in the saying, "I am boiling with rage."

Waynbaum's Theory and Exposure Effects

How can the vascular theory of emotional expression explain the exposure effect? We are dealing with a simple difference—the difference between a novel stimulus and a familiar stimulus. It has been known for over twenty-five years that there are hard-wired responses to novel stimuli, the so-called orienting reflex. The orienting reflex occurs automatically to novel stimuli, and it is manifested in a variety of autonomic changes.

Consider the orienting reflex in terms of Waynbaum's theory. What happens during an orienting reflex? What happens when a person sees something new? The person pays attention, concentrates, and looks at the object harder, and, when concentrating, one furrows eyebrows, makes a face, and fixes the eyes. Generally, the face exposed to a novel stimulus is different from one confronting something familiar. If it is the case that familiar objects induce a facial expression that alters blood circulation to the brain in a way that produces effects on the appropriate neurotransmitters, it is possible that different subjective states are associated with these facial gestures. The internal state of concern here is one that leads the subject to say "I like it" or "I don't like it." The person is, of course, very often not aware of what is happening. Nevertheless, the physiological mechanics and hydraulics of this encounter are such that they provide information to the individual about the nature of the stimulus. The reaction produces certain subjective effects such that the individual experiences certain states. This view of affect and of reactions to familiarity and novelty is quite different from the classical cognitive view. The theory based on Waynbaum's ideas would suggest that many of our preferences are unconscious and stem from a subjective state that has arisen from the expressive action of our facial muscles. Expression was always thought of as something that happens at the very end of an emotional episode, not as a necessary or a significant antecedent having causal consequences in the emotional process. But if Waynbaum's work is taken seriously, it is possible to consider emotional elements in preference and choice in a different way.

How can the vascular theory be useful in consumer behavior research? It is, of course, assumed that affective reactions to products and to marketing stimuli are quite significant. They are especially significant in influencing memory. What is it about affect that makes one remember an item better? Perhaps it is the person's expression. Perhaps it is the particular expression one forms on seeing an advertisement that induces a certain emotional state. The state and the gesture are retained in memory; the bodily gesture will later serve as an additional cue that is reinstated when one tries to recall the product or an aspect of the product, an advertisement, or the like. So it is possible for affective components to influence memory of advertising.

Emotional expression can also affect preferences. If we somehow can make the individual smile when looking at a product, thereby making the individual feel good, his or her attitude might be influenced as well. Advertising is, of course, replete with techniques intended to produce just that. There are funny ads, ads showing happy events, ads showing success, joy, and satisfaction. Why do they have positive effects? Waynbaum's theory, in which it is assumed that facial and bodily movement can have subjective, hedonic consequences, may, at least in part, explain how this happens.

People do not react to objects in a passive way. They do not perceive something remaining motionless and expressionless. The face is one object that is perceived in a very active manner. A study by Dimberg (1982) had people simply look at photographs of faces. They looked at angry faces and happy faces. Electromyographic measures were taken from the corrugator and from the zygomatic muscles. Dimberg's results show that when a person looks at a happy face, he or she smiles too, and when the person looks at an angry face, he or she frowns.

So one can produce activity that accompanies information reception in a person's own face, and this activity can then have hedonic consequences that are not trivial. We do not yet know how important they might be, but they certainly do not appear to be trivial. The fact that repeated exposure to an object results in enhancing the subject's attitude or preference for this object turned out to be a very difficult problem. Mere repeated exposure is perhaps the most primitive means, the minimal means of producing a change in preference or in forming preferences, but it is a basic one. All other means of producing and changing preferences must be more complex than just showing something over and over again. If we do not understand these simple means, if it took us so much time to just begin having some hunches as to how exposure effects work, then the understanding and analysis of processes more complex than exposure must be even more difficult. It is hoped that research in consumer behavior will produce information that, together with the basic processes we are studying in psychology, will eventually reveal how preferences are formed and modified.

2
Emotion in the Consumption Experience: Toward a New Model of the Human Consumer

Morris B. Holbrook
Columbia University

I f the ratio between the importance of a topic and the attention it attracts from researchers working in an area is any indication of urgency, then emotion must rank as the aspect of consumer behavior most urgently in need of investigation. We all recognize emotional phenomena as pervasive components of human behavior in general and consumer behavior in particular. Yet, like the way in which weather reporters treat problematic news about hurricanes and tornadoes, we dutifully note the key role played by emotion in consumers' lives without doing very much about it. Thus, we acknowledge the impact of emotions in shaping and reflecting consumption experiences but fail to undertake systematic study of these important emotional phenomena.

A similar bias has prevailed in our parent discipline of psychology where the psychoanalytically oriented clinicians have tended to focus on the negative emotions (anxiety, depression, guilt) at the expense of their more positive counterparts (love, joy, exhilaration), whereas the behaviorists have eschewed the mentalistic bias they find implicit in studies of mediating thoughts and feelings. The resulting failure to deal adequately with emotional phenomena has troubled a growing number of psychologists (Beloff 1973; Daly, Lancee, and Polivy 1983; Dienstbier 1979; Lazarus, Kanner, and Folkman 1980; Plutchik 1980). Unfortunately, if psychological work on emotion lags behind that on other areas, the gap is even more dramatic in the study of consumer behavior.

As one step toward closing this gap, this chapter explores the role of emotion in the consumption experience. I begin with a general consideration

The author thanks Rajeev Batra, Eric A. Greenleaf, and several anonymous reviewers for their helpful comments on an earlier draft of this chapter. He also gratefully acknowledges the support of Columbia Business School's Faculty Research Fund. Request for reprints should be sent to Morris B. Holbrook, 510 Uris Hall, Graduate School of Business, Columbia University, New York, NY 10027.

of emotion's neglected importance to human affairs in general and to consumer behavior in particular. After thus motivating the discussion, I turn to an examination of the emotional process in consumer behavior, viewing the consumption experience as a complex system composed of three stages: consciousness, emotion, and value. As the central stage in this C–E–V system, emotion entails multiway interactions among physiological, cognitive, behavioral, and experiential components. This focus on the central role of emotion leads me to an investigation of emotional content as reflected by various approaches to taxonomy and classification. Here, I review some potentially useful typologies that distinguish among different types of emotion. I then extend these views on process and content to the specific context of consumer behavior by offering some introspective illustrations and anecdotal evidence concerning the nature and importance of consumer emotions. I conclude by describing three recent empirical applications concerned, respectively, with consciousness, emotion, and value and undertaken with the help of various colleagues interested in the role of emotion in the consumption experience.

Emotion and the Behavior of Human Consumers

Man As Machine

Scientists of every era tend to view human nature as one more manifestation of the principles governing their favorite machine. Thus, in the time of Descartes, the analogies between humans and the delicate workings of precision clockwork appeared inescapable. Later, Freud's hydraulic model of the personality owed much to the ethos surrounding the development of modern plumbing. More recently, these earlier views of *man as pocketwatch* and *man as toilet* have yielded to an increasingly ubiquitous conception of *man as computer* (Neisser 1963; Simon 1967).

Man As Computer

The doctrine of *man as computer* has permeated all branches of psychology. When extended to consumer behavior, this *man as computer* model regards consumption as a series of rational decisions wherein the buyer processes information to make brand choices that result in purchase outcomes. To the extent that emotion is considered at all, it is viewed as an intervening variable that helps to explain additional variance in buying choices (Holbrook and O'Shaughnessy 1984; Tybout and Hauser 1981). Usually, emotion (in all its complexity, richness, and variety) disappears and is replaced by some information-processing representation of *affect* (narrowly conceived). Thus, for example, the familiar multiattribute attitude model (in its expectancy-value or adequacy-importance formulations) deals with only one aspect of emotion (namely, favorable predisposition, liking, or approach tendency). As noted by Hochschild (1983), this narrow conception of affect ignores the remainder of the emotional spectrum (love, hate, fear, anger, joy, sorrow, and so on).

As one instance of the deeply entrenched information-processing, decision-making view of *consumer as computer,* let us turn to a brief capsule history of what I shall call the C–A–B paradigm. This C–A–B framework exemplifies the neglect of emotion in consumer research while also suggesting a perspective I intend to take as the point of departure for my subsequent attempt to build emotion into a coherent view of the consumption process.

The C–A–B Paradigm

For many years, consumer researchers have played relatively minor variations on a theme that can be traced all the way back to Plato's distinction among cognition, affect, and conation. For example, Howard's original model (1963) of buyer behavior incorporated a flow of effects in which cognitive variables (information seeking) determined affective responses (state of predisposition) that, in turn, produced conative or behavioral effects (choice process and purchase). With support from the ubiquitous hierarchy-of-effects concept (Lavidge and Steiner 1961), this notion of a causal flow from cognition to affect to behavior (C–A–B) dominated subsequent modifications of Howard's basic theoretical framework. Thus, Howard and Sheth (1969) modeled the flow of effects from *brand comprehension* to *attitude* to *intention/purchase;* Howard (1977) renamed these variables *brand identification, attitude,* and *intention/purchase;* and Howard (1983) stripped this model to the bare bones while still maintaining the progression from *identification* to *attitude* to *intention/purchase.*

Numerous other consumer researchers have borrowed and extended the basic C–A–B paradigm. For example, Andreasen (1965) described a flow of effects from *beliefs* to *feelings/disposition* to *select[ion].* Nicosia (1966) portrayed similar links from his *Field One* to *Field Two* to *Field Three.* Engel, Kollat, and Blackwell (1973) proposed a chain of relationships from *information processing* to *alternative evaluation* to *purchasing outcomes.* More recent modelers focus on such C–A–B variables as *internalized stimuli, decision processes,* and *choice outputs* (Zaltman and Wallendorf 1979); *information search, evaluation,* and *purchasing processes* (Loudon and Della

Bitta 1979); or *perception of stimuli, brand evaluation,* and *intention to buy* (Assael 1981).

Problems and Epicycles in the C–A–B Paradigm

Many researchers have pointed to problems with the C–A–B paradigm and, explicitly or implicitly, have indicated the need for modifications or extensions thereof. First, Krugman (1965) has suggested that, in the case of low-involvement products, a consumer may move directly from awareness to purchase without engaging other cognitive or affective processes in between. Second, Zajonc (1980; Zajonc and Markus 1982) has argued that cognitive and affective processes may constitute separate and independent systems so that affective responses may not necessarily entail prior cognitions—or, at least, not at the conscious level (Lazarus 1982). Third, several consumer researchers propose that additional affective responses involving attitude toward the advertisement (A_{ad}) may also serve as mediators that intervene between cognitions and behavior (Batra 1984a; Batra and Ray 1983b; Holbrook 1978; Lutz, MacKenzie, and Belch 1983; MacKenzie and Lutz 1983; Mitchell and Olson 1981; Moore and Hutchinson 1983; Shimp 1981; Zinkham, Gelb, and Martin 1983). Fourth, Ahtola (1985) and Batra (1985) distinguish between utilitarian and hedonic components of affect, (A_u) and (A_h). Fifth, various features-perceptions-affect-behavior models treat objective product characteristics or brand features (F) as determinants of cognitions or beliefs (Holbrook 1981; Huber 1975; Neslin 1979; Tybout and Hauser 1981). Sixth, by using such objective features (or suitable proxy variables) to gain identifiability for nonrecursive models, some investigators include the role of feedback effects such as those resulting from halo bias due to affective overtones that influence perceptions (Beckwith and Lehmann 1975; Holbrook 1983b; Holbrook and Huber 1979; Reibstein, Lovelock, and Dobson 1980).

Conceptually, these modifications and extensions amount to little more than adding epicycles onto the basic C–A–B framework. Thus, (1) Krugman, (2) Zajonc, (3) attitude toward the ad (A_{ad}), (4) utilitarian affect (A_u) versus hedonic affect (A_h), (5) feature effects (F), and (6) halo bias could be presented, respectively, as:

1. $C \longrightarrow B \longrightarrow A$

2. $C: \quad A \longrightarrow B$

3. $C \begin{array}{c} \nearrow A \searrow \\ \searrow A_{ad} \longrightarrow \end{array} B$

4. $C \begin{array}{c} \nearrow A_u \searrow \\ \searrow A_b \nearrow \end{array} B$

5. $F \longrightarrow C \longrightarrow A \longrightarrow B$

6. $F \longrightarrow C \rightleftarrows A \longrightarrow B$

Such epicycles serve as concessions to empirical reality that permit retaining the dominant C–A–B paradigm. By adding new variables, arrows, and loops to the basic C–A–B scheme, we cling to our conventional conceptions of cognition, affect, and behavior so that we can recycle the same framework for one more round of service.

Disenchantment with the C–A–B Paradigm

Recently, however, several commentators have expressed dissatisfaction not so much with the arrows and loops in the revised and extended C–A–B scheme as with the nature and purpose of the traditional cognitive, affective, and behavioral variables themselves (Holbrook and Hirschman 1982). Briefly, the C–A–B model serves as a proposed explanation of buying behavior and focuses on purchase decisions or brand choices. If we were to ask *why* consumer researchers have devoted so much attention to this decision-making or choice-modeling perspective, one answer might be that, often if not always, we have tried to serve the needs of marketing managers whom we regard as especially concerned about the determinants of sales or market share (Holbrook 1985). In our eagerness to help and to please such real or imagined practitioners, we focus on trying to explain the phenomenon in which they show the most interest—namely, buying behavior. Accordingly, we adopt the decision-oriented viewpoint implicit in the C–A–B paradigm.

However, real questions arise as to whether consumers generally do make purchase decisions (Olshavsky and Granbois 1979) and as to whether such brand choices are of primary importance to consumers themselves. Recalling Alderson's distinction (1957) between *buying* and *consuming* and Boyd and Levy's exploration (1963) of the consumption system, one observes that purchasing decisions constitute only a minor part of the overall consumption experience (Woods 1981). The fact that this minor part may be of particular concern to marketing managers should not necessarily guide our focus as consumer researchers. Unquestionably, *marketing* research (intended as relevant to practitioners) should reflect the managerial perspective. By the same logic, however, one might expect *consumer* research (to the extent that it constitutes a distinct field of inquiry) to represent the perspective of consumers (Holbrook 1985).

I believe that, from the consumer's viewpoint, the components of the conventional C–A–B model, as typically conceptualized and measured, are unnecessarily and perhaps misleadingly narrow. In the hands of most consumer researchers (including much of my own work, by the way), cognition (C) consists mostly of beliefs or perceptions (sometimes strung together into complex semantic networks or other elaborate representations of memory). Affect (A) is narrowly conceived by these same consumer researchers (still including me) as a simple bipolar continuum running from positive to negative and roughly synonymous with Osgood, Suci, and Tannenbaum's evaluative dimension (1957) or with Fishbein and Ajzen's attitude (1975), that is, good/bad, like/dislike, pleasing/displeasing, favorable/unfavorable, etc. Behavior (B), as already indicated, is typically treated as synonymous with the purchase decision or brand choice. These conventions, widely maintained in consumer research, have greatly facilitated the measurement and testing of C–A–B models. Indeed, such measurement and testing has grown so sophisticated that one suspects it may have reached its limits in accounting for consumption phenomena. Here, I echo broader charges leveled by Giorgi (1970) at the positivistic bent that has long dominated research in psychology, with a resultant emphasis on empiricism, quantification, and prediction and a corresponding tendency toward reductionism and determinism. However great our enthusiasm for the methodological refinement that characterizes measurement and tests of the C–A–B schema, one wonders whether the narrowness or tightness of its definitions may not screen out some equally important aspects of the consumption experience.

Like Giorgi (1970), I am concerned about the phenomenological experiences that characterize everyday behavior, much of which involves consumption activities. I am well aware that such consumption experiences may exert feedback effects through satisfaction on subsequent purchase decisions and brand choices (Howard and Sheth 1969; Oliver 1980). However, I do not regard such sales results as an adequate reason, from the *consumer's* perspective, for studying consumption experiences. From the consumer's viewpoint, regardless of any managerially relevant effects on buying outcomes, the consumption experience constitutes an important component of social welfare and the quality of life that deserves study in its own right (Andrews and Withey 1976; Scitovsky 1976). This concern has led to the focus on the *hedonic* aspects of consumption (Hirschman and Holbrook 1982) or on consumer *fantasies, feelings, and fun* (Holbrook and Hirschman 1982), but the glimpses of the consumption experience adumbrated in those earlier treatments require further extension and elaboration. This chapter provides such a development, with particular emphasis on the neglected role of emotion.

The Role of Emotion in a Broadened View of the Consumption Experience: An Expanded C–E–V Paradigm

The work by Holbrook and Hirschman (1982) preserves a clear parallel between their experiential focus and the conventional C–A–B paradigm—that is, between fantasies–feelings–fun and cognitions–affect–behavior. The key differences in our approach involve a broadening of the basic building blocks of the model and a shift in purpose from the explanation of brand choices to the representation of consumption experiences. In line with the latter purpose, we provide an enlarged scope for the role played by emotions in our conceptualization of the three key components in consumer behavior. This enlarged role encompasses the emotional aspects of cognition (as in fantasies or other dreamlike states of consciousness), the full subjective experience of affect (as in emotional feelings), and the behavioral expression of emotion (as in attaining various types of value such as fun). The wide range of relevant phenomena helps alert us to the breadth of consumption experiences encompassed by our expanded view of consumer behavior.

From this perspective, the conventional conceptions of *cognition, affect,* and *behavior* in consumer research—as narrowly conceived in two decades of work on the C–A–B model—have rendered these terms inadequate to express the expanded meaning intended by the broadened view of the consumption experience advocated here. I am well aware that some psychologists already do employ such terms as *cognition* and *affect* in their broadest senses (perhaps contributing to some confusion in the psychological literature itself). However, I believe that such enlarged meanings for these terms in consumer research have been forever precluded by their long history of inveterately narrow usage by C–A–B theorists.

Accordingly, in what follows I shall replace the terms *cognition, affect,* and *behavior* with *consciousness, emotion,* and *value* in what I shall call the C–E–V model. The C–E–V model differs from the C–A–B paradigm in its attempt to encompass the full range of phenomena in the consumption experience. Specifically, in this view, the consumption experience involves three phases (consciousness, emotion, and value) that are linked by the over-arching concept of emotion and that expand on the older parallel concepts (cognition, affect, and behavior). Thus, I intend to extend the C–A–B model into an enlarged C–E–V schema directed toward better representing the nature of consumer behavior. This expanded view should reveal emotion as one (and, perhaps, *the*) key linking pin that holds together the consumption experience.

As one example of the mediating process by which emotion shapes value in the consumption experience, consider Hochschild's treatment (1983) of consumers' responses to the service provided by an airline. Hochschild clarifies the extent to which the emotional labor of the flight attendants encourages a cheerful and secure flying experience in the face of anxieties that might otherwise escalate into a dread fear of air travel. Thus, the steward(ess)'s friendly smile and accommodating style become part of the basic aeronautic service and convey a feeling of contentment like that of being entertained in someone else's home: "Home is safe. Home does not crash" (Hochschild, 1983, p. 106).

Summary: Consumer As Human

In sum, as Cary Grant told us long ago in the film *Mr. Blandings Builds His Dream House* (1948), the time has come to end our neglect of emotional phenomena, to renounce their stepchild treatment as constructs that only help to explain variance in purchasing decisions, and to recognize their importance as key components of the consumption experience. For Mr. Blandings, one buys, builds, or inhabits a house with love. In a speech to his lawyer and friend (played by Melvin Douglas), Blandings (Cary Grant) speaks passionately about the role of product intangibles not measurable on a slide rule. He compares his dream house to a fine painting, one bought for love, whose value cannot be gauged on a monetary scale. He characterizes home finding as something you do with your heart and not your head:

> You just don't understand business. . . . Look, you can't measure everything on a slide rule. This house has certain intangibles. . . . Now let me explain something. . . . Muriel and I have found what I'm not ashamed to call our dream house. It's like a fine painting. You buy it with your heart, not your head. You don't ask how much was the paint, how much was the canvas. You look at it, and you say "it's beautiful, I want it." And if it costs a few more pennies, you pay it—and gladly—because you love it, and you can't measure the things you love in dollars and cents. Oh well, anyway, that's the way I feel about it.

I have already mentioned Hochschild's treatment (1983) of the flying experience. Other anecdotal and empirical examples of emotions in consumption will appear later. Meanwhile, it should suffice to reiterate that feelings such as love, joy, anger, and fear do not just matter because of their ability to account for incremental variance in brand choices. Rather, they matter because of their complete infusion into the consumption experience, broadly conceived. Our experience as consumers encompasses both positive feelings (joy, love) and their negative counterparts (sadness, disgust). These emotional dimensions of consumption bear directly on our quality of life as people and citizens. They raise questions concerning social welfare, public policy, and the commonwealth that transcend any presumed relevance they may bear to purchasing decisions of interest to business managers. Whatever the impact of emotions on brand choices and market share, their role in our lives as consumers makes them important subjects for study in their own right.

Psychologists have increasingly recognized that the reductionistic treatment of people as machines neglects their most important characteristic—namely, their humanity (Denzin 1984; Giorgi 1970; Hochschild 1983; Seamon 1984). In this light, the model of consumer as computer must give way to a more comprehensive view of human nature. Certainly, it is not consumers' capacities to process information and make decisions that renders them distinctively human. Rather, the phenomena that distinguish consumers from machines lie in their capacity to experience emotions. We can build computers that think and choose and act. But, as Rey (1980) points out, we do not regard such machines as people. Machines are not persons because they feel no emotions. Emotions make people human.

Emotion and the C–E–V Model of the Consumption Experience

Considerable confusion has surrounded attempts to define emotion and to explain the way it works. This confusion appears in the laundry lists of inconsistent definitions that sometimes appear in the literature (for example, Kleinginna and Kleinginna 1981) and has prompted the call for better integrated, more comprehensive frameworks (for example, Plutchik 1980, p. 84). I shall attempt to provide such a framework in the area of consumer behavior by drawing on the work of numerous psychologists (for example, de Rivera 1977; Izard 1977; Mandler 1975; Plutchik 1980; Strongman 1978), sociologists (for example, Hochschild 1983), and philosophers (for example, Lyons 1980; Rorty 1980; Solomon 1976). Briefly, my proposed conceptualization views emotion in the consumption experience as the central link in a system of interacting components that comprise a multifaceted dynamic process represented by the aforementioned C–E–V model involving consciousness, emotion, and value.

In this chapter, I depart from an earlier, more restrictive definition (Holbrook and O'Shaughnessy 1984) by regarding emotion as encompassing a wide range of phenomena that entail four components to be described later (physiological responses, cognition, behavioral expression, and feelings). Here, I intend to exclude as little as possible from the sphere of emotional phenomena and, indeed, to emphasize that emotion interpenetrates into such other closely related aspects as consciousness and value.

Inputs

The outlines of the proposed model of emotion in the consumption experience appear in figure 2–1. This model follows Lazarus (Lazarus, Averill, and Opton 1970) and Mehrabian (1980; Mehrabian and Russell 1974) in distinguishing inputs from the *person* and from the *environment*, but it adds a third general type of input—namely, those resulting from *person–environment interactions* involved in determining the relevant consumption *situation* (Denzin 1984; de Rivera 1977; Kahn 1984). Following Holbrook and Hirschman (1982), personal inputs comprise *general customer characteristics* (demographics, socioeconomics, psychographics) and *resources* (time, energy, money). Following Holbrook (1983a), environmental inputs entail a contrast between *significate* (an object, such as the physical brand or product itself) and *sign* (a symbolic unit used to designate this object, such as an advertisement, some other promotional message, or indeed any communi-

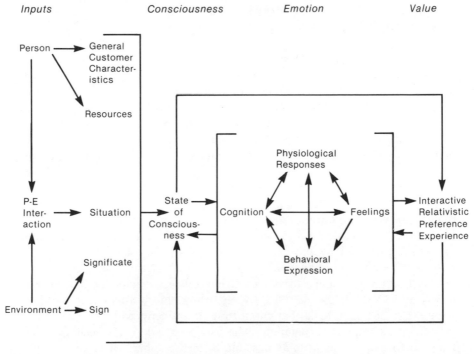

Figure 2–1. C–E–V Model of the Consumption Experience.

cation from one's social environment [Howard and Sheth 1969; Langer 1942; Morris 1946; Ogden and Richards 1923]). (For a review of the social aspects of emotion, see Denzin 1984.) Together, these inputs affect a system of interacting components encompassed by the C–E–V framework. I discuss each of these—particularly the second, most central focus—in more detail.

Consciousness

The phenomena of consciousness have posed numerous intractable problems for both philosophers and psychologists (Jaynes 1976). I use the term *consciousness* to cover a wide range of unaltered or altered mental states varying along a continuum from unconscious to subconscious to conscious awareness (Hilgard 1980) and subsuming various forms of diminished consciousness (Jaynes 1976). Hence, the consumer's consciousness includes not only beliefs about product attributes (the conventional preoccupation of the C–A–B modelers) but also a variety of fantasies, daydreams, imagery, subconscious thoughts, and unconscious mental processes (Holbrook and Hirschman 1982).

In broadening the sphere of cognitive activity in this manner, I also hope to sidestep the controversy between Zajonc (1980; Zajonc and Markus 1982) and Lazarus (1982) by acknowledging that some sort of cognitive process generally precedes and feeds into an emotional response, even if that mental activity occurs at a subconscious or even an unconscious level. Hence, somewhat paradoxically, my use of *consciousness* encompasses conscious, subconscious, and unconscious mental phenomena. (I also recognize the importance of both unaltered and altered states of consciousness, but shall not dwell on the latter in the present discussion.)

Operationally, I define consciousness as a verbal or nonverbal reaction to informational inputs from the person, the environment, or the person–environment interaction. In the case of signs such as advertising, for example, this definition would encompass the extensive work on psychophysiological measures of attentional activation (for recent reviews, see Holbrook and O'Shaughnessy 1984; Kroeber-Riel 1979, 1982; Olson and Ray 1983; Stewart and Furse 1982; Watson and Gatchel 1979; Weinstein 1982) as well as the verbal measures proposed by Wells (1964; Puto and Wells 1984), Batra (1984a, Batra and Ray 1983b), Schlinger (1979), and others (Holbrook and O'Shaughnessy 1984). Later, I shall present an example of such verbal measures used to assess emotional responses to television commercials (attitude toward the ad). As conceptualized here, consciousness precedes and partially determines emotion in the consumption experience. In other words, I focus on the dependence of emotion on consciousness. However, one should also recognize the possible feedback loops (figure 2–1) wherein emotion affects the attentional and perceptual processes that underlie various conscious states (for a review, see Ray and Batra 1983).

Emotion

As the central construct of primary interest, emotion itself involves a set of interacting components (physiological responses, cognition, behavioral expression, feelings). These components appear as key elements in a number of influential theories and parallel Strongman's classification (1978) of theoretical emphases into the physiological, the cognitive, the behavioral, and the experiential. Generally, individual theorists have tended to omit at least one of the four interacting components. For example, the following authors have focused primarily on the three components indicated:

Author(s)	Focus
Lazarus, Averill, and Opton (1970)	physiological response, cognitive appraisal, motor–behavioral action–expression
Mandler (1975)	arousal, cognitive interpretation, consciousness
Izard (1977)	neural activity, facial/postural expression, subjective phenomenological experience
Strongman (1978)	physiological effects, behavioral effects, subjective effects
Lyons (1980)	abnormal physiological changes, beliefs and evaluation, feelings

Combining these perspectives suggests the system of interacting components shown in figure 2–1. This four-component system constitutes emotion proper. It results in outputs in the form of value experiences and exerts feedback effects on consciousness.

In some ways, the C–E–V model resembles the familiar stimulus–organism–response (S–O–R) model (compare Mehrabian 1980; Mehrabian and Russell 1974). An important extension, however, is that the mediating emotion is itself viewed as an interacting system with *no necessary causal priority among the four components*. Rather, as indicated by the double-headed arrows, they exert effects on one another in a reverberating network of mutual interrelationships (Denzin 1984; Giorgi 1970). In this respect, the present schema follows Izard's treatment (1977) most closely but draws heavily on the other references cited above and further elaborated on in the discussion of individual components below.

Physiological Responses. In an early theory of emotion, James (1890) stressed the physiological component by proposing that perception leads directly to bodily changes that are in turn experienced as the relevant emotion. This general viewpoint has led to decades of research on such psychophysiological indices of arousal as circulation (pulse rate, blood pressure, blood volume), sweat-gland changes (galvanic skin response), muscular tension (muscle potential), and electrical brain activity (alpha blocking). Appropriate measures involve the use of electrocardiograms (EKGs), psychogalvanometers (GSRs), electromyograms (EMGs), and electroencephalograms (EEGs). Good reviews appear in discussions by Grings and Dawson (1978), Hassett (1978), Kroeber-Riel (1979), and Lang, Rice, and Sternbach (1972). See also chapter 4 by Cacioppo et al.

Though all these indices represent activity in the autonomic nervous system (circulation and sweating) or in the central nervous system (musculature and brain waves) and though these aspects of arousal are clearly implicated in emotion, the arousal–emotion linkages have proven to be a highly refractory subject for study. Indeed, many researchers now regard the evidence on psychophysiological changes underlying emotion as disappointing (Strongman 1978, p. 54). This disillusionment stems from two primary sources: (1) the various physiological indices of arousal show only weak intercorrelations so that arousal cannot in any sense be regarded as a unitary event (Grings and Dawson 1978; Plutchik 1980; Strongman 1978); (2) with few exceptions such as Ax's work (1953) with blood pressure and muscle tension; Mason's work (1975) with hormonal responses; Clynes' work (1980) with sentographic indications of finger pressure; and Ekman, Levenson, and Friesen's work (1983) with heart rate and finger temperature, there appears to be no unique correspondence between particular physiological states and different subjective emotions. Investigators continue to search for such patterns, but the accumulated evidence still supports Grings and Dawson (1978) and Plutchik (1980) in their discouraging assessments of the limited chances for finding one-to-one correspondences between physiology and subjective emotional experience.

A more plausible and comprehensive approach to the role of physiology has emerged from the position proposed by Schachter (1971; Schachter and Singer 1962) and largely adopted by Mandler (1975) and others (Hochschild 1983; Lyons 1980). Briefly, Schachter viewed arousal as a necessary but not sufficient condition. Such arousal, in his view, received its emotional label as the result of cognitive interpretation. Schachter and his colleagues demonstrated this effect in a series of experiments in which arousal was manipulated directly by injections of epinephrine. Given the presence of this physiological basis, the emotional experience tended to depend on the subject's cognitive interpretation of the surrounding experimental context (for example, the presence of a euphoric or angry confederate). Though specific details of Schachter's work have received criticism and have often resisted replication (Dienstbier 1979; Reisenzein 1983), his conceptualization based on an arousal–cognition interaction has exerted a strong influence toward the recognition of cognitive labeling as a key component of emotion. Further indication of the role of cognitions comes from Valins's work (1966) on nonveridical physiological feedback. When supplied with phony information on pulse rate, subjects provide their own appropriate self-explications.

Cognition. Emphasis on the role of cognitive interpretation or labeling is closely associated with the work of Arnold (1960; 1970), who argued strongly for a cognitively based theory of emotion. This cognitive approach has proven congenial to a number of subsequent theorists (Averill 1980; Hochschild 1983; Lazarus, Averill, and Opton 1970; Lazarus, Kanner, and Folkman 1980; Lyons 1980; Mandler 1975; Plutchik 1980; Strongman 1978).

Philosophically, one can demonstrate that cognition (conscious, subconscious, or unconscious) must precede arousal (Lazarus 1982). Thus, the assertion "you are a fool" will produce violent anger only in someone capable of understanding English, whereas a grizzly bear will fail to elicit the appropriate fear response if it is mistaken for a cow (Delgado 1966). The cognitivist claim goes considerably beyond this quasi-tautological position, however, in that it argues for a structural model of the emotional process something like that shown in figure 2–2.

The cognitivistic structural model (figure 2–2) represents an attempt to synthesize the arguments of Arnold, Lazarus, Lyons, Mandler, Plutchik, and Strongman. Thus, for example, Arnold (1960) describes a process wherein

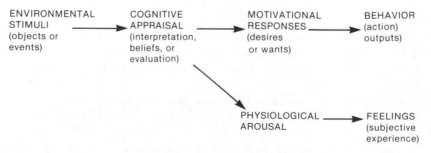

Figure 2–2. Cognitivistic Structural Model of the Emotional Process

cognitive appraisal (evaluation of a stimulus situation as good or bad) results in an action tendency (toward the good, away from the bad). Mandler (1975) emphasizes that the cognitive appraisal results in *both* action outputs *and* physiological arousal. A similar position is taken by Lyons (1980), who emphasizes the role of belief-based evaluations in shaping desires or wants as well as the physiological changes that result in subjectively experienced feelings.

This cognitions-based model provides a hierarchic account of the emotional process that errs in much the same way that Lavidge and Steiner's hierarchy of effects (1961) errs as an account of consumer communication—namely, by disregarding feedback effects wherein later stages affect earlier stages of the model. Specifically, one must assume that actions and feelings exert feedback effects on cognitive appraisal (Kleinginna and Kleinginna 1981). For example, the aforementioned processes of cognitive labeling may be explained by causal attribution (Dienstbier 1979). However, by the time one has added such complicating feedback loops, the system of fully interacting components shown in figure 2–1 appears to be the more parsimonious yet general formulation.

Behavioral Expression. The behavioral expression component of figure 2–1 includes such overt manifestations as body postures, nonverbal gestures, and facial expressions (Denzin 1984, de Rivera 1977, Sudnow 1979). Postures and gestures have, of course, received detailed study in the literature on kinesics and body language (Birdwhistell 1970). However, the nonverbal communication of greatest concern to emotion theorists is that which occurs via facial expression.

Calling on a tradition that extends back to the work of Charles Darwin, the role of facial expression has received sustained attention from Tomkins (1962, 1963), Ekman (for example, Ekman and Friesen 1975; Ekman, Levenson, and Friesen 1983), and Izard (1977). The latter researcher describes numerous studies, many of which explore the role of facial muscles via electromyographic measures. The role of facial expressions is well established as a cross-cultural phenomenon. More important in the present context, however, is the role played by facial expression in the communication of emotional reactions within (as opposed to between) organisms. This intraindividual communicative role refers to the feedback process whereby we receive information from our own facial musculature as a basis for further cognitive interpretations, subjective feelings, or physiological responses. (For a more detailed discussion, see chapter 4 by Cacioppo et al.)

Feelings. Finally, the emotional system involves a subjective, phenomenological, experiential component that may be designated *feelings* (Denzin 1984; de Rivera 1977; Giorgi 1970; Izard 1977; Lyons 1980; Nowlis 1970;

Strongman 1978). Researchers have referred to such phenomenological experience as "lived consciousness" (Denzin 1984, p. 108) or the "life-world" (Giorgi 1970, p. 222). Recognition of this component of the emotional process requires the researcher to face up to some tough methodological issues. Weinrich (1980) has commented on the problems raised by the need to study the subjective phenomena involved in an emotional experience. Indeed, in an effort to render such observations tractable, the researcher is generally forced to rely, often with embarrassment, on some form of verbal report (Strongman 1978). Plutchik (1980) tends to distrust such verbal reports. By contrast, Strongman stresses the hope that verbal data can be collected systematically and analyzed scientifically.

As we shall see, much of the work toward a taxonomy of emotions requires some such faith in a possible rapprochement between phenomenology and empirical methods (for example, de Rivera 1977). This point will gain clarity in the next section's discussion of emotional content and its classification. First, however, I shall round out the description of the consumption experience by mentioning value, the output of the C–E–V system. Here, I focus on the effects of emotion on value though, once again, one should also recognize possible feedbacks from value to the other constructs (figure 2–1).

Value

As previously noted, the central emotional processes may result in the output of value. Elsewhere, I have defined value as an *interactive relativistic preference experience* (Holbrook 1984a; Holbrook and Corfman 1984). Specifically, value involves an *interaction* between some subject (such as a consumer) and some object (a thing or event such as a product or service). It is *relativistic* in at least three senses, being *comparative* (based on a ranking of one object against another), *personal* (differing among people), and *situational* (depending on the context in which an evaluation occurs). It entails a *preference* (some relatively more or less positive affective response). Finally, it pertains not to an object itself but rather to the *consumption experience* resulting from its use (extrinsic value) or appreciation (intrinsic value).

This concept of value roots the key output of the C–E–V model in the consumption experience rather than in the C–A–B model's focus on the purchase decision or brand choice. In this view, value involves preference and therefore ties directly to the positive–negative affective polarity of emotion. Thus, emotion and value intermingle closely in the C–E–V framework.

Drawing on the theory of value or axiology, Holbrook (1984a) developed a typology of value in the consumption experience based on the following three distinctions: (1) *extrinsic* (resulting from use in a means–ends relationship) versus *intrinsic* (resulting from the appreciation of some experience for its own sake); (2) *self-oriented* (concerned with one's self-interest) versus *other-oriented* (concerned with the reactions of other people or other parts of the cosmos); (3) *active* (derived from the manipulation of some object) versus *passive* (derived from the responsive appreciation of some object). The resulting typology appears in table 2–1. It distinguishes among eight types of value (with a parenthetical example provided for each). Holbrook and Corfman (1984) tested the top portion of this typology in an experiment designed to manipulate consumer judgments of convenience, fun, beauty, and quality. They found that the first three value judgments tended to vary with the factors intended to manipulate them independently, but that quality appeared to serve as a more global value judgment intervening between perceived convenience, fun, or beauty and a still more global measure of overall preference. Other researchers (for example, Denzin 1984; Hyde 1983) have focused more on the bottom portion of the typology involving the other-oriented aspects of socially centered emotions that underlie such types of value as success, reputation, virtue, and faith.

Classification of Emotional Content

The preceding section examined the dynamic structure of the consumption experience (consciousness, emotion, and value) and has argued for the view of emotion as a central complex composed of four interacting components (physiological responses, cognition, behavioral expression, and feelings). This section examines the content or substance of the emotional subsystem and inquires into the dimensions that underlie the classification of emotions and the types of emotions that may be distinguished. The discussion begins with a consideration of different ways in which emotion taxonomies may be built and then inspects the results of these different approaches.

Table 2–1
Typology of Value in the Consumption Experience

		Extrinsic	*Intrinsic*
Self-oriented	Active	Efficiency (convenience)	Play (fun)
	Passive	Excellence (quality)	Esthetics (beauty)
Other-oriented	Active	Politics (success)	Morality (virtue)
	Passive	Esteem (reputation)	Religion (faith)

Source: Data from Holbrook, 1984a.

Classification of Emotional Typologies

Much of the work on emotion has moved toward the classification of emotional content according to one or another kind of typology. Indeed, this general impetus toward identifying different types of emotional content appears to be one main commonality among an otherwise diverse set of emotion researchers.

The resulting emotional typologies may themselves be classified according to two dimensions that underlie their manner of construction. First, one may distinguish between those typologies whose basis is primarily *conceptual* and those derived more on the basis of *empirical* data. Second, the more *systematically* developed typologies contrast with those that appear to be more *nonsystematic* in origin. Combining these two distinctions yields the classification of emotional typologies shown in table 2–2.

The table distinguishes four types of emotional taxonomies. The first involves simple *enumeration* or a conceptual but nonsystematic listing of salient emotions that come to mind upon reflection. The second retains the primarily conceptual focus of enumeration but adopts a more systematic approach to *logical derivation*. The third moves from conceptualization to an empirical foundation but approaches data nonsystematically via some form of *data reduction*. Finally, the fourth combines the virtues of systematization and empiricism to engage in *theory development and testing*. These four types of emotional taxonomy have all appeared widely in the literature, as discussed in the paragraphs that follow.

Typologies Based on Enumeration

From time immemorial, thinkers about emotion have shown a tendency to list what they regard as basic emotional types (Plutchik 1980, p. 131). Thus, for example, Descartes identified six (love, hatred, desire, joy, sadness, admiration), Spinoza isolated three (joy, sorrow, desire), and Hobbes listed seven (appetite, desire, love, aversion, hate, joy, grief). Along similar lines, Gaylin (1979) has described twelve types of feeling (anxious, guilty, ashamed, proud, upset, tired, bored, envious, used, touched, moved, and good). Such enumerative listings appear to have stemmed largely from impressionistic

Table 2–2
Classification of Emotional Typologies

	Conceptual	Empirical
Nonsystematic	Enumeration	Data reduction
Systematic	Logical derivation	Theory development and testing

reflections. Recently, however, more carefully developed enumerations based in part on the role of facial expressions have been offered by Izard (1977; Izard and Buechler 1980), Tomkins (1980), and Ekman and Friesen (1975; Ekman, Levenson, and Friesen 1983):

Author(s)	*List of Primary Emotions*
Izard	interest, joy, surprise, sadness, anger, disgust, contempt, fear, shame/shyness, guilt
Tomkins	interest or excitement, enjoyment or joy, surprise or startle, distress or anguish, fear or terror, shame or humiliation, contempt, disgust, anger or rage
Ekman	happiness, surprise, sadness, fear, anger, disgust

Typologies Based on Logical Derivation

The logical derivation of typologies involves a systematic conceptualization of key underlying dimensions. For example, Arnold (1960) distinguished (1) between beneficial and harmful object-appraisals and (2) among situations with object present, object not present, and object present or not. These distinctions produced the following classification of basic emotions:

Object	*Beneficial*	*Harmful*
Present	delight, joy	sorrow, sadness, anger, dejection
Not present	wanting, desire, hope	aversion, daring, fear
Present or not	love, liking	hate, dislike

Sometimes the pursuit of systematic conceptual classification can uncover types of emotions (or other phenomena) that might otherwise escape attention (Holbrook 1984b). For example, Millenson (1967) identified three general types of emotion based on the onset–termination of positive–negative reinforcement. Systematic cross-classification suggests strongly that a fourth type (shown in parentheses) should also have been included:

	Positive Reinforcement	Negative Reinforcement
Onset	pleasure	apprehension
	elation	anxiety
	ecstasy	terror
Termination	annoyance	(relaxation)
	anger	(relief)
	rage	(deliverance)

De Rivera (1977) appears to have pursued the method of logical derivation further than any other psychologist engaged in the study of emotions. Based on five distinctions (one involving three as opposed to two categories), he derives a 2 × 2 × 2 × 3 × 2 or 48-celled classification. This typology permits an extremely fine-grained representation of emotional content.

A similarly detailed typology of emotion emerges from philosophical work in which Solomon (1976) introduced the following key distinctions:

1. Positive evaluation versus negative evaluation (p. 267);

2. Outer-directed versus inner-directed versus ranging or bipolar (pp. 254–256);

3. Only human object versus human or other object (p. 258);

4. Narrow scope versus broad scope versus ranging scope (p. 257).

My own cross-classification of these distinctions yields the detailed typology shown in table 2–3. Whenever possible, I have filled each cell of the typology with examples drawn from Solomon (with appropriate page references shown parenthetically). Where good illustrations did not appear among Solomon's descriptions, I have supplied my own suggestions (as indicated by the absence of parenthetical page references).

The approach to typology construction via logical derivation deserves our attention—both as a challenging exercise that may uncover hitherto neglected types of emotional experience and as an appropriate vehicle for detailed description. However, both de Rivera's typology and the Solomon–Holbrook taxonomy indicate a key problem associated with using logical derivation as the basis for classification schemes. Specifically, the process of logical division can continue indefinitely with no clear rules to indicate when it should stop. By the time one has generated a 36- or 48-celled typology, one may feel bewildered by the resulting complexity and may begin to long for the greater parsimony that might result from the data-reduction approach.

Table 2–3
Complex Conceptual Typology of Emotion

		Positive Evaluation (Good or Gain)		Negative Evaluation (Bad or Loss)	
		Only Human Object	Human or Other Object	Only Human Object	Human or Other Object
Outer directed	narrow scope	respect (358)	worship (369)	indignation (331)	shame (363)
	broad scope	trust	faith (310)	envy (307) resentment (352)	anxiety (288) despair (299)
	ranging scope	admiration	gratitude (316) hope (328)	contempt (291)	anger (285) fear (312) frustration (315) sadness (359)
Inner directed	narrow scope	self-respect (361)	vanity (367)	embarrassment (304) remorse (350)	regret (349)
	broad scope	self-esteem (361)	innocence (333)	guilt (319)	depression (295)
	ranging scope	self-satisfaction (361)	pride (347)	anguish (289)	recrimination
Ranging or bipolar	narrow scope	friendship (313) love (338)	enjoyment	hate (324) jealousy (335)	pity (343)
	broad scope	humanitarianism	joy (336)	enmity	sorrow
	ranging scope	good will	contentment (293)	ill will	discontent

1324

Typologies Based on Data Reduction

Numerous researchers have pursued the data-reduction approach to classification construction by undertaking cluster or factor analysis on some type of verbal emotional scales. Historically, this work owes its origins to the semantic differential methodology developed by Osgood, Suci, and Tannenbaum (1957). Variations on this approach have subsequently been conducted by, among others, Block (1957), Beldoch (1964), Daly, Lancee, and Polivy (1983), and Nowlis (1970); but perhaps the most sustained efforts have been reported by Mehrabian and Russell (1974; Mehrabian 1980; Russell 1980) and by Davitz (1969, 1970).

Mehrabian's work builds directly on Osgood's repeated identification of three dimensions of meaning: evaluation, activity, and potency. The Mehrabian framework stresses three analogous dimensions of emotion—pleasure, arousal, and dominance—that together constitute the so-called PAD paradigm. Mehrabian and his colleagues argue that specific emotions may be regarded as positions on these three PAD dimensions. Based on extensive empirical work with verbal rating scales, Mehrabian (1980; Mehrabian and Russell 1974) produces voluminous evidence supporting the reliability and validity of his PAD conceptualization. Further, recent research suggests the usefulness of the PAD framework in representing consumers' emotional responses to such experiences as the enjoyment of success in playing video games (Holbrook et al. 1984; Mehrabian and Wixen 1983).

A less conventional and even more compendious data-reduction approach has been carried forward by Davitz (1969, 1970), who set out to compile a dictionary of emotional terms that would reflect "a consensual or social phenomenology" (1970, p. 252). His work with critical incidents and a checklist of 556 verbal items resulted in definitions of emotional terms based on those items checked by more than 33 percent of his respondents. Subsequent cluster analysis suggested a typology of emotion based on four important dimensions (activation, relatedness, hedonic tone, and competence), each with three subcategories (ranging from positive to negative).

Dimension	*Subcategories*
Activation	activation, hypoactivation, hyperactivation
Relatedness	moving toward, away, against
Hedonic tone	comfort, discomfort, tension
Competence	enhancement, incompetence/ dissatisfaction, inadequacy

Davitz (1969) provides plenty of conceptual links between his results and the general literature on emotion. However, his findings suffer from a problem typical of the data-reduction approach—namely, that the absence of a firm initial theoretical foundation lends the conclusions a somewhat ad hoc quality. This difficulty is largely avoided by an emotional typology based on more systematic theory development and testing.

Typologies Based on Theory Development and Testing

Plutchik (1980) appears to have offered the best-developed systematic and empirical basis for a theoretical classification of emotions. His approach combines systematization and empiricism toward the construction of a clearly conceived, research-supported emotional typology.

At the conceptual level, Plutchik adopts a "psychoevolutionary" theoretical stance in which the primary emotions perform key adaptive functions tending to aid species at all stages of evolution in their struggle for survival. In his view, this struggle necessitates the performance of eight basic functions: incorporation, rejection, protection, destruction, reproduction, reintegration, orientation, and exploration. To these eight basic functions correspond eight basic subjective and behavioral components according to the following parallelism:

Functional	*Subjective*	*Behavioral*
incorporation	acceptance	affiliating
rejection	disgust	repulsing
protection	fear	escaping
destruction	anger	attacking
reproduction	joy	cooperating
reintegration	sadness	crying for help
orientation	surprise	stopping
exploration	expectancy	exploring

In a further structural elaboration, these eight primary components may be regarded as pairs of polar opposites (acceptance–disgust, fear–anger, joy–sadness, surprise–expectancy) and arranged in a circular pattern or a circumplex (acceptance–fear–surprise–sadness–disgust–anger–expectancy–joy) within a conic shape in which height conveys intensity: acceptance (tolerance to adoration) vs. disgust (boredom to loathing), fear (timidity to terror) vs. anger (annoyance to rage), joy (serenity to ecstasy) vs. sadness (pensiveness to grief), and surprise (uncertainty to amazement) vs. expectancy (mindfulness to vigilance). More specific emotions are derived by mixing these primary emotions in various degrees—much as one might mix primary colors to obtain all possible hues. For example, joy blended with acceptance gives love; fear mixed with surprise yields awe; sadness combined with expectancy produces pessimism (Plutchik, 1980, p. 162).

Plutchik (1980) reports extensive research using the verbal rating scales of the so-called Emotion Profile Index (EPI). Data reduction by factor analysis suggests a circumplex structure of primary emotions with bipolarities that generally conform to his theory. Whereas individual details concerning specific emotions are not completely consistent from study to study, the overall pattern of findings conveys the impression of a well-supported conceptual scheme. Accordingly, Plutchik's eight primary emotions will be retained as a basis for the illustrations of consumer responses discussed in the next section and as the point of departure for some of the empirical applications in the section after that.

Some Introspective Illustrations and Anecdotal Evidence on the Role of Emotions in the Consumption Experience

The important role played by emotions in the consumption experience has not yet served as the subject for extensive empirical research. Indeed, besides the empirical applications discussed in the next section, few studies have undertaken systematic explorations of emotional phenomena (other than positive–negative affect) in consumer behavior (for recent exceptions, see Batra 1984a; Batra and Ray 1983b; Holbrook et al. 1984; Ray and Batra 1983). To say that this treatment of emotion by consumer researchers constitutes neglect would be an understatement. Yet we need not wait for extensive empirical results before offering a few intuitive observations concerning the place of emotion in consumption.

The manner in which emotions pervade the consumption experience is suggested by the following introspective illustrations of Plutchik's eight primary emotions (1980) within the consumption context:

Primary Emotion	Example in Consumption
Acceptance	Deep personal liking for your favorite talk-show host
Disgust	Discovering that you have just swallowed a large mouthful of sour milk
Fear	Eating your first mouthful of a canned tuna that was recently recalled because of a botulism scare
Anger	Realizing that the auto salesman sold you a car that gets eight miles per gallon in highway driving

Joy   Listening to the finale of Beethoven's Ninth
                       Symphony

Sadness   Being seven years old on Christmas morning
                       and finding out that your new video game does
                       not work

Surprise   Learning that the Dallas Mavericks have just beaten
                       the Boston Celtics in a four-out-of-seven series

Expectancy   Beginning to read the last chapter of an Agatha
                       Christie novel

As noted earlier, one expects that emotions such as those just listed will feed back upon subsequent purchase decisions in a manner that might build repeat buying (Beethoven recordings, murder mysteries), enlarge audience share (talk-show ratings), and boost attendance (basketball games) or, conversely, that might discourage future buying behavior (milk, automobiles, tuna, and video games). Equally or more importantly, as previously mentioned, one must regard the emotional components of consumption as themselves a fundamental part of the quality of life. They bear directly on social welfare and determine one's satisfaction with a personal lifestyle. On these grounds, they deserve more attention than they have thus far received from consumer researchers.

The most conspicuous anecdotal evidence for the importance of emotions in the lives of consumers has appeared in the recent work of advertising copywriters. Here, one observes considerable movement away from the kinds of factual claims requiring extensive documentation to forestall charges of deceptive advertising: more doctors recommend our brand of pain killer to their own children; after only three days' use, our toothpaste completely removes stains and cavities; gargling once a week with our medicinal mouthwash can cure arthritis, shrink hemorrhoids, and prevent asthma attacks; our cola drink contains three times as much flavor as the leading competitor. Such themes demand expensive empirical support and thereby discourage their use in advertising copy. In addition, however, a growing consensus appears to recognize the possibly greater effectiveness of emotional as opposed to factual advertising appeals—especially for some types of nontechnical, symbol-laden, intangible, or esthetic products. Holbrook and O'Shaughnessy (1984) refer to this strategic philosophy as the *contingency approach* and cite numerous adherents (Berger 1981; Bettman 1982; Golden and Johnson 1983; Gorn 1982; Hansen 1981; Holbrook 1978, 1983a; Petty, Cacioppo, and Schumann 1983; Puto and Wells 1984; Ray and Batra 1983; Shimp 1981; Vaughn 1980).

At the moment, I am concerned only with the emotional side of the contingency argument. From this perspective, testimonials from industry practitioners to the efficacy of emotion-based advertising appeals have recently proliferated in such publications as *Advertising Age* (for example, August 25, 1980, p. 1), *Marketing News* (for example, August 7, 1981, p. 10), and Ogilvy and Mather's *Viewpoint* (Riney 1981). Lawrence M. Light of BBDO summarized these signals by calling for a "return of the heart" in an "Era of Emotion" (*Marketing News,* September 19, 1980, p. 1).

The convictions behind these assertive endorsements of emotional advertising have apparently inspired a number of ad campaigns. Recall, for example, the emotional message carried by recent commercials for Coca-Cola ("Have a Coke and a smile"), Pepsi-Cola ("Get that Pepsi feeling"), Maxwell House ("Get that good-to-the-last-drop feeling"), General Motors ("Get that great GM feeling"), Belmont Park ("It's an unbeatable feeling"), Sealy Posturepedic ("Feeling so good it shows"), Remy Martin ("Arouse your sense of Remy"), AT&T ("Reach out and touch someone" or "He called just to say 'I love you, Mom' "), New York Telephone ("Millions of New Yorkers put their feelings on the line everyday. From tears to laughter, . . . New Yorkers express themselves on the phone"), Kodak ("Decorate your home with love"), Sergio Valente ("Jeans for the way you live and love"), Burlington Mills ("Never go to bed with a sheet you don't love"), Shure ("This revolutionary new phono cartridge . . . brings back the emotion of the performance"), Kenwood ("This system is . . . pure ecstasy"), Dim pantyhose ("For the sheer pleasure of it"), Mastoloni cultured pearls ("Mix business with pleasure"), Neiman-Marcus ("Live with a sense of pleasure"), American Express ("In addition to all the logical reasons for using the American Express card, there is now one that is unabashedly sentimental. . . . Coming to the aid of the Statue of Liberty"), and Saab ("One car you can buy where your emotions aren't compromised by your intellect"). Finally, contemplate the following scenario for what was perhaps the prototypical commercial in the new wave of advertising emotionalism:

> Mean Joe Green, champion defensive tackle for the Pittsburgh Steelers, stumbles from the football field looking dejected, defeated, devastated. A small boy follows along, visibly overwhelmed by timid but persistent adulation of the sports hero. Mean Joe brutally rejects the child's friendly advances until, in a moment of unsurpassed generosity, the lad offers the gridiron idol his bottle of Coca-Cola. As Mean Joe presses the cold bottle to his tired lips and drains its contents in one Herculean gulp, a rapturous smile transforms his weary face into an expression of uncontained pleasure. Overwhelmed with gratitude, the formerly surly ballplayer tosses the boy his precious sweat-soaked jersey, thereby conveying his rugged but sincere appreciation for the child's altruistic deed. The lad radiates pure ecstatic joy and exudes: "Gee, thanks, Mean Joe."

Empirical Applications

In describing some recent empirical applications investigating the role of emotion in the consumption experience, I draw on studies primarily concerned with addressing each stage of the C–E–V paradigm shown in figure 2–1. Specifically, the first stage represents the consumer's consciousness of informational inputs from such external agents as signs (for example, advertisements), significates (for example, products), and situations (for example, consumption contexts). Here, I shall focus on a study that adopts a broadened view of the emotional responses involved in *attitude toward the ad*. The second stage deals directly with emotions as a central part of consumption. Here, I shall describe one piece of research that investigates *emotional responses to the consumption experience*. The third category deals with emotions as determinants of value viewed as an interactive relativistic preference experience. Here, I point to an example of work aimed at distinguishing *types of value in the consumption experience*.

My empirical examples all pursue a macrolevel of analysis (as opposed to a microlevel) by examining consumption phenomena that occur across advertisements or among products or even over a range of objects (rather than for a particular ad, brand, or item). This macroview looks for general patterns of consumption behavior and thereby extends beyond the typical but somewhat parochial preoccupation with a single brand in some product category. Hence, I hope to encourage a broader concern for the full range of consumption experiences.

In choosing my three illustrations, I have drawn from my own research with various students and colleagues. I intend no implication that our work deserves preferential attention. However, I could find no other examples that come as close to providing macrolevel analysis of the three stages described earlier.

Consciousness As Attitude toward the Ad

Holbrook and Westwood (1983) reported data on 54 television commercials collected from 613 respondents recruited by shopping-mall intercepts. Small groups of respondents watched films containing subsets of commercials. They indicated purchase-likelihood intentions both before and after viewing; provided measures of recall, perceived confusion, and perceived unbelievability; and rated the ads on forty scales of emotional response. A subset of twenty-four emotional scales provided three-item indices of Plutchik's eight emotional types (1980), discussed above. These scores were all aggregated across respondents and were then analyzed across commercials.

Plutchik's eight emotions (1980) attained high reliabilities, with alphas ranging from .85 to .97. Moreover, when proximities among commercials (as represented by intercorrelations across the forty emotional scales) were submitted to multidimensional scaling (MDS), a two-dimensional space appeared to provide a good representation, with a correlation between input and output proximities of $r = .83$ (and only marginal improvements from adding further dimensions). Vectors introduced into this space to represent Plutchik's eight emotions showed generally good regression fits and suggested interpreting the MDS axes as (1) positive–negative (horizontal) and (2) serious–light (vertical). The MDS space for the fifty-four commercials (represented by Xs) and vectors for the eight Plutchik emotions (with regression Rs shown parenthetically) appear in figure 2–3.

The coordinates of commercials on MDS dimensions 1 and 2 were then used to develop an exploratory path analysis intended to explain advertising

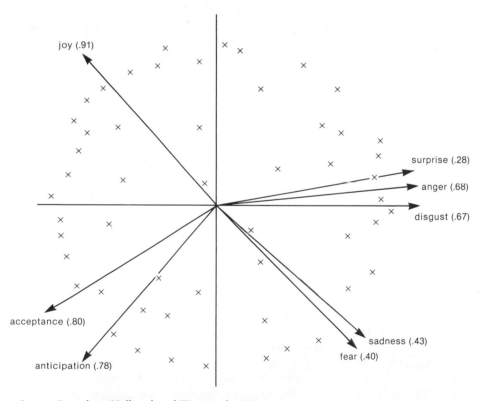

Source: Data from Holbrook and Westwood, 1983.

Figure 2–3. Commercials Space Based on MDS Scaling of Correlations among Commercials across Emotions.

perceptions (confusing, unbelievable) and effects (recall, intentions shift) via the intervening role played by the Plutchik emotions (acceptance, surprise, etc.). Results for this exploratory path analysis appear in figure 2–4. I emphasize that it doubtless incorporates considerable search bias and should therefore be viewed as illustrative rather than definitive.

The path diagram indicates that emotions (anticipation, surprise, acceptance, joy, and anger) and advertising perceptions (confusing and unbelievable) mediate the relationships between spatial positions (dimensions 1 and 2) and advertising effects (recall and intentions shift). Contrary to expectations, recall did not contribute significantly to the prediction of intentions shift. The two advertising effects are therefore represented by separate causal paths. This finding accords with results reported by Zielski (1982).

Each causal chain contains several intervening variables that help ac-

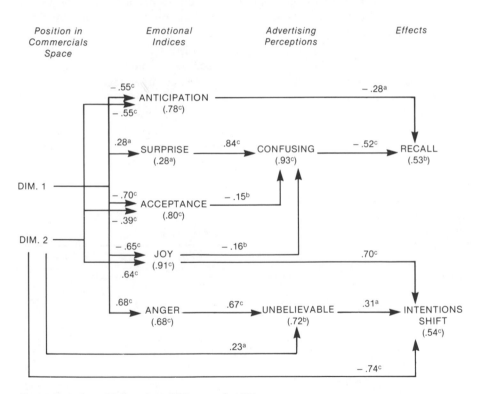

Soure: Data from Holbrook and Westwood, 1983.

Note: Path coefficients (β) appear above or below each arrow. Multiple correlation coefficients (R) are shown parenthetically under each dependent variable.

[a]$p < .05$; [b]$p < .01$; [c]$p < .001$.

Figure 2–4. Exploratory Recursive Path Analysis

count for the overall relationships between positions in the commercials space and advertising effects. Most of these mediating links make good sense intuitively: the negative effects of acceptance and joy on confusing ($-.15$ and $-.16$, $p < .01$) and of confusing on recall ($-.52$, $p < .001$) and the positive effects of surprise on confusing ($.84$, $p < .001$), of anger on unbelievability ($.67$, $p < .001$), and of joy on intentions shift ($.70$, $p < .001$). Two contradict intuitive expectations: the negative effect of anticipation on recall ($-.28$, $p < .05$) and, especially, the positive effect of unbelievable on intentions shift ($.31$ $p < .05$). Both counterintuitive effects are relatively weak. The first may be explained by a tendency for informative–intelligent–instructive ads to be relatively difficult to process and, therefore, hard to remember. The second suggests the intriguing possibility that unbelievability due to anger (insulting, annoying, irritating) may actually enhance persuasion (for example, by causing people to purchase a brand just to prove to themselves out of spite that its advertising is deceptive). Such a finding conforms to the long history of difficulty in demonstrating even the most straightforward hierarchy-of-effects relationships (Maloney 1963; Palda 1966). However, it might help to account for what some observers regard as an otherwise inexplicable barrage of annoying commercials that confront the television audience.

The overall relationships between spatial dimensions and advertising effects are further elucidated by an examination of the direct and indirect impacts of dimensions 1 and 2 on recall and intentions shift. These summary comparisons appear in table 2–4 and demonstrate that the overall correla-

Table 2–4

Summary of Direct and Indirect Effects of Dimensions 1 and 2

Dependent Variable	Type of Linkage	Effects of Dimension 1	Effects of Dimension 2
Recall	Direct	$-.078$	$-.050$
	Indirect via anticipation	.165	.157
	Indirect via surprise	$-.119$	$-.018$
	Indirect via acceptance	$-.051$	$-.035$
	Indirect via joy	$-.092$	.100
	Indirect via confusing	.037	.060
	Overall r	$-.138$	.214
Intentions shift	Direct	$-.626$	$-.725$
	Indirect via joy	.047	.392
	Indirect via anger	.126	.007
	Indirect via unbelievable	.126	.118
	Overall r	$-.327$	$-.208$

Source: Data from Holbrook and Westwood, 1983.

tions between dimensions and recall or intentions shift tend to be relatively weak (ranging in magnitude from $-.138$ to $-.327$) because the direct and indirect effects (and sometimes the indirect effects themselves) tend to work in opposite directions so as to cancel each other out. Thus, the weak negative relationship between dimension 1 and recall ($-.138$) results from the partial cancellation of some negative direct and indirect effects by some positive indirect effects (via anticipation and confusing). A similar cancellation process leads to a relatively weak overall correlation between dimension 2 and recall (.214). In the case of intentions shift, both dimensions exhibit strong negative direct effects ($-.626$ and $-.725$). However, these strong direct effects are largely counteracted by positive mediating links so that the overall correlations are greatly reduced ($-.327$ and $-.208$).

The substantive implications of table 2–4 (which are, of course, confined to a specific set of test commercials) are probably of less interest than the general manner in which they arose. Specifically, one notes the tendency for emotional mediators to work at cross-purposes. Thus, the same ad can unleash various conflicting emotions, any one of which might facilitate recall or intentions shift if working by itself but which tend to cancel each other out when working in consort. This tentative conclusion must be regarded as an exploratory finding. However, it does suggest a potentially fruitful topic for future research on consumers' emotional responses to advertising.

Emotional Responses to the Consumption Experience

Havlena and Holbrook (1985) have focused more directly on emotions prompted by various types of consumption experiences. For this purpose, they adapted procedures used in environmental psychology (for example, Mehrabian and Russell 1974) to collect inventories of introspective descriptions by asking twenty respondents to provide brief accounts of consumption experiences in eight categories: (1) esthetics; (2) athletics; (3) dining; (4) entertainment; (5) fashion; (6) hobbies; (7) religion; and (8) security. This procedure yielded a total of 149 experiential descriptions giving often quite colorful accounts of responses across a wide range of consumption situations (compare Levy, Czepiel, and Rook 1981). The following examples represent each of the eight categories:

1. I went to a Rolling Stones concert two years ago where I felt surrounded by the music which made me feel happy and energetic (almost high) for three hours. I felt transported to another world where the music just made me feel great and glad to be alive.

2. Two months ago, I tried to begin running again after a lapse of 1½ years, and I felt so heavy and out of breath that I ran only two blocks.

I was really depressed and sad about my physical condition and my neglect of my body.

3. Preparing breakfast for the family. I especially enjoyed the sounds of preparing the breakfast; listening to the eggs frying, bacon sizzling, and coffee percolating filled me with a sense of well-being. I felt warm, content, and loved.

4. The first time I played PAC-MAN was very exciting because I felt so close to the friend who was with me. Each time I squealed because I was about to get caught by the monsters, my friend squealed and hugged me. I was delighted and perfectly happy that we were so close and, at the same time, totally taken up in trying to get control over the game. I felt totally caught up in those few minutes and never wanted to stop!

5. When I wear my long white dress, I am transformed into a fairy tale princess. It is a very lovely dress but what makes it special is its power to create in my mind a picture of me as a tall, elegant, gorgeous creature (which I am not). I am suffused with self-confidence and joy.

6. What did it take to grow snowdrops? Not much. Buy the seeds. Bury them in dirt ½" deep in the fall. Sometimes, even when there is snow in April, the delicate snowdrops peek above the ground to herald the arrival of spring. Each year they surprise me. My heart skips a beat, and I smile.

7. Two years ago, marching with lighted candles at night with hundreds of people around the cathedral of Lourdes, France, chanting hymns gave me a great feeling of communion with others.

8. Having a Fichet lock installed on our apartment door a few months ago made me feel suddenly very secure and satisfied.

The full set of 149 experiential descriptions served as the units of analysis for the remainder of the study and were rated by two separate sets of ten content-analytic judges on (1) eight three-item Plutchik indices; and (2) three four-item Mehrabian PAD indices (hereafter referred to as *Plutchik's Eight* and *Mehrabian's Three*). As found in previous work, both types of emotion indices attained generally good levels of internal consistency (alpha)—as measured both by index reliabilities (averaged across judges) and by interjudge reliabilities (Holbrook and Lehmann 1980). Global averages for the two reliability measures were .74 and .91 for Plutchik's Eight and .88 and .93 for Mehrabian's Three, respectively.

The issue of convergent validity was explored by a variety of procedures, including the use of canonical correlation analysis (CCA) across experiential descriptions to determine Stewart and Love's index of redundancy (1968) in predicting each full set of scales as criteria using the other full set as predictors (see the references in Holbrook and Moore 1982). Here, since each set of scales contained different numbers of items (twenty-four for Plutchik's Eight and twelve for Mehrabian's Three), we also used adjusted squared canonical correlations to compute redundancies (Johnston 1972). The resulting adjusted redundancies in from one- to four-dimensional CCA solutions suggest a tendency for Mehrabian's Three (containing twelve items) to explain more variance in Plutchik's Eight (containing twenty-four items) than vice versa, though this tendency declines as we extract more dimensions (that is, pairs of canonical variates): (1) 47.7 percent vs. 38.0 percent; (2) 53.6 percent vs. 42.1 percent; (3) 56.7 percent vs. 51.2 percent; and (4) 59.1 percent vs. 53.7 percent. For example, in two dimensions, Mehrabian's Three accounts for 53.6 percent of the variance in Plutchik's Eight, whereas the reverse prediction attains an explained variance of only 41.2 percent. In other words, Mehrabian's Three (the PAD framework) appears to contain more information than Plutchik's Eight (the psychoevolutionary model) even though it contains fewer separate items. This otherwise surprising result follows from the fact that several of Plutchik's emotions show strong intercorrelations. Indeed, the previously discussed work on advertising effects suggested that Plutchik's Eight could be adequately represented by a two-dimensional space (Holbrook and Westwood 1983).

These findings tentatively imply that, in spite of their less systematic theoretical underpinnings, Mehrabian's Three (the PAD framework) may turn out to be more useful than Plutchik's Eight in investigating emotional responses to the consumption experience. The PAD scheme carries the additional advantage of cohering with Osgood, Suci, and Tannenbaum's dimensions of meaning (1957)—evaluation, activity and potency—already familiar to most consumer researchers. Moreover, it focuses attention on pleasure or positive affect, the primary hedonic component of many intrinsically motivated consumption experiences and a key aspect of value, to which the discussion now turns.

Types of Value in the Consumption Experience

In a study conducted at the macrolevel but prior to my formulation of the value typology shown in table 2–1, Holbrook, Lehmann and O'Shaughnessy (1983) distinguished between "using versus choosing" and suggested that the experiences characterizing the former might underlie the reasons driving the latter. Two independent, randomly assigned samples of British housewives (both with $n = 41$) rated fifty-three products on *either* (1) the salience of various reasons for purchasing in each product category (habit, picking easiest, liking, economic, technical, social, for others, reputation); *or* (2) perceived usage characteristics (specific–concrete/symbolic–abstract), use functions (objective–tangible/subjective–intangible), and user benefits (rational–intellectual/irrational–emotional). MDS analysis of correlations among products across reasons generated the two-dimensional products space shown in figure 2–5 with a correlational fit between input and output proximities of $r = .91$ (and little improvement from adding more dimensions). Mean usage-characteristic, use-function, and user-benefit scores from the second sample were regressed on product-position coordinates to obtain three vectors with fits of $R = .62, .69,$ and $.66,$ respectively (shown as one arrow in figure 2–5 because of nearly perfect overlap). These vectors align closely with the vertical dimension of the space so as to suggest that products toward the top versus those toward the bottom are distinguished by their tendencies to contribute toward extrinsic versus intrinsic or utilitarian versus hedonic value. This finding parallels Batra's results (see chapter 3), for differences across products in the relative predominance of utilitarian versus hedonic components of affect (see also Ahtola 1985). By contrast, the horizontal dimension of the products' space in figure 2–5 defied clear interpretation, thereby indicating the need for further research into the nature of use value across consumption experiences.

Accordingly, Holbrook, Huber, and Stinerock (1985) have undertaken a study in which housewives rate sixty-four consumption experiences on their tendencies to provide the eight fundamental types of value distinguished in table 2–1 (efficiency, fun, quality, beauty, success, virtue, reputation, and faith). One-half of the randomly assigned subjects rate the products based on their own conceptions of the value terms, whereas a second randomly assigned group of informed judges attempts to use value definitions based on the conceptualization shown in the table. Discriminant analysis of the informed judges' ratings produces an MDA space containing consumption experiences. Value vectors based on the mean ratings of the naive subjects indicate the manner and extent to which the space captures the value judgments typical of ordinary linguistic usage in our subject population.

At the time of writing, the work by Holbrook, Huber, and Stinerock awaits completion. However, I mention it here as one potentially promising direction for research on types of value in the consumption experience at the macro level.

Conclusion

The recital of intuitive arguments that consumer emotions matter, the listing of anecdotal observations concerning emotional advertising, or the summarizing of ongoing research on emotional aspects of the consumption experience does not by itself demonstrate that consumers are emotional, that emotional commercials are effective, or that research on consumer emotions will bear big bunches of fruit. These phenomena do serve, however, to re-

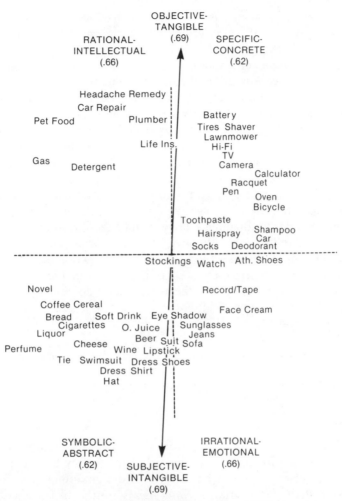

Source: Data from Holbrook, Lehmann, and O'Shaughnessy, 1983.

Figure 2–5. Usage-Characteristic, Use-Function, and User-Benefit Vectors in the MDS Products Space.

mind us that the role of consumer emotions constitutes a neglected but important aspect of the consumption experience, one still awaiting full exploration in the work of consumer researchers. This chapter has argued that emotions—and their place in consumption—help define our status as humans. Emotion appears to play a central role in the consumption experience (consciousness, emotion, and value), and its dynamic structure may be viewed as a system of four interrelated components (physiological responses, cognition, behavioral expression, and feelings). Its content may be classified in a number of ways, among which the most promising remains to be determined (though preliminary evidence seems to favor the PAD framework). Such typologies appear to possess heuristic value in describing intuitively plausible consumption phenomena. The importance of such phenomena receives anecdotal support from the claims made by advertising practitioners. These introspective illustrations and anecdotal observations combine with the aforementioned conceptual developments to serve as the basis for an ongoing stream of work devoted to studying emotional facets of the consumption experience, as indicated by three empirical examples.

Returning to *Mr. Blandings Builds His Dream House,* we recall that Cary Grant plays the part of a man who lets his heart rather than his head guide him in the purchase and construction of a new home. Throughout this film, Melvin Douglas (as Blandings' lawyer and friend) raises wise objections dictated by logic and reason. Ultimately, however, even Melvin must admit that Cary was right and that feelings may beneficially dominate thoughts in guiding some consumption experiences. In the end, with a touch of jealousy, Melvin realizes that in some things the heart should dominate the head, that he himself lacks those things, and that those may be the things most important to human happiness:

> You know, ever since this thing started, I've been the voice of doom about the whole project. . . . But when I look around at what you two have got here—well, I don't know—maybe there are some things you should buy with your heart and not your head. Maybe those are the things that really count.

On the same subject of architecture, an article by Goldberger (1980) described "a certain feeling . . . in the air" displayed by new design trends that stress the romantic, the whimsical, and the emotional aspects of the modern style. Perhaps "a certain feeling" is also in the air breathed by consumer researchers and will work soon to affect the architecture of our own discipline. Perhaps, instead of perpetuating the monumental edifice that we have built to the rational decision-making faculties of computerlike consuming automatons and instead of encouraging us to install still more theoretical ornaments and empirical curlicues on the superstructure of thought in consumer research, this new spirit may inspire us to tear away layers of glossy intellectual finish and empty academic wallboard to reveal the partly hidden emotional foundations that underlie the consumption experience, thereby acknowledging the role that this foundation of emotions plays in the lives of human consumers.

3
Affective Advertising: Role, Processes, and Measurement

Rajeev Batra
Columbia University

I n discussing the nature of cognitivism and its overwhelming reliance on a computerlike model of human information processing, Haugeland wrote:

> Perhaps the programmable computer is as shallow an analogy as the trainable pigeon—the conditional branch as sterile as the conditioned reflex . . . we should be as ready to follow up on partial failures (of cognitivism) as we are on partial successes. The clues could be anywhere. (1978, p. 225)

This volume testifies to the fact that, although computerlike models of consumer behavior have indeed been helpful and have taught us much, such models have also suffered from partial failures. Their inability to completely explain the processes and contingencies underlying advertising effects is one such area of disappointment. The clues indicated by these partial failures suggest a role for affect in models of advertising processing in which affect is not only the outcome of advertising processing but a determinant of such an outcome as well. Nonetheless, as will become readily apparent, the role of affective processes in this research area is clearly not to replace the role previously ascribed to more cognitive processing, but to form a vital supplement. The word *vital* is deliberate: modeling advertising processes while ignoring their affective components may well be like the staging of Hamlet without the ghost.

This chapter seeks to identify and build on clues about the role of affect suggested by previous research taking an exclusively cognitive perspective. The domain here is affect in advertising: its role, the processes and effects through which it works, and research on how such processes and effects can be measured. I try to be comprehensive but make no claims to being so; my

I gratefully acknowledge the contributions to this paper of Michael L. Ray, who collaborated in much of the research reported within. Morris Holbrook provided helpful comments on a preliminary draft, and the Marketing Science Institute provided funding for the studies discussed. This research was supported by the Columbia Business School's Faculty Research Fund. Address correspondence to Rajeev Batra, 512 Uris Hall, Graduate School of Business, Columbia University, New York, NY 10027.

own research, conducted with my collaborator Michael L. Ray, is mentioned more often than it deserves simply because it is typical of the research conducted by many and because it is the research with which I am most familiar.

In discussing affective advertising, I cover many individual source literatures, ranging from theories of preconscious attention to models of how neurochemicals and neurohormones shape our emotional states. In keeping with the objectives of this book, I will not be reluctant to stick my neck out and attempt to make connections where such theoretical integration promises to be fruitful. Books like this that not merely tolerate but indeed encourage the development of theory are rare indeed, and I would be wasting a valuable opportunity were I not to attempt such theory development.

There are some aspects of the role of affect in advertising that I do not review or develop here because they have recently been reviewed elsewhere (Ray and Batra 1983). A quick summary of these aspects is in order, however. Such research shows that people may pay greater attention to affective advertising because of the prominent role of affect in attention and perception. Once attended to, such ads may be processed more because—up to a point—arousal promotes information processing. Once processed, affective ad executions may lead to more positive judgments of the advertised message, since an affective frame of mind increases the likelihood of less critical processing. And such affective ad executions may be remembered better. Readers interested in these indirect effects of affective advertising should consult Ray and Batra (1983); here I primarily concern myself with the direct effects of advertising on brand attitudes, along with the processes preceding them.

The word *affect* is used interchangeably with *feelings* and *emotions*. As I discuss below, such use is often problematic and obscures important differences. For the moment, however, let us define *affect* as the sorts of feelings toward a stimulus that lead to relative preferences for that stimulus out of a class of similar stimuli. This initial definition means that (like Zajonc 1980) we are concerned here only with the kinds of affect involved in preferences, rather than the kinds that constitute emotions such as shame, guilt, and so forth. Those interested in a careful discussion of terminological alternatives should see chapter 2.

I begin by presenting an overview model of the role of affect in advertising that attempts a theoretical integration of current and prior research and identifies those areas where current research is supplementing earlier models of how advertising works. This model is hypothetical in that there are linkages shown that still require empirical support. I then sequentially discuss three areas of current research, that on affective responses, multicomponent brand attitudes, and the affective consequences of brand familiarity. Each of these sections discusses both theory and empirical research.

Role of Affect in Advertising: An Overview

Simply put, we are interested in studying the role of affect in advertising because we do not yet fully understand how advertising works. Consider, first, the inadequacies of traditional models of advertising effects.

Traditional Models

The Yale University research on persuasive communications (for example, Hovland, Janis, and Kelley 1953), the learning-hierarchy model of Colley (1961), the attitude-change model of Fishbein and Ajzen (1975), and the information-processing model of McGuire (1978), to mention just a few, all assume that advertising modifies brand preferences through the *comprehension of brand attribute assertions,* leading to changes in the stored beliefs one has about those brand attributes and the consequent effect on brand attitudes. McGuire, in fact, explicitly states that his model assumes that consumers approach advertising in a problem-solving mode, implying highly motivated processing of brand attribute assertions in the ad.

Such attribute processing, however, clearly does not occur in many ad reception situations. This is exemplified best by the processing of television commercials, the advertising medium most preferred by the top one hundred leading national advertisers (who typically spend over 60 percent of their advertising budgets through this medium). Their faith in television advertising is both surprising and foolish, because consumers rarely process television ads deeply (in the sense of thinking much about the attributes of the advertised product or service).

Evidence substantiating this statement is presented below, but common sense and intuitive support abound. After all, how much careful thought can consumers give to an advertiser's advocacy in a medium that has been derisively called "chewing gum for the eyes," "video valium," or worse, "the electronic nipple"? One researcher has gone so far as to argue that television viewing is predominantly a nonanalytic, right hemisphere activity since the right hemisphere of the brain does not get tired quickly and yet can serve a vigilance function should something important appear (Krugman 1980). Another has observational evidence that over 60 percent of all "looks" (uninterrupted viewing sequences) at television programming are but ten seconds long (Anderson 1983).

Such processing of television programming may indicate something very soporific about the nature of the medium itself, but the processing conditions for television advertising make the situation even worse. Television advertising is intrusive in the sense that most of it is not deliberately sought out by the consumer. The motivation to process such ads can therefore be expected to be low. The ads are usually short, most often but thirty seconds long, and embedded in program material; exposure to them is also, therefore, extremely rushed. Further, exposure to the ads occurs in a noisy, cluttered, strainful reception environment, where the content of the preceding and subsequent program material, not to mention the clutter of other ads, distracts from the processing of the currently screened ad. Finally, such ads offer material in a way that does not encourage ordered information retrieval or immediate information use.

Not surprisingly, given these processing conditions for the typical television ad (Wright 1981; Batra and Ray 1983a), consumers tend not to have many thoughts about the advocated brand and its attributes (Wright 1981, p. 276). These conditions may be somewhat less severe for the processing of print advertising, which gives consumers greater opportunity to process a message deeply (Krugman 1965; Wright 1974, 1981), and not all television advertising may be processed under the conditions depicted above, but the general point about the likelihood of thoughtful processing is clear.

Such thoughtful processing, however, is how traditional models assume advertising works. It is therefore not uncommon for some persuasion researchers to believe that such advertising can have little impact, and that the billions of dollars spent on it are largely wasted (for example, McGuire 1969, p. 227).

Let us assume, however, that the advertisers who continue to pump over $15 billion a year into television advertising know something we do not, and that it is not they who are mistaken; rather it is these traditional theories of how advertising works that are. This takes us, then, to the newer models of advertising effects.

Newer Models

Advertising does work in ways other than attribute processing, and there are models that specify minimal amounts of attribute processing. However, these models are themselves far from complete.

For example, following Krugman's initial characterization (1965) of most television advertising as being less involving, research showed that the hierarchy of effects typically found in such television advertising is one where messages tend to produce awareness-based behavioral change that precedes, rather than follows, changes in attitudes (Ray et al. 1973). Such low-involvement advertising was shown to work with a sequence of *effects* different from those assumed by the traditional models, where messages produced attitude change (after initial cognitive attribute learning changes), which then led to behavioral consequences.

In such a model, low-involvement advertising processing did not work by changing the attribute beliefs underlying brand attitudes. Instead, it propelled buying action by increasing awareness of the advertised brand, with such use then changing attitudes toward the purchased brand.

Within this low-involvement hierarchy, however, although the effects of behavior on attitude are readily interpretable in terms of attribution (Kelley 1967) and self-perception (Bem 1965) mechanisms, the earlier process link—that of advertising (awareness) inducing behavioral change—has not been adequately developed. Is affect entirely missing here?

One reason why such affect may not be missing is the mere-exposure effect researched in social psychology (Zajonc 1968). Research has long shown that repeated exposure to a stimulus does lead to the creation of a conditioned affect toward the repeated stimulus, provided some conditions are met (Harrison 1977; Sawyer 1981).

Another indication that affect is not entirely absent from this low-involvement hierarchy comes from recent research on two alternative routes to attitude change. (The section below discusses at length the relationship between affect and attitudes. For the moment, attitudes are defined as preference predispositions having both cognitive and affective sources.) Such contemporary two-route research suggests that changes in affect toward the advertised brand are not absent in low-involvement processing prior to purchase. Such changes in affect, however, are derived from sources other than the perceived value of desired brand attributes, as believed to be possessed by the advertised brand (the route of the traditional models).

Recent studies indicate that attitude toward the advertising execution itself leads to changes in brand attitudes, in addition to those caused directly by message arguments (Mitchell and Olson 1981; Gorn 1982). Similarly, research in social psychology has developed models of attitude change processes called *heuristic* and *peripheral,* to reference just two (Chaiken 1980; Cialdini, Petty, and Cacioppo 1981). Most of these models show that such attitude-change processes involve limited elaboration of message arguments, with persuasive effects stemming instead from such execution cues as source credibility, the number of arguments in the message (rather than their quality), source likability, and so forth.

Some of these studies, in fact, demonstrate clear interactions between involvement levels and attitude-change route: attitude-change attempts that use superior attribute arguments are more successful in high-involvement situations than in low-involvement ones, with the opposite result holding for source (message execution) cues (Chaiken 1980; Petty, Cacioppo, and Goldman 1981; Gorn 1982; Lutz, MacKenzie, and Belch 1983; Batra and Ray 1984a).

Parenthetically, let me note that the execution cues studied by social psychological research on the two routes to attitude change differ across studies, encompassing source credibility, source likability, and the number of arguments in the message. Indeed, some cues such as the number of arguments in the message have been used as the manipulation of the systematic route in one study (Chaiken 1980) and of the peripheral route in another (Petty, Cacioppo, and Goldman 1981).

For research into how affective advertising works, I suggest, the most relevant effects from this literature are those obtained through the likability of the execution. Although the credibility results apply primarily only to ads using testimonials, most affective or emotional ads rely on more common elements such as music, humor, and vignettes to create a warm and likable feeling, so that the source likability results are relevant to them (and to ads using attractive testimonial sources). In addition, whereas the literature on source credibility shows that credibility effects occur through cognitive response mechanisms (for example, Cook 1969; Sternthal, Dholakia, and Leavitt 1978), the research comparing source credibility and source attractiveness shows that attractiveness (likability) effects appear to be more involuntary and less cognitive in that they occur whether the source is identified at the beginning of the message or not (Mills and Harvey 1972; Norman 1976). Thus attractiveness effects would seem more applicable to research on affective advertising. For these reasons, and because the relevant research on *attitude toward the ad* (Aad) also stresses reactions of liking or disliking the ad, the results on source likability (for example, Chaiken 1980) are the ones I imply when I refer below to the heuristic or peripheral route.

An Integrative Model

By demonstrating that the attitudinal effects of source/execution likability are significant only under low levels of motivational involvement (Chaiken 1980; Gorn 1982), recent studies show that affect (liking for the source) *is* present in inducing attitude change toward the stimulus object or issue in low-involvement situations. This differs from earlier hierarchy research, which argued that purchase intentions in low-involvement situations were exclusively awareness driven (for example, Ray et al. 1973) and that ads had no effect on brand attitudes prior to changes in purchase intentions. The likability results also show, however, that the *source* of affect toward the brand may be different in high- and low-involvement situations. In high-involvement situations, it is the quality of message arguments that (through usual expectancy-value multiattribute mechanisms) drives (affective) attitude change; in low-involvement situations, the likability of the message execution itself can change attitudes toward the object or issue in the message.

Such likability research is obviously very useful, but it is not quite complete as a model of a route of attitude change, if by a route we mean not just an input–output link but also the process steps in between. This statement is better understood by reference to the cognitive response paradigm, which provides the process understanding for the thoughtful processing advertising models discussed above and for the central/systematic routes. In this paradigm, ads work by *first* inducing cognitive responses in the mind of the receiver, receiver-generated responses to message arguments and execution credibility; these responses *then* modify attitudes and, through them, behavioral intentions (Greenwald 1968; Wright 1973).

Even though the likability route lacks an analogous process component just yet, it does help us understand a clue (to use Haugeland's term above) from a partial failure of the cognitive response paradigm. Although that paradigm argues that few such cognitive responses are produced in low-involvement processing, thus leading to minimal attitude change, it does not address the question of what other—if any—mediating responses occur in such low-involvement situations.

Further, studies using cognitive responses have demonstrated that the three most commonly studied cognitive responses—support arguments, counter arguments, and source derogations—do not explain as much attitudinal variance in low-involvement attitude change situations as they do in high-involvement ones (Petty and Cacioppo 1979; Wright 1973). Such results lead one to suspect that some important mediating processes may be missing from the set of cognitive responses usually analyzed.

Since the referenced research on Aad and the two routes suggests that execution cues—especially (in the advertising context) execution likability—are major determinants of attitudes in such low-involvement situations, then the responses mediating these Aad/likability effects could be the responses missing from conventional cognitive response studies. I discuss evidence bearing on this below; for the moment, let me simply note the need to model such affective responses for the likability route.

Research on the mediating responses underlying the likability/Aad route could yield a model in which not only are there different *sources* of affect in high- and low-involvement situations, but also one in which these sources act through different kinds of mediating responses. However, in expanding the steps in the two-routes models, I could go even further by suggesting that these two kinds of sources of affect not only act *through* different kinds of mediating responses but also act *on* different kinds of attitudinal affect.

A recent stream of research, not yet integrated into models of advertising effects or into the two-routes literature, suggests that brand attitudes are not unidimensional but have two components: an affective one and a cognitive one (for example, Bagozzi and Burnkrant 1979; Bagozzi et al. 1979; Bagozzi 1981). If brand attitudes are modified through two different sources of affect—brand attributes and ad execution likability—it may be that these two sources modify the two attitudinal components differently. How this could occur is discussed at length later in this chapter.

An expanded model would extend the two-routes literature and integrate it with the model on two attitude components, but the expanded model would still not model the effects of brand awareness and familiarity high-lighted in the hierarchy-of-effects models of advertising response. To do this, one could next hypothesize that if brand familiarity does lead to increased affect toward the brand through mere-exposure effects, this effect should occur more through that attitudinal component that is differentially sensitive to ad execution influences, since both ad execution and mere-exposure influences represent classical conditioning mechanisms. (In the case of mere-exposure influences, although the creation of affect toward the ad due to exposure frequency is not based on classical conditioning but on other two-factor mechanisms involving novelty and tedium [see Harrison 1977; Sawyer 1981], the transfer of affect from the ad to the brand would be based on such conditioning.)

If execution likability is most important in influencing brand attitudes in low-involvement situations as shown in the two-routes research, then the attitudinal component more affected by this source should more strongly influence purchase intentions in low-involvement situations than the other attitudinal component. These hypotheses are embodied in the percentage-contribution model presented by Batra and Ray (1984a) in which the effects of the two attitude components on purchase intentions are expected to vary systematically with the level of involvement. (A similar model is presented by Lutz, MacKenzie, and Belch, 1983.)

This hypothesized integrated model of advertising processes and effects suggests not only that attitude change can stem from (broadly speaking) two different *sources* of affect but also that these two sources act *through* different mediating responses and *on two different components* of brand attitudes. There do seem to be two routes to attitude change. There probably is more to these routes, however, than just different sources of affect.

Further, in examining their involvement-mediated impact on purchase intentions, the percentage-contribution model also integrates these two routes with brand familiarity. It therefore brings together the hierarchy-of-effects and two-routes models, each of which is otherwise incomplete.

This integrative, overview model of advertising processes and effects works as follows. The vector of advertising influences includes message arguments, execution likability, and exposure frequency. These in turn create cognitive responses, affective responses, and brand familiarity, respectively. These three mediating processes then all act on two different components of brand attitudes, which in turn influence purchase intentions.

However, the relative importance of each route can be strong or weak, depending on the level of message response involvement in the situation. (Such involvement, discussed below, will itself be a function of the receiver's motivation, ability, and opportunity to process the ad in an attribute-based fashion.) In particular, the high-involvement route primarily consists of message arguments evoking cognitive responses that change cognitive attitudes and then purchase intentions. The low-involvement route, however, has ex- ecution likability generating affective responses that influence the affective attitudinal component and then purchase intentions. Additionally, in this low-involvement scenario, repetition frequency generates brand familiarity, which influences purchase intentions both directly (through salience mech- anisms) and indirectly (through mere-exposure influences on the affective attitudinal component). For a schematic representation, see Batra and Ray (1984a).

This, then, is the grand model suggested by previous and current re- search, integrating the cognitive and affective ways in which advertising seems to work. Note that this is still a hypothetical model in that certain linkages, especially those involving the two attitude components, still require empirical verification. Note also that this model ignores the Aad construct, restricting itself to effects on brand attitudes only. (If included, the Aad construct would be affected by both attribute and affective processing and would influence both attitude components; see Batra and Ray, 1984a, and Lutz, MacKenzie, and Belch, 1983.)

I turn now from this overview to a discussion of selected elements: af- fective responses, the two attitude components, and the familiarity–affect link.

Affective Responses

As researchers into advertising processes and effects are well aware, the cognitive response paradigm is perhaps the most frequently used approach to modeling consumer responses to advertising. Since its development by Greenwald (1968) and Wright (1973), the idea that consumer acceptance of advertising depends much more on cues generated by the message receiver than on the receiver's learning of the content in the ad has won wide accep- tance. In contrast with the earlier Yale paradigm (for example, Hovland, Janis, and Kelley 1953) of Ostrom (1981), the consumer response paradigm (1) focuses on the message receiver's production tasks, not on inferential capabilities; (2) is multivariate in nature, simultaneously considering differ- ent responses; (3) considers not just quantitative indicators but the qualita- tive characteristics of different responses; and (4) stresses long-term memory storage and retrieval, not just temporary information-based reactions.

Not surprisingly, this paradigm has since become very popular; recent examples include the work of Belch (1982) and Toy (1982) to mention just a few. Researchers in marketing and social psychology have used cognitive responses as independent, moderating, or dependent variables in various persuasion research contexts, including repetition effects (for example, Ca- cioppo and Petty 1979b; Calder and Sternthal 1980), the effects of issue involvement on message processing (Petty and Cacioppo 1979), and distraction effects (Petty, Wells and Brock 1976), among many others. Reviews of such research can be found in Wright (1980) and Petty, Ostrom, and Brock (1981).

Although the number of contexts in which such cognitive responses have been studied has grown, the number of responses studied still tends to remain the same as that studied by Wright (1973): support arguments, counter arguments, and source derogations. However, there are exceptions. Beaber (1975) introduced the category of simple affirmations and disaffirmations, Cacioppo and Petty (1979b) used neutral, irrelevant thoughts, and Belch and Lutz (1982) introduced source bolstering and repetition-related thoughts.

Given the spate of research suggesting that low-involvement attitude change processes rely primarily on execution cues rather than message arguments, researchers have now begun to investigate the idea that the mediating responses generated by such execution cues are execution or communicator related, rather than responses to message arguments (such as support and counter arguments). Research in this vein includes the coding schemes adopted by Chaiken (1980), Petty and Cacioppo (1979), and Lutz, MacKenzie, and Belch (1983). Typically, such research models support as well as counter arguments as the mediators of the central route of attitude change—that using message arguments—and communicator–execution-related thoughts (positive and negative) as the mediators of Aad and the heuristic–peripheral route.

Such research is valuable and has helped give source derogations and source-bolstering thoughts the attention they deserve. In an advertising context, however, even more complicated classification schemes are likely to be required because ads are not pallid statements of positions on issues, such as those studied in most social psychological research but instead are extremely complex messages that combine attribute statements with music, humor, affectionate vignettes, story elements, role portrayals, and the like. As a consequence, the vector of consumer responses to real commercials is far more complex than typically studied; such complexity is apparent in ad agency research on viewer responses to television advertising (for example, Wells, Leavitt, and McConville 1971; Schlinger 1979).

I believe that consumer responses to ad executions go beyond an evaluative reaction toward the commercial that is evoked by message execution style (such as positive reactions typically coded as source-bolstering thoughts and negative reactions coded as source-derogation or source-discounting thoughts). Ads are not merely liked or disliked; they also generate moods and make us feel a certain way. Affective ads can make us happy, sad, or warm in addition to making us admire and like them. The moods and feelings they evoke are internal states not necessarily directed toward the ad. To use a distinction often made by theorists on emotion (for example, Clore and Ortony 1983), moods and feelings are state emotions, whereas thoughts and feelings toward the ad are object oriented and need to be coded separately.

It thus seems reasonable to study moods and feelings evoked by ads in addition to the commonly studied categories of source bolstering and source discounting. However, we are faced with major problems in developing a coding scheme for use in the classification of such ad-evoked moods and feelings. The literature on emotional categories is large (for example, Plutchik 1962; Nowlis 1965; Davitz 1969; Izard 1977; Pribram 1980; Russell 1980), and it is impossible to find universal agreement on a set of basic emotional dimensions. Nowlis, for example, based on research using the Mood Adjective Check List, found about twelve basic emotional unipolar dimensions, whereas Russell argued that only two bipolar dimensions exist. The task is made more difficult because many of the emotional categories such as egotism, shame, and guilt identified in the literature have little to do with advertising, though they could, of course, emerge in certain contexts.

My interpretation of this literature is available in Batra and Ray (1984b), and interested readers should also see the typologies discussed by Holbrook (chapter 2) and by Holbrook and O'Shaughnessy (1984). Our analysis of this literature, however, led us to work with four positive dimensions of affective response to commercials that we thought parsimoniously represented the typologies and factor analytic results of earlier research.

1. Feelings of an upbeat mood evoked by music, humor, and similar ad elements. Following the moods literature (Nowlis 1965), this dimension has been variously called *surgency, elation, vigor,* or *activation.* We use the acronym SEVA to code such responses.

2. Feelings of quiet and relaxed pleasantness. Again, following the moods literature, we call this dimension *deactivation.* Wells, Leavitt, and McConville (1971) detected a similar dimension in feelings evoked by cosmetics commercials and called it *sensuousness.*

3. Feelings of heartwarming, moving tenderness. Using the term used for this dimension in the moods literature, we call this dimension *social affection.*

4. Feelings of motivational, appetitive desire to buy or consume the advertised brand or category. Such feelings are evoked primarily by food ads, especially when the ad sells the product through its *sizzle.* Since such feelings relate to the advertised product, we combined them with support arguments for the purposes of subsequent analysis.

Other classification schemes for affective responses are possible (for example, Holbrook and Westwood 1983; Stout and Leckenby 1984), but this is the one we believe is most representative and parsimonious. Note that these four dimensions are in addition to the commonly studied ones of support and counter arguments, source derogations and bolstering, and neutral and irrelevant thoughts. A summary of the coding scheme is presented in table 3–1.

To determine whether these categories of affective responses evoked in consumers by likable ad executions had any effect at all on brand attitudes, after coding categories of source bolstering and source derogation were taken into account, we selected forty ads (real, thirty-second, television commercials) for study. Since we wanted to investigate the relative influence of such affective responses on brand attitudes and intentions under different types of advertising situations, especially situations varying on dimensions of involvement, we chose these ads from ten product categories, five each from (pretested) high- and low-involvement product categories. We then varied the extent to which the respondent had prior knowledge and use experience with the brand in the ad by using two different brands per product category. Finally, for each brand we selected two different ad executions, one apparently affective and the other rational.

These forty ads thus comprised five replications of a 2 × 2 × 2 design, varying product category involvement, brand use, and ad execution style. Since it seemed difficult to get each respondent to view the eight ads implied

Table 3–1
Cognitive/Affective Response Categories

Name	Description
Support arguments	Reasoned/simple affirmations of message arguments
Counter arguments	Reasoned/simple disaffirmations
Execution discounting	Challenges to execution credibility, other execution derogation
Execution bolstering	Positive references to elements, style, realism, and so forth
Feelings of surgency, elation, vigor, and activation (SEVA)	Upbeat feelings from music, humor, other elements
Feelings of deactivation	Feelings of ad being soothing, relaxing, pleasant
Feelings of social affection	Ad felt to be warm, touching, and so forth
Distractor thoughts	Ad-evoked thoughts irrelevant to message (for example, of surprise, curiosity about ad elements, of other ads)
Other	Ad content playback, subsequently generated thoughts

by a full-factorial design, we used a half-factorial design and had each respondent view four ads. For these ads, the respondents gave us retrospective verbal protocols yielding cognitive and affective response data as well as data on brand attitudes, intentions, and so forth.

Multiple regression analyses indicated that the affective response category of social affection did appear to influence brand attitudes overall in equations that also included source bolstering and derogation, support and counter arguments, and so forth. Furthermore, when the sample was split into two subsamples (based on each respondent's individual level of product category involvement for each ad shown using actual levels and not those assumed based on the pretest), the regressions showed that, in the low-involvement sample, feelings of surgency, elation, vigor, and activation became significant predictors of brand attitudes and intentions in addition to the already mentioned social affection affective response category.

These results suggest that the feelings of social affection are somehow more intense than those of SEVA, which is a lighter mood possessing attitudinal consequence only in low-involvement conditions. It is also interesting to note that feelings of deactivation do not, in the aggregate, appear to influence either brand attitudes or intentions; Wells, Leavitt, and McConville (1971) found that such feelings (which they called *sensuousness*) lowered rather than raised day-after recall.

Finally, while on the subject of this study, I should add another interesting result: model comparison tests examining the statistical significance of the incremental variance explained by these three affective response categories (compared to models using the other five response categories only) found these responses added significantly to explained variance only in the low-involvement subsamples of the data. Without these three affective response categories, the attitudinal variance explained by other (traditional) categories was higher in the high-involvement samples than in the low, a result that replicates the findings of Petty and Cacioppo (1979) and Wright (1973); with these three categories, it was actually higher in the low-involvement sample than in the high.

Although these results provide no direct evidence that these affective responses mediate the effects of ad execution likability, they do suggest that such moods and feelings represent mediators of affective advertising impact, in addition to the source-bolstering and discounting thoughts researchers have usually studied. Such a suggestion is supported by analyses of covariance results that examined alternative possible causal sequences; such analyses indicated that these affective responses first influence attitude toward the ad, then brand attitudes, and finally purchase intentions (see Batra and Ray 1984b).

The existence of these affective responses, however, also yields the added bonus of better understanding the meaning of involvement in an advertising context. As argued in the overview model above, the level of involvement in the advertising situation is the major variable in the contingency approach suggested here.

Message Response Involvement

Typically, involvement is considered a motivational, predispositional construct, and research demonstrating the interaction of involvement with attitudinal route has used the term in this sense. Experimental manipulations of involvement have reflected this by being ones in which the personal consequence of the issue, to the respondent, are varied (for example, Petty and Cacioppo 1979b). Since such manipulations have produced the referenced interactions with attitudinal route, this motivational involvement is widely considered to be the mediating variable of interest.

A case can be made on theoretical grounds, however, that—in the context of variables mediating the way in which advertising works—it is inappropriate to consider only this motivational variable as the involvement construct of interest. This theoretical case uses two main arguments.

First, Petty and Cacioppo (1979b) demonstrated that the mechanism mediating the effects of high issue involvement on attitudinal route is the *amount* of cognitive responses the respondent produces about the advocated message response position. High motivation to respond increases the number of cognitive responses produced. For a strong argument message, these are predominantly support arguments, whereas for a weak argument message they are largely counter arguments. Such high motivation to respond thus increases the impact of argument strength on message acceptance, which otherwise has a weak influence.

We thus have a situation where variable X (motivational involvement) moderates variable Z (attitude change) through the mechanism of variable Y (cognitive response production). The theoretical importance given to X is not threatened if X and Y are perfectly correlated, with X being a necessary and sufficient condition for Y. In such a case, we have a discriminant validity problem about the boundaries between X and Y. If, however, Y is also produced by a variety of other variables, such that Z is likely to follow with Y from antecedents other than X, then X is potentially of only secondary importance. This is known as the "intervening variables problem" (Ellsworth 1977, pp. 614–615).

We do have evidence—and this is the second argument in the theoretical case—that the amount of cognitive response production (Y above) is, in fact, a function of more than just the motivational antecedent (X). The respondent's ability and opportunity to respond to the message (in an attribute-based fashion) are also important antecedents.

The ability factor encompasses respondent knowledge and prior-use experience (see Roberts and Maccoby 1973), whereas the opportunity factor includes the number of arguments in the message (for example, Calder, Insko, and Yandell 1974) and media mode (Krugman 1965; Wright 1974, 1975, 1981). This three-antecedents view of cognitive response production is now standard in the cognitive response literature (for example, Wright 1975; Petty 1981).

If the moderating effects of interest, then, are caused by cognitive response production and if such response production is a function of three antecedents acting in concert, then it seems clearly inappropriate to treat one of these three antecedents of response production (the motivation to respond) as the involvement construct of interest. It seems to make more theoretical sense to make the response process itself the involvement construct of interest, with the motivation, ability, and opportunity to respond the antecedent factors of interest and the attitudinal route the consequence of relevance. Following earlier suggestions (Batra and Ray 1983b), the response process itself is called *message response involvement*. For details on this construct and its measures, see Batra (1984a), who also provides evidence that the moderating effects shown by the motivation antecedent extend to the ability and (to some extent) the opportunity antecedent.

Conceptually and nomologically, greater levels of such message response involvement should imply greater effort (compare Houston and Rothschild 1977; Greenwald and Leavitt 1984). It follows that if one were to attempt an operational index of the level of message response involvement in terms of some combination of the different kinds of mediating responses ads can evoke, then the responses in the index should require greater effort to generate.

Evidence exists not only that the production of support and counter arguments requires high levels of motivation (Petty and Cacioppo 1979b) and that such motivation induces greater self-reported respondent effort (Chaiken 1980) but also that affective responses require low-effort levels to create. Most of this evidence is indirect and comes from research showing emotions and moods to be contagious and the transfer of such moods and emotions as involuntary. Reviews of such literature are available in Izard (1977, pp. 106–107) and Zajonc (1980). Studies by Schachter (1971) and Nowlis and Nowlis (1956) show that in the presence of euphoric (angry) actors we tend to become euphoric (angry) and that the majority mood of a social group affects the mood of all its members. In Izard's words, "emotion is catching" (1977, p. 106), and according to Zajonc "affective reactions . . . occur without effort" (1980, p. 156). Both Zajonc (1980) and Leventhal (1980, p. 193) argue that emotional and mood changes precede complex cognitive reasoning.

It therefore seems reasonable to argue that if message processing tends to consist primarily of relatively effortless affective responses, then that viewing episode should be considered less involving than one in which a large number of support or counter arguments are generated. This differential-effort criterion supports the suggested operationalization of message response involvement in terms of the number (or proportion) of support or counter arguments generated. For further discussion and evidence regarding this and other nomological criteria, see Batra (1984a).

To sum up, when the motivation, ability, and opportunity to produce support and counter arguments is high, attitude change occurs primarily through the central route presented in the overview model above. When such antecedents are low—in Petty and Cacioppo's terms (1979b), when the "elaboration likelihood" is low—such support and counter argumentation will not occur, and affective responses generated by a likable ad execution will be the major determinants of attitude change. Batra (1984a) presents evidence suggesting the production of support and counter arguments overrides the influence of affective responses generated on attitudes and purchase intentions, although measurement difficulties make those results suggestive rather than conclusive. We turn now to the second building block of the overview model: the two components of brand attitudes.

Two Components of Attitudes

The second way current conceptions of affect may be incorporated into models of how advertising works is the idea that brand attitudes have two distinct, empirically distinguishable components. The models of attitude structure most frequently used today are the unidimensional models of Fishbein and Ajzen (1975) or variants thereof. These models argue that attitudes consist only of affect, with such affect being derived from constituent attribute beliefs evaluated in an expectancy-value fashion (that is, having an exclusively cognitive origin) and leading to action tendencies. Such a unidimensional conception relies heavily on the identification by Osgood, Suci, and Tannenbaum (1957) of a primary evaluative dimension to concept ratings and on tests of construct validity using the Campbell and Fiske (1959) criteria by Ostrom (1969) and Kothandapani (1971).

Such unidimensional conceptions reject alternative multicomponent views of attitude structure, which hold that attitudes *simultaneously* consist of cognitive, affective, and conative elements (for example, Katz and Stotland

1959, Rosenberg and Hovland 1960). Triandis (1971, 1977) theorized that behavioral intentions are not a function of a unidimensional attitude construct but of expectations of consequences (measured on good–bad and valuable–harmful scales) and affect (measured on scales of enjoyable, interesting, and pleasant).

Empirical evidence supporting multicomponent conceptions can be traced back almost thirty years; Osgood, Suci, and Tannenbaum (1957, pp. 62, 70, 71) identified clusters of scales within their attitudinal evaluative dimension that differentiated between types of goodness. Ten years later, Komorita and Bass (1967) factor analyzed student attitudes to various issues and found clear evidence for factors called *functionally evaluative, affective–emotional,* and *moral–ethical.* More recently, studies by Bagozzi and colleagues (Bagozzi 1978, 1981; Bagozzi and Burnkrant 1979; Bagozzi et al. 1979) have found evidence for the convergent and discriminant validity of a two-component model of attitudes, using confirmatory factor analysis techniques. Their analysis suggests that attitudes have an affective and a (multidimensional) cognitive component, both leading to behavioral intentions.

Despite such theory and evidence, most studies of attitude formation and change continue to follow the Fishbein–Ajzen paradigm using a unidimensional attitude construct—even studies investigating two different routes to attitude change. I believe the evidence at hand calls for researchers to model and measure the two components separately, to make possible tests of the hypothesis that the two routes work on two different components. Tests of such a hypothesis will then give the attitude-component literature the nomological network it has so far not really developed and (potentially) greatly enrich our understanding of how advertising works and how its effects can be assessed.

Before examining the role of the two routes in influencing the two components, however, we need a better understanding of what they are and how they are formed.

The Two Components: Characteristics

I hypothesize that one attitude component, here called *utilitarian affect,* would be affect toward the brand based on an appraisal of the brand's instrumentality in delivering constituent attributes. The other, here called *hedonic affect,* would be an approach–avoidance feeling—a *hedonic tone*—toward the brand as a unified entity.

Before I proceed further, a word on terminology. The conceptualizations presented here of *utilitarian affect* and *hedonic affect* resemble the cognitive and affective distinctions by Bagozzi and colleagues (Bagozzi 1981; Bagozzi and Burnkrant 1979; Bagozzi et al. 1979). Their terminology is not used since a case could be made that *both* components are, in an information-processing sense, cognitive. As Lazarus (1982) and Watts (1983) pointed out in their responses to Zajonc (1980), even basic emotional responses require some primitive cognitive operations; other theorists on emotion, such as Clore and Ortony (1983), make the case that emotional labeling has to be an act involving a cognitive situation appraisal. Further, even if affective reactions are preconscious, the domain of cognitive science clearly includes preconscious operations, such as those involved in visual pattern recognition and the production of language. For discussion on whether the domain of cognitivism includes moods and emotions, see the debate between Haugeland (1978) and Pylyshyn (1980).

Terminological quibbling aside, what is important are the differences conceptualized between the two components. Both could, in some abstract sense, be considered brand attributes, one physical and the other psychological or inferential. Myers and Shocker (1981), for example, classify brand attributes into physical characteristics, benefits, and imagery when discussing the different kinds of scaling techniques appropriate for each. However, such abstraction would obscure important differences in what causes them, their situational influences on purchase intentions, how long they last, and so forth.

The utilitarian component, as conceptualized here, would be based on physical brand attributes and constructed in a bottom up fashion. This attitude component would thus be formed on the basis of a person's expectancy-value computations involving the object's attributes and would be formed in a manner similar to the current Fishbein–Ajzen formulation, as operationalized through the *adequacy importance* versions currently used in marketing (compare Cohen, Fishbein, and Ahtola 1972; Mazis, Ahtola, and Klippel 1975).

The hedonic component, on the other hand, would be created by phenomena other than the valuation placed on the brand's attributes—phenomena such as the conditioning of affect from likable ad executions (Mitchell and Olson 1981; Gorn 1982), from affect developed from ad frequency mere-exposure effects (Zajonc 1968; Harrison 1977; Sawyer 1981), from individual-specific nonutilitarian consumption and use effects (Hirschman and Holbrook 1982), from affective reactions to packaging, and would be brand specific (Srinivasan 1979) instead of being based on constituent attributes. Some aspects of such hedonic attitudinal affect presumably involve a gestalt, configural appraisal of the stimulus object, going beyond the assessment of the utility contributed by each individual attribute.

Note, though, that in this conceptualization not all ad-created psychological attributes would create hedonic affect. A *delivers status* image, for example, is considered here to be an attribute used in the computation of utilitarian affect. Hedonic affect specifically refers to a feeling that a brand is, in some sense, friendly, pleasant, and warm. As *Time* magazine pointed out (July 11, 1983), IBM's Charlie Chaplin Tramp ad campaign for its personal computer had the effect of giving the company, previously seen as efficient and reliable but also cold and aloof, a human face, thus creating a friendlier image for the company and its products. It is in this sense that hedonic affect is conceptualized here.

Such a distinction—between an evaluative affect based on constituent properties of the stimulus (or delivered outcomes other than a direct enjoyable/warm feeling) and a *pure* affect that is the primary approach–avoidance reaction of the subject to the stimulus—is made most eloquently by Zajonc (1980). In a similar vein, Holbrook and Hirschman (1982; Hirschman and Holbrook 1982) emphasize the multisensory, emotive, and often fantasy-based and symbolic experiences that accompany consumption, pointing out that these hedonic aspects are ignored by the usual multiattribute derivation of affect.

Decomposability

Since the hedonic component is conceptualized as being configural, brand specific, and not based on component attributes, it is also hypothesized as being subsequently nondecomposable into component attributes. The origin of the utilitarian component, on the other hand, implies greater decomposability into component attribute sources in later attitude change episodes.

Such differential decomposability could have the following interesting implication. If the initial attitude toward a brand is based on nondecomposable hedonic affect, fewer individual beliefs should then be available (Tversky and Kahneman 1973) for change in subsequent attitude-change episodes, and such attitudes subsequently may be very difficult to change through belief-based attitude change attempts. This may help explain the well-known perseverance effects of initial attitudes in certain experiments (Ross, Lepper, and Hubbard 1975) and may suggest strategies through which brands may inoculate their attitude franchises from competitive attacks (Batra and Ray 1983a). The current frustration among Democrats in their inability to attack President Reagan on the issues—and their oft-quoted complaint that he is a "Teflon President," one from whom all attacks seem to bounce off—seems to prove this point if you believe the president's appeal is based on his friendly personality and not his specific policies. As Abelson et al. (1982) have shown, political voting preferences also are based on a pure affective dimension, in addition to trait beliefs and judgments.

Note, however, that although under this perspective hedonic affect would be subsequently nondecomposable, not all nondecomposable affect existing toward a brand would be formed through the sources here attributed to that component. One could form an attribute-based utilitarian affect, use a brand, retain an overall affect, but forget the origin of such affect. The crucial point here is that although nondecomposable affect could have (originally) decomposable sources, affect created through a brand-specific route will *never* be decomposable.

Formation, Effort, and Permanence

In a single-exposure advertising context, the hedonic component would be based partly on the respondent's liking for ad *execution* elements, whereas the utilitarian component would be based on the respondent's appraisal of the *arguments* in the ad about the attributes of the product being advertised. Earlier, I argued that the two-routes literature could be expanded by positing that, although message arguments in the ad evoke cognitive responses of support and counter argumentation, ad execution likability evokes affective responses characterized by certain moods and feelings. I can now extend that even further and suggest that the evoked cognitive responses primarily influence the utilitarian attitude component, whereas the affective responses primarily influence the hedonic component.

It was also pointed out above, however, that moods and emotions are contagious and that affective reactions are relatively effortless. The hedonic attitude component, one would therefore expect, should be relatively more *effortless* to form (*primary,* to use Zajonc's term [1980]). It may, however, be more difficult to verbalize. In contrast, the utilitarian component would seem to require, in its formation, greater processing effort, making the creation of such utilitarian affect more voluntary. If hedonic affect is more involuntary and easier to form, one would expect it, rather than the utilitarian one, to be the primary influence on purchase intentions in situations in which the consumer does not process ads deeply. I have therefore suggested elsewhere (Batra and Ray 1984a) that the two components influence purchase intentions differently, depending on the degree of involvement with which the ad was processed. The percentage contribution for the utilitarian component should be greater in high-involvement situations; opposite predictions hold for the hedonic component. (Lutz, MacKenzie, and Belch, 1983, test a similar hypothesis, although theirs deals with a less effortful Aad dimension rather than a hedonic component of brand attitudes.)

If it is true that the utilitarian component requires more processing effort to form, then it should also be true that intense processing leads to a deeper memory trace (compare Craik and Lockhart 1972). This, in turn, should show greater temporal stability than the more easily formed hedonic component, which should be more transient. Thus the hedonic component should show greater decay over time compared to the utilitarian component. (Note that I am talking here of affect created prior to purchase and use.) Chaiken (1980) did, in fact, find that the decay rate of attitude change created by a many-arguments source was lower than that for attitude change created by source likability. She did not, however, measure the differential decay of the two attitude components separately or their possibly differential relationship to the two kinds of message sources.

I have therefore arrived at a fairly elaborate set of interlocking hypotheses about what the two attitude components represent, how they are formed, and what they lead (or fail to lead) to. As a historical note, it may be that the distinction between these two components was not totally lost on Fishbein and Ajzen, who nonetheless chose to ignore it for empirical reasons. In a footnote in their book, they wrote:

> The terms "affect" and "evaluation" are used synonymously throughout this book. Although it might be argued that there is a difference between a person's judgment that an object makes him feel good and his evaluation that the object is good, there is little evidence to suggest that a reliable empirical distinction between these two variables can be made. (1975, p. 11, footnote 2)

It is important that their objection to such a two-component conceptualization is one of measurement, not theory. As mentioned, Bagozzi (1981 and earlier) demonstrated that such an empirical distinction can be made, after measurement error is explicitly modeled. Measurement is not quite a settled issue, however, nor is the theory, as the following results from two recent studies (Batra 1984b; Batra and Ray 1984a) suggest.

Issues of Measurement and Theory

Previous work (for example, Bagozzi 1981) has suggested that semantic differential measures of affect can be reliably used to measure hedonic affect, whereas utilitarian affect could be measured through belief-based Likert, Guttman, or Thurstone attitudinal scales. However, it should not be assumed a priori that all semantic differential measures of affect measure the hedonic component.

This is evident from the study by Burnkrant and Page (1982). Following Bagozzi's recommendations, cognitive attitudes were measured by Likert scales, whereas affective attitudes were measured by semantic differential items of good–bad, harmful–beneficial, helpful–troublesome, and worthless–valuable. Using these operationalizations, tests found that although these two attitude components each achieved convergent validity, they failed to achieve discriminant validity; further, the cognitive component predicted the affective component quite well.

Whereas the Burnkrant and Page (1982) conclusion was that the two components could not be discriminated between, a plausible rival hypothesis is that the specific semantic differentials used in their study to measure the affective component reflect nothing more than the same cognitive component, leaving open the possibility that other semantic differential scales might measure the affective component quite well. Additionally, since semantic differential scales are extremely easy to administer, it would be interesting to see if semantic differential scales could be developed to measure both the affective (hedonic) and cognitive (utilitarian) components.

In a pilot study bearing on this question, I asked fifty-nine working women to rate four brands (Pepsi, Listerine, Comet Cleanser, and Cadillac) on each of sixteen different semantic differential items. These sixteen items all loaded highly on the evaluation attitudinal factor identified by Osgood, Suci, and Tannenbaum (1957). To ensure adequate domain sampling, eight were selected because of their high likelihood to be hedonic (for example, agreeable–disagreeable; pleasant–unpleasant), whereas the other eight were expected to be utilitarian (for example, beneficial–harmful, useful–useless). These selections were merely tactical and were meant to ensure that both factors had a chance of emerging in the data; they were not intended as tests of hypotheses in a formal sense.

These data were first subjected to (exploratory) common factor analysis, both orthogonal and oblique, using all sixteen items. This analysis was performed to provide indications of which items to drop from subsequent analysis, either because they loaded inconsistently across products or because they did not load highly on the major factors. Ten of these sixteen were then used in initial confirmatory factor analyses, which offered rotationally unique solutions that were statistically testable in measurement models with (the best) three, four, and five observed variables per factor. Since the three-indicator models fit best, these were finally used in detailed confirmatory factor analyses.

I will not provide details here (see Batra 1984b), but some results are important. First, the various analyses all strongly suggested a two-factor structure. One factor, here identified with the hedonic construct, loaded heavily on pleasant–unpleasant and related items. The second, here identified with the utilitarian construct, loaded heavily on useful–useless and related items. (See table 3–2 for a sample factor loading matrix.) This two-factor structure was tested in a confirmatory factor analysis in which discriminant validity between the two components and convergent validity for each of the two components were established (see Batra 1984b for certain technical caveats).

Second, three items that are commonly used to indicate overall, unidimensional attitudes (like–dislike, good–bad, and positive–negative) tended to load differently depending on the brand. In the aggregated all-brands subsample, and for Cadillac and (to some extent) Listerine, they loaded almost equally on both factors; whereas for Pepsi they loaded highest on the hedonic factor and for Comet highest on the utilitarian factor. Most dra-

Table 3–2
Affective Factor Structure: All Four Brands Merged

	Orthogonal (Varimax)		Oblique[a] (Factor Pattern)	
	Factor 1	Factor 2	Factor 1	Factor 2
Unrotated variance explained	75.4%	16.4%		
Pleasant–unpleasant	0.852	0.188	0.922	0.061
Agreeable–disagreeable	0.806	0.427	0.852	−0.206
Nice–awful	0.753	0.396	0.757	−0.192
Harmonious–dissonant	0.593	0.196	0.640	−0.026
Sociable–unsociable	0.515	−0.063	0.543	0.220
Positive–negative	0.645	0.510	0.626	−0.345
Like–dislike	0.583	0.468	0.544	−0.321
Good–bad	0.544	0.628	0.487	−0.502
Useful–useless	0.143	0.795	0.006	−0.803
Beneficial–harmful	0.044	0.704	−0.035	−0.731
Important–unimportant	0.211	0.684	0.078	−0.666
Meaningful–meaningless	0.159	0.563	0.009	−0.556
Intelligent–unintelligent	0.324	0.489	0.264	−0.422

Note: n = 236. Common factor analysis; total variance explained (of 2 factors, Eigenvalue $\geq$ 1) = 91.8 percent.
[a]After rotation with Kaiser normalization.

matically, the good–bad item was closest to the hedonic cluster for Cadillac and Pepsi but was closest to the utilitarian cluster for Comet and Listerine.

The implications of this inconsistency are discussed further below, but it is interesting to note that Osgood, Suci, and Tannenbaum themselves found that the nature of the items that loaded highest on their *evaluation* factor changed, depending on the concept(s) being rated on those semantic differential items (1957, pp. 77, 187, 326). The authors observed this instability to be systematically greater when the concepts had "high emotionality" (pp. 180, 302). In some of these cases, a factor called *receptivity* or *sensory adiency* (orientation) apparently became very important (pp. 64, 180, 326).

In fact, in those cases where the concepts (stimuli) rated were largely denotative rather than connotative in character, the proportion of total scale variance extracted by the first three factors explained a very low percentage—less than one-third—of the variance in judgments (p. 47). (Connotative descriptions of a class are those that list the attributes that define the class; denotative descriptions are those that identify the population of objects within a class that may be so designated without reducing this membership to component attributes. See Snider and Osgood (1969, p. 86) for Osgood's own definition.)

Because of such instability, the items like–dislike, good–bad, and positive–negative were dropped from further analysis since the objective was to develop scales to measure the two attitude components that could be used confidently for any product. By dropping these three items, the category–scale interaction problem was considered overcome, and the study proceeded. Based on the results of this prestudy, it appeared that the best two-item scales to measure the hedonic and utilitarian components would be, respectively, pleasant–unpleasant and nice–awful (Cronbach alpha 0.90) and useful–useless and important–unimportant (alpha 0.76). These best two-item scales correlated 0.44 ($p< = 0.001$, $n = 236$).

In a subsequent study (Batra and Ray 1984a), the following expectations pertaining to the two attitude components were tested: (1) Was the utilitarian component differentially sensitive to the support and counter argumentation evoked by message arguments, and was the hedonic component differentially sensitive to the affective responses evoked by ad execution likability? (2) Were purchase intentions driven more by the utilitarian attitudinal component in high-message-response-involvement situations but more by the hedonic component in low-involvement situations?

I will not repeat the details of this study and analysis here; suffice it to say that data were subjected to causal modeling using path coefficients estimated through LISREL (Jöreskog and Sörbom 1981). What is of interest here are not the results of those analyses, because they were plagued with measurement difficulties, but the measurement difficulties themselves.

We found, first, that the scales used to measure the two attitude components correlated much more highly among themselves when respondents rated brands after seeing ads, as in this study, than when no ads were shown, as in the prestudy (the r now was 0.77). A speculative explanation may be that in the presence of advertising stimuli a respondent may activate in long-term memory both a prior affect node (compare Bower 1981) and prior semantic belief and value nodes, such simultaneous activation creating greater congruence than would exist in the absence of such stimuli (I am indebted to Richard Bagozzi for suggesting this).

Given the high correlations between the two components, it was not surprising that they did not relate as differently as expected to the different kinds of mediating responses, and this made the subsequent tests of hypotheses problematic, although we did attempt to conduct them after adjusting for the relationships observed in the data.

What is of interest here, however, is that the relationships between the two attitude scales and the affective and cognitive responses appeared to vary with the product category. We had used ten different product categories, so we computed the partial correlations between the two attitude scales and two aggregates of mediating responses: the net valence of support and counter arguments, and the net valence of source bolstering, source discounting, and the three mood–feeling categories presented in the beginning of this chapter.

Given the small sample sizes at the level of the individual product category, only six of the thirty-two relationships were significant at 0.10 or less. Yet they are intriguing. It appears, for example, that in one case affective responses increase the perceived utility of the brand advertised, rather than create feelings of pleasantness toward the brand itself—affective responses increase the perception of certain long-distance phone call services as being useful and important. In some others, however, such affective responses increase the feelings that the brand advertised is pleasant and nice (frozen pizzas, ready-to-eat cereals). In still other cases, it is responses affirming (on balance) attribute superiority, through support and counter arguments, that lead to enhanced feelings of pleasantness toward the product (for example, instant chocolate drinks).

Some of these interactions could be measurement artifacts caused by low scale reliability, but then again they may indicate something fundamental about the two attitude components. It was hoped during the prestudy that the deletion of inconsistently loading items would remove such interactions, but that obviously turned out to have been hoping for too much. Nor are such interactions unprecedented. As described above, they emerged extensively in the work of Osgood, Suci, and Tannenbaum (1957), surfaced again in the study by Komorita and Bass (1967), and appeared again in Calder and Sternthal (1980), the only marketing study in recent years to have used a two-component model.

Such interactions suggest that it may be wrong to view each brand (or product category) as having both attitude components in equal measure; at a minimum, there may be a brand by ad execution interaction. More importantly, the data—admittedly imperfect—seem to suggest that attitudes for some products may be primarily hedonic but utilitarian for others. Positive advertising content, both arguments and source likability, may reinforce this product-dominant component: hedonic for fun foods such as pizzas and for self-indulgent, multisensory products such as shampoos, and utilitarian for long-distance phone call services and automatic dishwashing machines. (Very similar results are reported by Holbrook, Lehmann, and O'Shaughnessy, 1983.) Moreover, some kind of haloing process might then raise the appraisal of a brand on the other attitude component as well.

A somewhat similar conceptualization has recently been suggested by Wells (1980), who classified products along an intrinsic approach–avoidance continuum. Wells argued that advertising for approach products, which are intrinsically enjoyable (such as foods, beverages, clothes, vacations, new cars) tends to be likable itself, such that for these products sales are related to a liking for the ad. Avoidance products, on the other hand, are those that would not be bought if they did not help the consumer do something, such as cleaning products, insurance, denture adhesives, proprietary medicines. For these products, Wells hypothesized an inverse relationship between liking the ad and sales.

Such conceptualizations and evidence suggest that the utility from eating pizzas may simply be the hedonic pleasure that comes with its consumption, and the hedonic effect of an affective phone service ad may simply be an enhanced perception of the useful role of telephones in our daily lives rather than a feeling of friendliness towards the commercial-sponsoring company. The same measuring instruments may thus measure different affects for different types of products, and such differential measurement may be most problematic in experiential products. Such a view finds support from a variety of sources.

It is consistent with the fact that Osgood, Suci, and Tannenbaum found such concept–scale interactions to be highest when the concepts had high emotionality (1957, pp. 180, 302), when a factor called *receptivity* or *sensory adiency* became very important. It also is consistent with the emerging views on hedonic consumption (Holbrook and Hirschman 1982; Hirschman and Holbrook 1982). Such views argue that for many products and services—especially services—consumption is multisensory, emotional, and often full of fantasy and fun, and that such affective payoffs are poorly captured by multiattribute constructs equating affect with the evaluation of physical attributes.

It is also consistent, in a fashion, with the functional theories of attitude (Katz 1960; Smith, Bruner, and White 1956), which argue that attitudes can serve different functions for different stimuli. Among the functions that these theories believed attitudes served were instrumental (utilitarian) and value-expressive. (Hedonic pleasure is certainly an important value—some would allege a dominant one—in contemporary society.) Attitudes could thus be utilitarian for some products and hedonic for others.

We still have no complete model of attitude structure, and the complications just introduced make it more difficult to confidently model the linkages between the advertising vector of the overview model and the two attitude components. Perhaps we should begin asking a different set of questions. Perhaps the discussion needs to shift from a universal model of attitude structure to a more situational one, with hedonic, utilitarian, and even moral (compare Komorita and Bass 1967) components, purposes, and measures. Individual differences would also be important (compare Hirschman and Holbrook 1982).

Certainly, at a minimum, much more attention needs to be given to multiproduct and multidomain research, with any analysis simultaneously examining attitude factors, products (or situations), and individuals by means of techniques such as three-mode factor analysis (Tucker 1964, 1966). Such an analysis, by simultaneously examining three dimensions, should improve our understanding of what sorts of individuals tend to have what sorts of attitude dimensions for what sorts of products in what sorts of situations. Only through such analysis can we develop measurement instruments for the attitude components that can be used confidently across products, situations, and individuals.

After such basic methodological research is complete, we can begin to research the nomological network developed for the hedonic and utilitarian components earlier in this chapter. We can then investigate whether the cognitive responses evoked by advertising argumentation primarily influence the utilitarian component, with the likability-generated affective responses influencing the hedonic component more. We can test how the two attitude components drive purchase intentions across product categories and across levels of message response involvement. We can compare the relative effort required to form the two components, their decay rates over time, and their possibly differential susceptibility to attitude-change attempts. We can study whether actual product use creates utilitarian rather than hedonic affect or whether, again, these effects interact with the nature of the product category. From all this, perhaps, will emerge (1) an understanding of fundamental ways in which attitude structures differ across product classes; and (2) knowledge that can then be used to understand how advertising does, and should, work differently across such product categories.

The possibilities are exciting, and the research agenda large. The fundamental insight, however, is that we seem to be dealing today with attitudes not as unidimensional affect, but with attitudes as differently sourced affects. It is with the modeling and measurement of such affects, in all their complexity, that future research must concern itself.

On Familiarity and Affect

The third element, after message arguments and execution likability, in the vector of advertising influences in the overview model presented above was exposure frequency. Exposure frequency was presented as generating brand familiarity, which then influenced purchase intentions both directly (through heightened brand salience) and through the hedonic attitudinal component. Of all the processes in the overview model, this one is perhaps the least understood, although it has been speculated on for at least the last twenty years. What is particularly interesting is the relationship between such exposure-generated familiarity and attitudes.

As mentioned earlier in this chapter, the low-involvement hierarchy of effects, suggested by Krugman (1965) and reported by Ray et al. (1973), suggests that repetition-induced changes in awareness directly lead to changes in purchase intentions in low-involvement situations, with changes in attitudes following, rather than preceding, such movements in purchase intentions. This view suggests that affect is entirely absent from the effects of repetition on purchase intentions. It has been suggested earlier (for example,

Batra and Ray 1983a), however, based on the voluminous literature on mere-exposure effects (Zajonc 1968; Harrison 1977; Sawyer 1981), that repetition might create mere-exposure kinds of affect for the advertised brand, which then drive purchase intentions. The idea makes intuitive sense; its confirmation, however, requires substantial theoretical and methodological groundwork, as will become apparent below.

Importance

Some hypotheses studied in the Batra and Ray (1984a) paper involving the two attitude components have already been mentioned. In addition to those hypotheses, that study also explicitly modeled brand familiarity in an attempt to integrate the two attitudinal route models with the low-involvement hierarchy of effects. Brand familiarity was conceptualized as an index of differential brand awareness reflecting degrees of experience with the brand, ranging from past exposure to advertising through current use. Among other questions asked was: Does brand familiarity influence purchase intentions more strongly in low-involvement situations than in high-involvement ones?

It did, in fact, appear that brand familiarity was the most important determinant of purchase intentions in the low-involvement sample. Its direct path coefficient was a significant 0.23, rising to 0.52 after the indirect causal effects through the attitude components were considered. This total effects coefficient of 0.52 was much high than the 0.31 for the high-involvement sample, suggesting again that brand name familiarity plays a much greater role in driving purchase intentions in low- rather than high-involvement situations.

In a subsequent repetition study (Batra and Ray 1984c), we again found that brand familiarity and brand name (ad) recall correlated much more strongly with brand attitudes and purchase intentions in low-motivation/ability (= low involvement) conditions than when those antecedents of support and counter argument production were at high levels. These findings also correspond with the higher recall-attitude relationships under low-involvement (rather than high-involvement) conditions found by Beattie and Mitchell (1984).

Given the importance of brand awareness and familiarity in driving purchase intentions in low-involvement advertising situations, it becomes both important and interesting to understand the mechanisms by which such influence works. Not surprisingly, one turns first to proffered explanations of just how the "mere-exposure" effect occurs. Many explanations exist, and I review them briefly below, but it seems that further research is warranted on the links between awareness and familiarity on the one hand and affect on the other.

Explanations

Sawyer (1981) reviewed many of the competing explanations in detail (*response competition, expectancy arousal, opponent process theory,* and so forth). After rejecting as incomplete those explanations involving experimental demand artifacts and classical conditioning, his review suggests support for theories of optimal arousal and two-factor theories. These theories argue that exposure creates both habituation and learning, positively related to affect, and tedium, negatively related to affect, such that the net exposure–affect relationship is the inverted U-curve typically found in mere-exposure research.

Within this observed inverted U-curve relationship, it is easy to understand why tedium may create negative affect after a certain number of exposures, purely because of stimulus irritation and wearout. It is less obvious *why* learning and habituation should create positive affect.

The link between learning and affect was investigated by Petty and Cacioppo (1979), who offered a cognitive response interpretation of the inverted-U effect in terms of the production of support arguments (increasing, then decreasing) and counter arguments (decreasing, then increasing) in response to repetition. Similar results were found by McCullough and Ostrom (1974) and Calder and Sternthal (1980). As Petty and Cacioppo (1979) point out, however, all these studies confound the effects of repetition with those of greater time to think, which would lead to greater learning in the rising part of the inverted-U curve and would suggest that recall of ad content, rather than mediating response production, may be the cause of such repetition-induced affect.

In their covariate analyses checking the learning-leads-to-liking rival hypothesis, however, Petty and Cacioppo find no such effect, and therefore conclude that only the cognitive response explanation finds support. I would like to suggest that this test may be incomplete. In their tests, Petty and Cacioppo operationalized learning by measures of recall. I would like to put forward the notion that the liking phase of the mere-exposure effect is not due to conscious (recall-evidenced) learning but to some kind of preattentive recognition.

A discussion of recall versus recognition can be found elsewhere (for example, Bagozzi and Silk 1983), and Zajonc himself (1980) discusses the issue in great detail when trying to understand the mere-exposure effect. The weight of the evidence suggests some kind of preconscious recognition, occurring at the semantic level, that is responsible for the mere-exposure effect. In addition to what Zajonc (1980) has already written, it should be pointed out that models of human attention have long posited (for example, Treisman 1969) that a system for preattentive recognition has to exist in human memory systems in order for us to explain human attentional processes. Such recognition would be semantic, not merely physical (as in Broadbent 1958), because of evidence from dichotic listening experiments that attention shifts from one ear to the other based on continuity of meaning, not merely changes in physical cues. Late-selection models of attention like those of Treisman (1969) thus posit that as stimuli enter the sensory channels they are preattentively matched with semantic stores for relevance, and that attention is then allocated to different stimulus sources. Such evidence for semantic processing early in the analysis of incoming stimulus information is one reason why Baddeley (1978) faults Craik and Lockhart's notion (1972) of a hierarchy of depth of processing.

I mention this not just to point out that tests of the learning-leads-to-liking hypothesis should be done with measures more sensitive than those of conscious content recall but also to mention a rather reductionist (and very speculative) explanation of why familiar stimuli (familiar at the preconscious matching stage) should evoke positive affect. The argument is reductionist because it is neurological; it is speculative because there may be no way to test it.

According to Pribram (1978) and Luria (1973), quoting the work of Sokolov, Vinogradova and others, the amygdala and frontal cortex of the forebrain are associated with phasic arousal responses to novel stimuli, which play major roles in this learning-affect link. In a natural learning situation, stimuli are learned (habituated to) because their initial novelty creates a natural orienting (arousal) reaction; such arousal interrupts ongoing activity and leads to a forced discrimination (= learning) of the stimulus. This arousal (viscero-autonomic) response thus comes from unfamiliar stimuli.

Imagine, then, that a repeated stimulus is recognized preattentively (as per Treisman's model). Such preconscious recognition creates arousal *as long as the stimulus has not been totally learned,* that we experience as liking. This last link is even more speculative; it turns out that the amygdala, which is responsible for such preconscious recognition, orienting, and habituation, also happens to be the *control center* for the endorphin neurohormones that give us our subjective feelings of pleasure and liking (Pribram 1980).

After learning is total, however, tedium—negative affect—begins to set in. This explains why more complex stimuli, taking longer to learn, are liked longer (Harrison 1977). Liking may increase with repetition because the arousal from each exposure may be added on to earlier stored liking, perhaps involving storage and retrieval mechanisms similar to those suggested by Bower (1981).

If the true mechanism is even remotely like the one I have outlined, the implications for researchers are primarily those of measurement. It may be, for instance, that mere-exposure effects should be measured on the scales developed to measure hedonic affect rather than on the kinds of agreement scales used by Petty and Cacioppo (1979). Such suggestions obviously warrant research, but it is interesting to note that Harrison (1977, p. 58), in his review, did point out that conclusions as to whether or not the mere-exposure effect did emerge seemed to depend on the specific measures used. In particular, results obtained differ for like–dislike and good–bad scales, and it seems important to understand these differences by means of the two-attitude components literature discussed in the last section.

Interestingly enough, and speaking historically, it would appear that when Krugman developed his low-involvement hierarchy of advertising effects he treated the effects of awareness on purchase intentions in more than purely cognitive terms. In a somewhat neglected paper ("The Learning of Consumer Likes, Preferences, and Choices," which echoes views on familiarity going back to Titchener), he writes:

> Marketers would like to think that their products were indeed better and that consumers believed them to be better. What is often the unrecognized case, however, is that their product is neither liked nor considered better, but chosen only because it is adequately "good" *and* for the pleasure of its recognition (that is, sheer familiarity). (1968, p. 223).

Here, one should note the suggestion made elsewhere (Batra and Ray 1984a) that the two components of attitudes may not work additively in the choice context; overall preferences may not simply be the sum of the utilitarian and hedonic components. Instead, the two components may come into play at different points in the choice process (assuming they are in disagreement). For example, hedonic affect, or mere-exposure affect (if they are different), may play an important role in tie-breaker decisions at the last node in a hierarchical, elimination-by-aspects type of choice model (compare Tversky 1972). Krugman seems to have had something similar in mind, judging from the quotation above.

In all honesty, though, our knowledge of how familiarity works in the advertising-effects context is so limited that we must admit that the processes may not involve affect of any kind at all. Differential brand awareness may simply propel preferential choice on the basis of purely cognitive effects: I may choose the first brand that comes to mind, and more heavily advertised brands will obviously be more available and salient (compare Tversky and Kahneman 1973; Taylor and Fiske 1978). Alternatively, the fact that the brand advertises heavily and is familiar may lead consumers to believe that it must be a market leader and therefore superior. Mitchell and Olson (1981) have discussed such inferential belief formation processes, and economists such as Nelson (1974) and others have discussed such phenomena in terms of consumers searching for quality information and advertisers signaling to them such product quality. Finally, as modeled recently by some theorists, increasing familiarity with a brand may influence attitudes by reducing the uncertainty associated with that brand's attributes. It is interesting to note that although much recent research has investigated the impact of increasing amounts of brand information on the cognitive structure used by consumers to organize that information, there has been no research on analogous effects on the affective structure toward that brand.

In short, the relationship between ad familiarity, brand familiarity, hedonic affect toward the brand, and brand choice is still a fertile area for research. If we can understand the process by which advertising repetition has its effects, we may be able to develop ways in which advertisers could reduce their levels of repetition without reducing advertising effectiveness (for example, Batra and Ray 1984c). It would appear, however, that although it is appealing theoretically to conceptualize the effects of familiarity as done in the overview model, much research is required to refine these hypotheses and to make possible their empirical verification.

Conclusion

I conclude as I began: the information-processing paradigm, with its model of man as computer, has indeed yielded valuable insights into consumer behavior, but there are partial failures and clues that we can ignore only at our peril. Fortunately, the recent surge of interest in affect's role in various areas of consumer decision making, of which this book is part, indicates that such is not going to be the case. In the advertising area, certainly, there is no paucity of theoretical models that not only incorporate but also give prominent roles to affective phenomena.

Perhaps we are going too fast. Perhaps such theory-building is not the need of the hour. Perhaps basic measurement issues need to be addressed first or at least simultaneously. Consumer research has a long tradition of using paper-and-pencil measures. Will such measures capture the subtle shades and nuances of affect that our theories postulate? Will verbal protocols be successful in adequately capturing mediating affective responses? Will attitude scales succeed in measuring effortless and involuntary hedonic affect? Will we ever be able to measure the preconscious recognition that apparently underlies the mere-exposure effect?

Given the problems with physiological measurement (Watson and Gatchel 1979; Stewart and Furse 1982) and the potential of nonverbal paper scales such as those using affect thermometers (Abelson et al. 1982) and happy faces (Meyer-Hentschel 1983), it is too early to say that radically new measures are needed. But perhaps it is not too early to suggest that in this age of affect it is the area of measurement that is the next frontier.

Only after such basic methodological research, which would leave us with valid and reliable measures of affective responses, multiple attitude components, and brand familiarity, could we really begin to research the nomological network speculated on in this chapter. We could then begin to study, for example, how the multiple-attitude components relate to cognitive and affective responses, brand information and use experiences, and purchase intentions; how the ease or difficulty with which they are formed get modified and then decay; and how these relationships are contingent on the nature of the product category and the nature of the advertising processing situation. Such research should bring a more complete understanding of how advertising is processed and a more balanced assessment of the role of cognition and affect in that processing.

4

Properties of Affect and Affect-laden Information Processing As Viewed through the Facial Response System

John T. Cacioppo, Mary E. Losch, and Louis G. Tassinary
University of Iowa
Richard E. Petty
University of Missouri-Columbia

> The great German philosopher, Immanuel Kant, likened the human mind to a glass that imprinted its shape on whatever liquid was poured into the glass . . . [unfortunately] he neglected a major filtering mechanism, the innate affects, which necessarily color our every experience by producing a unique set of categorical imperatives, which amplify not only what precedes and activates each affect but also the further responses that are prompted by affect (Tomkins 1984, pp. 193–194).

> [T]here are many circumstances in which the affective reaction *precedes* the very cognitive appraisal on which the affective reaction is presumed to be based (Zajonc and Markus 1982, p. 125).

T heory and research on consumer behavior for nearly four decades have been influenced strongly by motivational notions of needs, drives, and rewards (Dichter 1964). With the growth of the cognitive perspective, the processes of encoding, storage, and retrieval became increasingly important topics of research, and the image of the consumer was upgraded to depict an information-integrating, decision-making organism whose primary purpose was to maximize life's comforts given limited processing and economic resources. Ill-considered actions on the part of consumers were no longer attributed to archaic urgings trapped in a civilized world but

Preparation of this chapter was supported by National Science Foundation No. BNS 82–17096 and BNS 84–14853. We are especially grateful to Alan Fridlund for comments on a preliminary draft. Address correspondence to John T. Cacioppo, Department of Psychology, University of Iowa, Iowa City, Iowa 52242, or to Richard E. Petty, Department of Psychology, University of Missouri, Columbia, Missouri 65211.

rather to errors in information processing and decision making resulting from the failure of a generally adaptive cognitive rule or heuristic.

Illustrative of the cognitive approach to consumer behavior is the wealth of research on multiattribute models, information integration, and cognitive responses to persuasion (for example, Zaltman and Wallendorf 1979). The premise underlying each of these theoretical approaches is that people's beliefs and cognitions about a product or recommendation determine their susceptibility or resistance to the appeal. In addition, individuals' retrospective verbal reports about their reactions to stimuli (for example, advertisements, products) or thought listings have been viewed as harboring information about the psychological foundations of attitudes and behavioral dispositions (Fishbein and Ajzen 1975; Petty, Ostrom, and Brock 1981).

The importance of the cognitive perspective for understanding consumer adaptability, versatility, and cultural variability should not be underemphasized. The thesis of this chapter, however, is that by focusing solely on a *cognitive* consumer we overlook the rudimentary and perhaps predominant forces underlying consumer behavior (compare Holbrook and Hirschman 1982).

Consider a case frequently encountered in research on attitudes using the thought-listing technique. Although the retrospective self-report data obtained using the thought-listing technique have been termed *cognitive responses* since Greenwald's influential chapter (1968), one can reasonably question whether this label captures the psychological foundations of responses such as "bull" written in bold, dark strokes across the thought-listing form (Miller and Baron 1973). One could view responses of this sort as a short-hand notation indicating that the individual had completed a detailed analysis of the appeal, possessed innumerable counterarguments, and decided not to list and elaborate on them for the experimenter, undoubtedly for good reason. On the other hand, the comment "bull" might *not* be the conclusion reached by individuals after thinking about the issue or the arguments for a particular recommendation; rather it might reflect the essentially emotional foundation underlying the person's reaction to the appeal (Cacioppo and Petty 1982; Petty and Cacioppo 1981). The articulation of retrospective verbal reports clearly relies on cognitive processes, and we and others therefore have viewed cognitive response data as the consequence of information processing (Cacioppo, Harkins, and Petty 1981). This is not to suggest that cognitive processes are the most rudimentary psychological act on which people's sentiments and actions can arise, but only to acknowledge that cognitive response data are at best an indirect index of both rudimentary affective and basic cognitive processes. It is noteworthy, for instance, that the only dimension along which thought-listing data have been related reliably to attitudes and behavioral inclinations is the polarity dimension (see reviews by Cacioppo and Petty 1981c; Wright 1980).

The effective antecedents of consumer behavior have been highlighted by recent research on attitude conditioning. This research indicates that affective features of advertisements having no intrinsic link to the merits of personally inconsequential products can nevertheless have subtle effects on consumer behavior. For example, Gorn (1982, Experiment 1) asked students to rate advertisements for new pens. Students were exposed to a light blue pen accompanied by background music from a popular album and a beige pen accompanied by a less well-liked excerpt of classical music; or the light blue pen accompanied by the disliked music and the beige pen accompanied by the popular musical excerpt. Results revealed that when subjects were later given the opportunity to choose between the two pens, they were more likely to select the pen that had been accompanied by the liked music even though they could not articulate this contingency. Of course, the inability of subjects to articulate the contingency does not mean that cognitive processes were absent; instead, it illustrates that affective manipulations can have subtle effects on consumer attitudes and behavior.

Petty and Cacioppo (1981, 1984, in press) have outlined an elaboration-likelihood model of attitude change in which simple affective cues are viewed as being more powerful determinants of attitudes when motivation and/or ability to process issue-relevant information is low than high. Consistent with this general framework, Gorn (1982, Experiment 2) exposed subjects to two different ads for a pen. One ad was attribute oriented, providing relevant information about the pen, whereas the other ad featured pleasant music rather than information. Before viewing the ads, half of the subjects were motivated to think by being told that their task was to advise an advertising agency as to whether or not it should purchase advertising time on television. Subjects in this condition were also told that they would later get to choose a three-pen pack of one of the advertised brands as a gift. Thus, the personal consequences of the subjects' evaluations were reasonably high. A second group of subjects was provided little reason to scrutinize the ads carefully. They did not expect to advise the ad agency and were not told about the free pen gift prior to ad exposure. About one hour after ad exposure, subjects were given a choice between the two brands of advertised pens. Seventy-one percent of subjects in the high-consequences condition chose the pen advertised with information, as compared with 37 percent in the low-consequences condition.

Finally, in an important study in which higher-order cognitive processes were even less obviously involved, Kunst-Wilson and Zajonc (1980) exposed subjects to a series of ten irregular polygons. The stimuli were presented tachistoscopically at a duration sufficiently brief that subjects could not discriminate the shapes to which they had been exposed from a comparable set of distractor shapes. Subjects, however, were significantly more likely to prefer the shapes to which they had been exposed than those not seen previously. These data have been interpreted as evidence that people "can like something or be afraid of it before we know precisely what it is and perhaps even *without* knowing what it is" (Zajonc 1980, p. 154).

The recent interest in the role of affect, therefore, may stem in part from research extending to or beyond the limits of the cognitive perspective (compare Zajonc 1980). Several other sources of impetus should be noted, however. Work in evolutionary biology and the neurosciences on adaptive but phylogenetically primitive systems for energizing and guiding behavior suggests that a system of evaluation and response exists that is tied less closely to the stimulus than is the reflex system but that is less flexible, adaptive, and reliant on neocortical nuclei than is the cognitive system as generally conceived (compare Izard, Kagan, and Zajonc 1984; Scherer and Ekman 1984). Conceptions of an affect system, such as Tomkins' characterization (1962, 1963, 1981, 1982) of it as a primary innate biological motivating mechanism that can interact with the reflex and cognitive systems in guiding behavior, fit well with these observations.

In addition, the very nature of the cognitive system—such as the variability in consumer attitudes and responses it potentiates across situations and individuals through learning and discrimination and the resistance to change it poses within situations and individuals through the establishment of dynamic cognitive structures—can place severe limits on the impact of any given cognitive appeal. These limitations contrast with the more universal, even if more transient, impact on consumer attitudes and behaviors one can expect from invoking the cruder (that is, less discriminating) affective system of evaluation (Petty and Cacioppo 1984; Zajonc 1980). It is interesting to note in this regard that advertisers, who are concerned with making a powerful impression on consumers rather than accounting for a small but statistically significant and predictable portion of variance in consumer response, appear to be returning to emotional appeals (Holbrook and O'Shaughnessy 1984).

The reexamination of the role of affect, therefore, portends advances in understanding consumer behavior. The reliance on cognitive analogies, paradigms, and measures to study affect may prove inadequate, however. Models that reduce affect to but one more attribute of a concept within a semantic network may match neatly with data obtained in cognitive paradigms (see review by Clark and Fiske 1982), and these formulations account well for the refined emotions that Tomkins (1981) termed *affect complexes* (for example, pride). But these conceptualizations fail to fully comprehend some of the distinguishing properties of affect, such as the similarities between its manifestation in neonates and adults, its automatic activation and pervasive influence, and its apparent dominance over thoughts and actions.

> One speaks of "being in the grip" of a strong emotion and that seems a particularly apt figure of speech. . . . One experiences a loss of control, a sense of functioning on a more primitive and less reflective level (Winton, Putnam, and Krauss 1984, p. 195).

To be sure, one can incorporate these properties into cognitive models (Lazarus 1984). However, the issue is not whether cognitive terminology can be developed to describe these behavioral phenomena, but rather whether theoretical clarity is gained by adopting a framework in which the affect and cognitive systems are jointly responsible for the evaluation of the environment, intraorganismic regulation, preparation of action, and communication of intention.

In this chapter, we adopt the position that consumer behavior can be more fully understood by accepting the premise that the cognitive system is not the only one with behavioral significance. Justification for this premise is elaborated on elsewhere; our purpose here is to examine advances in the objective assessment of ephemeral affective states.

Affect is not viewed here as being reducible to verbal report (Valins 1966) or physiological reaction (Meyer 1933) but rather as a system with motivational, perceptual, cognitive, physiological, motor expressive, and subjective manifestations. As Campos and Barrett (1984) note, individual differences, inhibitory testing conditions, and developmental changes make it unlikely for a given episode of an emotion to result in changes across all these modes of expression. Hence, until more is known about the parameters governing the operation of the affect system, experimental analyses should be employed that accommodate affect being elicited by multiple situational and imaginable events and manifesting in multiple and somewhat independent ways.

What might be the properties of this multilevel affect system? Consider pain phenomena. The argument regarding whether or not perceptual–cognitive processes are fundamental to affect has been based in part on arguments regarding the temporal relationship between stimulus recognition and feeling. It is interesting to note, therefore, that (1) sensory afferentiation can influence pain afferentiation at the level of the spinal cord; (2) the perception and recognition of the stimulus may actually precede the experience of pain due to differences in the transmission speeds of the differential neural circuits (that is, the afferents) responsive to the sensory and the pain features of a stimulus; and (3) the experience of pain can nevertheless develop independently of the perception and recognition of the stimulus (compare Melzack and Wall 1965). Affect and cognition need not rely on different afferents (as is the case for pain and sensation) but simply different neural circuits to suggest a comparable case may exist with regard to affect. Hence, the argument regarding the temporal precedence of affect and cognition may be moot.

Despite the capability of pain to develop independently of one's cognitive registration and appraisal of the eliciting stimulus, it is equally clear that the interpretation of the stimulus *can* have dramatic effects on physiological and psychological reactions. Evidence for this notion can be found in studies on topics ranging from cognitive dissonance (Zimbardo et al. 1969) to the predictability of highly noxious stimuli (Abbott, Schoen, and Badia 1984). It may be that, in the cases of both pain and affect, extended attributional processes are especially likely to emerge and modulate behavior when the cause of the pain or the affect is unknown.

Several additional parallels between the properties of pain and affect are noteworthy. As is the case for affect, the mechanisms for the registration of and response to pain do not depend on the verbal system and, indeed, exist in neonates and in nonprimates. Moreover, in a subset of pain and affect phenomena, a stimulus with specific features (for example, a sharp instrument, a bitter gustatory stimulus) impinging on the organism can evoke a reaction with strong motivational properties. Among the likely consequences are autonomic changes, a redirection of information processing, and behavioral adaptations.

Pain is usually a transient experience, but it can become chronic and subtly influence the information people seek and the manner in which they think about and respond to this information. Affect, too is generally conceived as a state rather than a trait, but affective states can be extended in time to become moods and can influence cognitive processes (Bower 1981; Gilligan and Bower 1984). As in the case of affect, pain tends to evoke stereotyped behavioral reactions and those aspects of the reaction that are observable act as powerful social stimuli (for example, Lanzetta and Orr 1980, 1981; Orr and Lanzetta 1980; Vaughan and Lanzetta 1980). Finally, through learning, pain can be evoked by the mere presentation of a conditioned stimulus. For instance, Rook (1984) argues that pain that persists into chronicity (defined as six months' duration and not responding to medical treatment) is best viewed as having "come under the control of cues and consequences in the environment. It is no longer a sensory event, but has become part of one's habits and life-style" (Rook 1984, pp. 476–477). Similarly, numerous studies have illustrated the power of a conditioned stimulus to evoke affect (for example, Gorn 1982; Lanzetta and Orr 1980; Ohman and Dimberg 1984; Zanna, Kiesler, and Pilkonis 1970).

The heuristic value of this analogy derives from its suggestions regarding the response properties of affect and from its argument for the plausibility of a partial independence in origin and function between the cognitive and affective systems of evaluation. It also underscores the suggestion that although the cognitive system is largely responsive for the vast flexibility, variability, and adaptability of human behavior, affect—like pain—may be capable of exerting a pervasive, motivating, and directive influence on what people attend to, encode, think about, retrieve, and seek. Silvan Tomkins put it as follows:

> The affect system is . . . the primary motivational system because without its amplification, nothing else matters, and with its amplification, anything else *can* matter. It thus combines urgency and generality. It lends its power to memory, to perception, to thought, and to action no less than to the drives (1984, p. 164).

Underscored, too, is that one of the most important characteristics of affect is its involvement of the somatovisceral apparatus (compare Knapp 1983).

Whereas debates have raged in consumer behavior regarding the utility of electrodermal responses, pupillary responses, heart rate, and the electro-encephalogram for studying affect (for example, see reviews by Petty and Cacioppo 1983; Stewart and Furse 1982), important advances for measuring hidden feelings have been the studies made in reading facial expressions. To illustrate, previous research has seldom found discriminable autonomic manifestations of distinctive emotional states (but see Ax 1953; Ekman, Levenson and Friesen 1983). However, there is now considerable evidence to support postulating a tight link between qualitatively different facial expressions and distinctive emotional states. This evidence has come from a variety of sources and includes support for: (1) Darwin's notions (1872) regarding their evolutionary history and adaptive utility (compare Ekman 1972, 1982a); (2) the capacity of facial expressions to serve as social stimuli (for example, Englis, Vaughan, and Lanzetta 1982; Lanzetta and Orr 1981; Orr and Lanzetta 1980; Sorce et al. 1981); and (3) the existence of the associated movements accompanying intrapersonal processes such as silent language processing and emotion (see recent reviews by Ekman and Oster 1979; McGuigan 1978; Zuckerman, DePaulo, and Rosenthal 1981). In the next section, we examine the rationale for investigating affect and its relationship to verbal processes by monitoring the facial response system.

Facial Response System

The face is the site for the major sensory inputs (vision, olfaction, audition, gustation) and for the major linguistic output (speech). It is a multisignal, multimessage response system capable of tremendous flexibility and specificity (Ekman 1982a; Ekman and Friesen 1975). This system imparts information in a variety of ways. "Static facial signals" in Ekman and Friesen's terminology represent relatively permanent features of the face, such as bone structure and skin pigmentation. "Slow signals" represent changes in the appearance of the face that occur gradually over time, such as the development of permanent wrinkles and changes in skin texture. "Artificial signals" represent exogenously determined features of the face, such as eyeglasses and cosmetics. Finally, "rapid signals" represent phasic changes in neuromuscular activity that may lead to visually detectable changes in facial appearance.

We are concerned here with rapid signals, for they are the most important in the expression of emotion and the production of speech. Ekman and Friesen (1975) suggested that among the types of messages transmitted by the rapid facial actions are (1) emotions—expressions paralleling reportable states such as happiness, sadness, anger, disgust, surprise, and fear; (2) emblems—symbolic communicators such as the wink and pseudo-emotional expressions; (3) manipulators—self-manipulative associated movements such as lip biting; (4) illustrators—actions accompanying and highlighting speech such as a raised brow; and (5) regulators—nonverbal conversational mediators such as nods or smiles (see review by Fridlund, Ekman, and Oster in press).

With regard to rapid facial actions, a further distinction can be drawn between motor activities under the control of afferent input (reflex activity) and those directed by a central program (involuntary and voluntary activity). In a reflex, the output to a unimodal stimulus is unimodal, and effector output does not alter receptor input (Gallistel 1980). In a reflex model of an action sequence (for example, walking), each response generates a new sensory state that in turn evokes the next response in the sequence. Although reflex activity is integrated into the majority of mammalian motor activities and is important for the accurate performance of complex patterned movements, it does not appear to dominate motor activity. Instead, studies indicate that a *central program* model better represents the control of most repetitive or patterned movements. By *central,* we simply mean that the response is influenced primarily by neural activity descending from the brain, and this term is used in contrast to *cognitive* because it is more general. We do not mean to suggest by this term that peripheral mechanisms and feedback are unimportant. Welford (1974), for instance, proposed a three-stage central mechanism: input is analyzed and briefly stored in the first stage; the signal is related to a response (or inhibition of a response) in the second; and the selected response is executed in the third. This formulation has since been revised to cast the first two stages as feedback dependent (Glencross 1977). Thus, in this model, the new sensory state set by each response can influence, but does not determine, the next response.[a]

Movements controlled by a central program can occur in a stereotyped fashion and may have a *reflexive* appearance, but, strictly speaking, they constitute behavioral units rather than reflexes. For instance, Weiss (1950) has demonstrated innate, centrally programmed response sequences in studies involving the surgical rearrangement of neuromuscular connections in nonmammalian vertebrates. In an illustrative study, transplanting the limbs of larval salamanders in a position opposite to their original resulted in the salamander walking backward in situations where salamanders normally walked forward. Interestingly, this inappropriate behavior proved resistant to change in the face of environmental reinforcers.

Consistent with Weiss's observations regarding learning, Eibl-Eibesfeldt (1972) among others noted that each species has inborn predispositions to respond that can facilitate or impair learning. Specifically, Eibl-Eibesfeldt suggested that phylogenic adaptations are found on the receptor side, first in capacities of the sense organs, and second in the animal's ability to react with stereotyped behavior patterns to a subset of the perceived stimuli. These unconditioned stimuli are often configurative and highly specific. Moreover, because they unlock a behavior pattern, Eibl-Eibesfeldt has referred to them as *key stimuli*.

The preceding observations regarding motor programs are interesting given the evidence that emotional and articulatory facial actions are based on behavioral units that are operational at or shortly after birth (for example, see reviews by Fridlund, Ekman, and Oster in press; Steiner 1979). This

---

[a]To note that human nature includes reflexes and innate, highly stereotyped predispositions to respond is not to argue that human behavior is genetically determined or driven by an ex-machina force. Willis and Grossman (1977), for instance, note that the cat is able to walk adequately immediately after the entire brain above the subthalamus is removed, whereas the primate cannot. This finding has been attributed to the greater encephalization of motor control in primates than in nonprimate species. It is worth emphasizing, therefore, that there is less than complete independence among behavioral systems, but then the tissues of the brain and the rest of the body obviously constitute an organic, interdependent unit. As Claude Bernard noted when discussing this thesis in the domain of physiology:

> We really must learn then that if we break up a living organism by isolating its different parts, it is only for the sake of ease in experimental analysis and by no means in order to conceive them separately. Indeed, when we wish to ascribe to a physiological quality, its value and true significance we must always refer to this whole and draw our final conclusions only in relation to its effects in the whole. Physiologists and physicians must, therefore, always consider organisms as a whole and in detail in one and the same time without ever losing sight of the peculiar conditions of all the special phenomena whose resultant is the individual (1927, p. 91).

evidence includes the following: (1) the vast majority of the discrete facial actions visible in adults can be detected in newborns (Oster and Ekman 1978); (2) imitation of specific facial actions (for example, mouth opening, tongue protrusion) may occur as early as two or three days following birth (Meltzoff and Moore 1977); (3) studies of the facial actions of anencephalic neonates, hydrocephalic neonates, full-term neonates, congenitally blind adolescents, mentally retarded adolescents, and normal adolescents have revealed discriminable facial expressions to pleasant (for example, sweet), neutral (for example, distilled water) and unpleasant (for example, sour) gustatory and olfactory stimuli (see Rosenstein and Oster 1981; Steiner 1979); (4) neonatal smiling occurs nonrandomly, primarily during REM sleep, and appears to reflect periodic, endogenous fluctuations in CNS activity (compare Fridlund, Ekman, and Oster in press); (5) reliable social smiling in an alert infant occurs as early as the third week (Wolff 1963); (6) congenitally deaf children born to deaf parents exhibit cooing at about three months, and they exhibit babbling—including well-articulated speech sounds such as *pakapakapaka,* laughter, and sounds of discontent similar to those of the hearing population—at about six months (Lenneberg 1967); (7) the phonemic repertoire with which children begin is similar across cultures, although the acquisition of a particular language subsequently reshapes this repertoire (Anisfeld 1984); and (8) large variations in environmental conditions leave the age of onset of certain speech and language capabilities relatively unaffected, suggesting that maturational changes are important (Lenneberg 1967).

The existence of rudimentary, possibly innate motor programs, of course, does not preclude the development through learning of complementary and/or more comprehensive motor programs for governing facial actions. As Glencross noted:

> During the early stages of skill acquisition, the executive system may monitor the response stage almost continuously, combining the unitary subroutines or units of action on the basis of incoming information. However, as competence is acquired, the executive system can combine predictable sequences of action and form larger units of action. These larger units are temporally integrated by the executive system, which at the same time is receiving and processing sensory feedback about the ongoing response. . . . The operation of such feedback mechanisms as those described above has a further significance in that the one motor program can be used to achieve a variety of related outcomes. (Glencross, 1977, pp. 26–27)

Moreover, voluntary movements appear to be characterized by the deliberate, reportable act of initiating movement (Willis and Grossman 1977). Once the movement is started, it is possible for it to be carried out by centrally programmed or reflex motor mechanisms. Hence, specific, innate motor programs serve as the building blocks for more complex and flexible expressions and behaviors, which themselves can become automated components of more complex patterns of volitional expression and action (Jackson 1958). Note too, however, that the development of comprehensive motor programs need not entirely mask the effects of primitive affective processes on rudimentary motor responses.

To summarize thus far, within rapid facial actions, one can distinguish (1) reflex actions under the control of afferent input; (2) rudimentary reflex-like or impulsive actions accompanying emotion and less differentiated information processing (for example, orienting reactions) that seem controlled by innate motor programs; (3) adaptable, versatile, and more culturally variable spontaneous actions that seem mediated by learned motor programs; and (4) malleable voluntary actions. Thus, certain movements, particularly of the facial muscles, are viewed as undemanding of a person's limited processing capacity, free of deliberate control for their evocation, and associated with (though not necessary for) rudimentary emotional and symbolic processing. Learning undoubtedly contributes to the development of these responses, but there are inborn predispositions on which the learned responses are based.[b]

Facial Actions and Affect Displays

The distinctions among the types and neural control of facial movements may hold some general interest to consumer researchers because they have implications for how affect is conceived (for example, Tomkins 1962, 1963) and suggest circumstances in which particular facial configurations can serve as objective and continuous markers for fundamental cognitive and affective processes. Based on the neural substrate of facial actions, for instance, one can postulate several psychophysiological connections.

First, as noted above, rudimentary expressions of emotion (for example, happiness, disgust) have been documented in anencephalic neonates, hydrocephalic neonates, full-term neonates, congenitally blind adolescents, mentally retarded adolescents, and normal adolescents. Ekman and Friesen (1975) have outlined the movements of facial landmarks that characterize surprise, fear, disgust, anger, happiness, and sadness, and blends of these emotional reactions (for example, happy surprise). In disgust, for instance, the brows

---

[b]It is interesting to note that corresponding distinctions have been made in theories of emotion. Both Zillmann (1978) and Leventhal (1984), for instance, discriminate between innate affective reactions, conditioned emotional responses, and emotional states that are based on more differentiated associative processes (for example, inferences).

are drawn down, lowering the upper eyelid, the lower eyelid is raised but not tensed, the nose is wrinkled, the cheeks are raised, and the upper lip is raised. In a smile associated with happiness, the cheeks and lower eyelid are again raised and relaxed, but the corners of the mouth are drawn back and up, a wrinkle runs down from the corner of the nose to the edge beyond the mouth, and the brows are not drawn downward (Ekman and Friesen 1975). The drawing of the brows downward and together is achieved by the contraction of the *corrugator* and *depressor supercilii* muscles, whereas the drawing of the corners of the lips back and upward is achieved primarily by the contraction of the *zygomatic major* muscle (see figure 4–1), and the actions of those three muscles are among the most important discriminators of positive and negative emotional expressions (Fridlund and Izard 1983; Schwartz 1975). Indeed, over a century ago Darwin (1872, p. 222) observed that furrowing of the brow was frequently linked with "something difficult or displeasing encountered in a train of thought or action." Elementary affective processes, therefore, can be expected to have associated movements in selected facial muscles even in the absence of clearly noticeable and distinctive expressions of emotion.[c]

Second, crying, cooing, babbling and, subsequently, articulation involve the actions of the perioral musculature. For instance, bilabial consonants (for example, *b*, *p*, *m*) are articulated by bringing the lips together, and labiodental consonants (for example, *f*, *v*) are articulated by bringing the lower lip against the upper teeth (Anisfeld 1984; Lenneberg 1967). The *orbicularis oris* muscle controls the closing and pursing of the lips (see figure 4–1), and McGuigan (1970, 1978), Sokolov (1972) and others have suggested that silent language processing might therefore have associated movements in the perioral region. These movements, therefore, may be informative regarding the extent of verbal processing.

Third, it is noteworthy in light of the preceding review regarding the

---

[c]The term *associated movements* is used here in its technical sense to refer to movements that normally occur as part of the total pattern of motor activity but are perhaps not necessary to performance of the basic activity. Our use of this term is not meant to imply that proprioception from somatic events has no emotional or behavioral significance, rather that a consideration of their role is not relevant to the present discussion. For instance, Cartwright-Smith (1979) measured forearm strength as people squeezed a dynamometer while relaxing their facial muscles, contracted their facial muscles (that is, grimaced), relaxed their foot, or contracted their foot. Results revealed that subjects showed the most strength when they grimaced and the least strength when they relaxed their facial muscles. To examine experimental demands in the setting, a second group of subjects were given the experimental instructions and were asked to specify the ordering of the cell means expected by the experimenter. Cartwright-Smith found that these subjects failed to specify the correct ordering of means. Although the theoretical mechanism underlying this phenomenon needs to be explored (for example, classical conditioning, excitation of the hypothalamus) and studies of this type do not bear directly on the principles discussed in this chapter, Cartwright-Smith's observations illustrate that the effects of proprioception from affect displays are an interesting area of inquiry in their own right (see also Petty and Cacioppo 1983; Zajonc and Markus 1982).

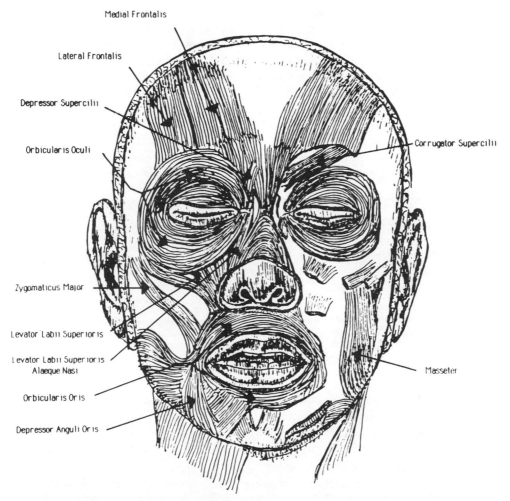

Medial Frontalis

Lateral Frontalis

Depressor Supercilii

Orbicularis Oculi

Corrugator Supercilii

Zygomaticus Major

Levator Labii Superioris

Levator Labii Superioris Alaeque Nasi

Masseter

Orbicularis Oris

Depressor Anguli Oris

Source: Modified and redrawn from figure 351 in Sobotta, J., and H. J. Figge. 1968. *Atlas of Human Anatomy,* Vol. 1, *Atlas of Bones, Joints, and Muscles,* 8th ed. New York: Hafner.

Figure 4–1. Facial Musculature. Superficial Muscles are Depicted on the Left, and Deep Musculature is Exposed on the Right.

hierarchical control of facial actions that part of the *experience* of emotion is the reported feeling that one can lose, or actually loses, self-control (Izard 1977; Scherer and Ekman 1984). If in fact emotional experiences may range from being *reflexive*—characterized by the perception of a loss of control and the rapid recruitment of facial actions—to *reflective*—characterized by a sense of predictability and control—then it is reasonable to expect reflexive emotional facial expressions (for example, disgust in response to the smell of rotten eggs) to be more explosive and stereotyped in appearance and to be more difficult to disrupt than reflective emotions (although expression of the former are still subject to being masked or inhibited).

Finally, although the preceding suggests connections between facial actions and affect, it should be emphasized that these connections are variable. As Ekman and Friesen (1975; Ekman 1982a) have noted, rapid facial actions serve a variety of functions, including the expression of emotion, articulation, eating and drinking, the regulation of oral and nasal respiration, gustation and olfaction, and the protection and lubrication of the eyes. Moreover, the meaning of an action in any single facial region is likely to be ambiguous. Disgust, anger, annoyance, seriousness, intense concentration,[d] and punctuating a word or phrase nonverbally can each lead to a drawing of the brows downward or together with corresponding activation of the corrugator muscle. Thus, temporally and spatially patterned facial actions provide the rich repertoire for the facial messages.

With these connections outlined, we now turn to a discussion of methodological issues in research on affect and the facial response system.

Methodological Issues

Judgmental Procedures

Psychological research on rapid facial actions has been pursued using various methods (see review by Ekman 1982b). The simplest technique is to have subjects make *selective judgments* regarding the nature and strength of the psychological state underlying a given facial display (for example, Sackeim

---

[d]Darwin (1872) posited that activity over the corrugator region was an indicant of generalized disturbance, cognitive or affective, in addition to negative affect. He noted, for example, that the brows could be observed to be drawn inward and downward during tasks requiring concentration, and he argued that this could not be taken as an indicant of negative affect because people sought and enjoyed tasks requiring intense concentration. Alternatively, these data can be interpreted as follows: (1) difficult tasks require that individuals identify and focus their attention on task-relevant information to the exclusion of tangential, more readily accessible information; (2) failure to exclude the irrelevant information constitutes a failure to perform the task in the manner to which the individuals aspire, and this evokes an unpleasant affective state; (3) the unpleasant affective state is displayed in increased activity over the corrugator region *and* provides a motivational booster to process the available information discriminantly (that is, to concentrate). In other words, the greater the concentration, the more evident the activity over the corrugator region, but it may be the negative affect evoked by the individual's endangered aspirations regarding task performance that pushes concentration and enhances activity over the corrugator region. Formulations such as opponent process (Solomon 1980) and cognitive dissonance (Festinger 1957) make it conceivable that intense concentration can be both predicated on an unpleasant affective reaction and yet ultimately become a rewarding activity.

and Gur 1978). This technique provides an indirect, subjective measure of facial actions and has demonstrated value. Ekman (1972), for instance, showed that people from various backgrounds and cultures could reliably identify the facial displays associated with the emotions of happiness, sadness, fear, anger, disgust, and surprise.

A second procedure involves measuring the *signal vehicles* (that is, specific changes in facial appearance) that convey the message. Ekman and Friesen's Facial Action Coding System (FACS) (1978) for scoring all "action units" that people are capable of seeing in the human face (for example, AU 4 = brows lowered and drawn together) is the most comprehensive measurement tool falling under this approach:

> Our interest in comprehensiveness was motivated not only by the diverse applications we had in mind, but by an awareness of the growing need for a common nomenclature for this field of research. . . . A constraint in the development of FAC was that it deals with what is clearly *visible* in the face, ignoring invisible changes (e.g., certain changes in muscle tonus), and discarding visible changes too subtle for reliable distinction. In part, this constraint on measuring the visible was willingly adopted, based on our interest in what could have social consequences (Ekman and Friesen 1976, p. 59).

The differences between these procedures do not reside only in what raters are asked to do. As Ekman (1982b) notes: (1) null findings with subjective judgment and positive findings with a sign vehicle measurement system such as FACs suggest that the raters were insensitive to actual differences in facial responses; (2) positive findings with subjective judgment and null findings with sign vehicle measurement suggest the latter is somehow faulty—perhaps due to being incomplete, unreliable, or insensitive; and (3) null findings with both measurement procedures may occur because the facial stimulus was ambiguous or unrepresentative, the actions too fleeting or subtle to be detected using either method, or "the face simply does not provide information about the topic being studied" (Ekman 1982b, p. 48).

Early research on facial expressions relied on drawings and still photographs of faces, and null or unreliable findings were common (for example, see review by Ekman 1973). Static representations such as photographs, however, provide a limited and potentially misleading portrayal of facial actions. It can be difficult to determine, for instance, whether a forehead wrinkle represents a static landmark (that is, a slow signal) or a contraction by the frontalis muscles (that is, a rapid signal). The use of videotapes and comprehensive assessments such as Ekman and Friesen's FAC system (1978), which emphasizes the timing and intensity as well as the location of facial actions, has unmasked previously controversial or poorly documented conversational and emotional facial messages. Ekman and Friesen (1975, 1978) have identified the facial actions that distinguish the expressions of happiness, sadness, fear, anger, disgust, and surprise, and Ekman and Friesen (1975) suggested that "blends" of these distinctive facial actions (for example, facial actions characteristic of surprise accompanied by the drawing of the corners of the mouth back and upward) correspond to blends of emotional appearances (for example, happily surprised).

Moreover, assessment of observable facial actions following the induction of these diverse emotional states has revealed that the facial expressions accompanying pleasant and unpleasant emotional reactions could be distinguished, as to some extent could the intensity of these positive or negative reactions (Ekman, Friesen, and Ancoli 1980; see Fridlund, Ekman, and Oster in press). Finally, they found that a large portion of variance in people's observable facial actions could be attributed to what they termed *display rules*—that is, socially learned prescriptions for regulating expressions of emotion (Ekman 1972; Friesen 1972).

Electromyographic Procedures

It should be emphasized, however, that:

> Facial expressions are principally the result of stereotyped movements of facial skin and fascia (connective tissue) due to contraction of the facial muscles in certain combinations. Such contractions create folds, lines, and wrinkles in the skin and cause movement of facial landmarks such as mouth corners and eyebrows (Rinn 1984, p. 52).

It is these folds, lines, and wrinkles in the skin and the movements of facial landmarks, not the neuromuscular impulses underlying these facial actions, that are measured when photographs and videotapes are analyzed. Measurement of the underlying neuromuscular impulses, therefore, may provide information not available using other procedures.

Each muscle consists of millions of individual muscle fibers housed in connective tissue and is innervated by a specific motor nerve. The motor nerve, in turn, consists of millions of nerve fibers that arise from discrete populations of motor neurons in the spinal cord and brainstem. (The area where a neural fiber actually terminates on a muscle fiber is called the motor end plate.) These motoneurons have differential critical firing thresholds, such that progressively larger motoneurons are added to, or progressively smaller units are subtracted from, the total output of a motoneuron pool as the neural input to the neurons is increased or decreased, respectively (Henneman 1980).

When a particular motoneuron is depolarized, a neural impulse travels to the end-plate region, and the chemical transmitter acetylcholine is released. The acetylcholine initiates a self-propagating electrical impulse, or muscle action potential (MAP), that traverses the muscle fiber and activates the physiochemical mechanism, which causes the fiber to contract. The acetylcholine is quickly eradicated by the enzyme acetylecholineserase, and MAP activity and muscle fiber contraction cease without additional neural activity.

Whenever a MAP passes along a muscle fiber, an electrical potential is created that can be measured at the skin. The greater the MAP activity, the greater the total voltage measurable at the skin. Needle electrodes inserted into the muscle or surface electrodes placed on the skin over muscle regions allow detection, amplification, and recording of these voltages; the resultant is called the electromyogram (EMG). (Interested readers should consult Fridlund and Izard 1983, for further discussion of these points.)

Small surface electrodes held into place by adhesive collars rather than needle electrodes are used in most psychophysiological research (for example, see Goldstein 1972; McGuigan 1979). EMG signals obtained from surface, in contrast to needle, electrodes do not allow precise determination of the source of the MAP activity since they reflect the MAPs from a cluster of heterogeneous motor units, perhaps from several proximal muscles, rather than the MAPs from a single unit or muscle. Although the details of the individual MAPs are lost in the surface EMG recordings, the discrete microvolt discharges from individual MAPs summate spatially and temporally during motor unit recruitment to yield an aggregate that, with proper placement and amplification, can indicate the action (or inaction) of motoneuron pools in facial muscle (for example, perioral) regions. Frequency analyses of the raw EMG signals obtained from surface recordings have thus far proven no more sensitive to psychological factors than the relatively inexpensive process of recording and analyzing the integrated EMG response (McGuigan et al. 1982; Sokolov 1972), although it has been useful in more traditional physiological investigations (for example, van Boxtel et al. 1983). Hence, the integrated EMG is the most common contemporary psychophysiological measure of the skeletal muscular system. The physiological observations of the lawful behavior of motoneuron pools supports the assumption that changes in the amplitude and form of the integrated EMG provides a reliable and valid index of changes in MAP activity (Lippold 1967; Cacioppo, Marshall-Goodell, and Dorfman 1983; Gans and Gorniak 1980).

The surface electrodes in EMG recording are placed in pairs over specific superficial muscle regions, as is shown in figure 4–1. Each person's facial size and musculature is slightly different, but the exact placement of electrodes can be determined unobtrusively while interacting with that individual. For instance, asking students how they feel about their sports teams almost invariably evokes a smile, which then can be used to identify fairly precisely where the *zygomatic major* muscle strip or smile muscle lies. Recordings from a variety of muscle regions can be obtained using this procedure.

The more fibers within a muscle that contract simultaneously, the greater the likelihood that overt muscle contractions will be exhibited. EMG recordings, however, can reveal MAP activity too small to evoke noticeable movements and/or whose corresponding muscle contraction is counteracted by contraction of an antagonist. In an interesting illustration of this principle, Ekman, Schwartz, and Friesen (reported in Ekman 1982b) simultaneously secured videorecordings and surface EMG recordings of individuals as they deliberately intensified the contraction of specific facial muscles *(corrugator supercilii* and *medial frontalis)*. Results revealed that (1) FACS and EMG recordings were highly correlated ($r = +.85$), but (2) reliable EMG signals emerged at levels of muscle activity substantially lower than could be reliably detected visually.

Ekman (1982b) also reported evidence suggesting that patterns of facial actions too subtle or fleeting to be reliably detected using visual scoring procedures may nevertheless leave an impression on observers carefully scrutinizing the person's facial expression:

> This study also showed that there are visible clues to muscle tension, measureable by EMG, when there is no movement. The person measuring the faces with FACS guessed which muscle had been tensed when they could not see any movement. . . . Analyses showed that when these guesses were correct—when the scorer predicted which muscle the performer was tensing, even though no movement was visible—there was a greater increase in EMG than when the guesses were incorrect (Ekman 1982b, p. 82).

Distinctive facial actions and expressions are not limited to interpersonal interactions, but can also reflect intrapersonal processes. People engage in covert oral behavior (for example, subvocalization, lip pressing) when silently reading (see reviews by McGuigan 1970, 1978; Sokolov 1972). Moreover:

> Whereas sounds and the body movements that illustrate speech are intermittent, the face even in repose may provide information about some emotion or mood state. Many nonverbal behaviors simply do not occur when a person is alone, or at least do so very rarely. For example, it would be unusual for someone to shrug or gesture hello when totally alone. Yet facial expressions of emotion may be quite intense even when a person is alone. They are not occasioned only by the presence of others. In fact, social situations can dampen facial expression of emotion (Ekman 1982b, p. 45).

To summarize thus far, facial EMG recordings seem to be capable of uncovering MAP activity in the human face even in the absence of visually quantifiable facial actions. More importantly, both cognitive (for example, semantic–messages vs visual–image information processing) and affective (for example, positive–negative) processes presumed to be fundamental to consumer behavior may be associated with discriminable (though not necessarily invariant) patterns of MAPs in the human face (Cacioppo and Petty 1981a). It may be possible, therefore, to study the role of cognitive and affective processes using a common methodology that does not require the individual to verbalize. In the remaining sections of this chapter, we review our research in this area. We conclude by noting the implications of our observations for conceptions of cognitions, affect, and attitudes.

Effects of Affect-laden Information Processing on Perioral EMG Activity

Most of the early psychophysiological research on facial EMG concerned the relationship between the activation of the muscles of articulation (perioral EMG) and information processing. Only recently has research focused on facial EMG and affect. Therefore, we begin by reviewing the earlier work on perioral EMG and information processing to examine the effects on facial EMG activity of information processing and to examine what effects mild variations of emotion have on perioral EMG activity. The empirical evidence to date is consistent with the notion that perioral EMG activity is related to information processing (see reviews by Garrity 1977; McGuigan 1970, 1978; Sokolov 1972) but the data are less clear regarding the validity and specificity of this relationship. Previous research has shown that silently processing linguistic materials (for example, reading) leads to greater EMG activity over the perioral region than silently processing nonlinguistic material (for example, music) and both tasks usually result in elevated perioral EMG activity relative to baseline measures (for example, Edfeldt 1960; McGuigan and Bailey 1969). The activation of the perioral muscles is also specific: (1) concomitant increases in EMG activity are not typically found indiscriminately or generally in nonoral muscle groups or in electrodermal responding when silently processing language material (for example, McGuigan and Tanner 1971; Sokolov 1972); and (2) the relative activation of muscles within the perioral (for example, tongue vs. lip) region has been shown to vary as a function of the phonetic characteristics (for example, *ta* vs. *ba*) of the material being processed (McGuigan and Winstead 1974). Finally, poor readers have been found to display greater perioral EMG activity when reading than good readers, though both display increased perioral EMG activity when silently reading difficult rather than simple text (for example, Edfeldt 1960; Faaborg-Anderson and Edfeldt 1958). Note, however, that the type of stimulus presented and/or the type of subject employed has been varied along with the extent of covert linguistic processing presumably manipulated. For instance, although poor readers show greater perioral EMG activity while reading than good readers, it is unclear whether this effect is caused by differences in the cognitive work involved in comprehending or in encoding the material, the manner in which the material is being processed, attentional differences in the readers, differences in self-monitoring between the readers, and/or differences in apprehension.

The instructional manipulations commonly used in cognitive psychology to study encoding operations provide an alternative procedure to study the associated movements of information processing. The paradigm involves presenting target words (for example, trait adjectives) to subjects while randomly varying the question pertaining to each trait word (Craik and Tulving 1975). In this paradigm, somatic responses attributable to features of subjects and stimuli are assigned to the error term and what generally remains is variance due to the instructional factor (the *cue question*), which serves operationally to pinpoint the predominant type of informational analysis operating during the target word presentation (compare Baddeley 1978; Cermak and Craik 1979).

Results of research in this paradigm have generally shown that the more semantic (that is, meaning-oriented) the cued analysis, the more likely subjects are to remember the stimulus word (see review by Craik 1979), although these effects are especially evident when semantic processes are cued both at the time of encoding and at the time of retrieval (Morris, Bransford, and Franks 1977; Tulving 1978). These data have been interpreted as indicating the existence of qualitatively different processes by which incoming information is related to one or more existing domains of knowledge (Cermak and Craik 1979; Craik 1979). The purpose of our initial study, therefore, was to determine whether perioral (*orbicularis oris*) EMG activity was higher when subjects performed tasks requiring that they think about the meaning and self-descriptiveness of a word rather than about the structural appearance of the word (Cacioppo and Petty 1979c). Furthermore, EMG activity over a nonoral muscle region (*superficial forearm flexors* of the nonpreferred arm) was recorded to determine whether task-evoked changes in EMG activity were general or specific.

Subjects were shown cue questions asking whether or not the succeeding trait adjective was printed in upper-case letters or whether or not the word was self-descriptive. Half the trait adjectives were printed in upper-case letters and half were printed in lower case; and half the trait adjectives were highly self-descriptive, whereas half were not at all self-descriptive. Subjects responded "yes" or "no" by pressing one of two buttons on a key pad. Cacioppo and Petty (1979b) found that (1) the self-referent task led to better recall than the structural task, replicating previous studies in social psychology (for example, Rogers, Kuiper, and Kirker 1977); (2) the self-referent task led to greater increases in perioral EMG activity than the structural task; and (3) EMG activity over a nonoral muscle group did not vary as a function of the orienting task. This latter effect renders it unlikely that subjects were generally more aroused or tense when performing the self-referent than structural task.

This orienting-task paradigm has also been used to investigate possible differences in the organization of domains of product and social knowledge. Studies have shown that product information and trait words are better recalled when rated for their descriptiveness of oneself or one's best friend than of people about whom one has little or no direct knowledge (for example, Bower and Gilligan 1979; Keenan and Baillet 1980). These data have been interpreted as indicating structural differences in domains of social and consumer knowledge in memory. As Ferguson, Rule, and Carlson (1983) note, the domains of knowledge (for example, one's self) accessed by tasks (for example, self-referent task) that produce relatively better recall of the incoming stimuli are thought to be characterized by greater elaboration (that is, more associates), integration (that is, stronger interassociative bonding), and/or differentiation (that is, more chunking of associates into distinct but related subsets). Ferguson, Rule, and Carlson (1983) further reported data from this paradigm using a between-subjects design showing that self-referent and evaluative orienting tasks yielded similar response latencies and levels of recall. They argued that (1) evaluation constitutes a central dimension along which incoming information is categorized and stored; and (2) both evaluative and self-referent tasks facilitated the use of the evaluative dimension and minimized the use of other irrelevant dimensions in processing incoming information. They concluded that, given the centrality of the evaluative dimension in the organization of memory, "no unique memorial status need be attributed to the self or familiar others." (Ferguson, Rule, and Carlson 1983, p. 260)

We have completed two studies on perioral EMG activity and information processing that bear both on the effects of information processing on perioral EMG activity and on Ferguson, Rule, and Carlson's analysis. In one study, subjects were exposed to sixty positive, neutral, and negative trait adjectives (Cacioppo and Petty 1981b). Each trait adjective was preceded by one of five cue questions that defined the processing task: (1) Does the following word rhyme with————(rhyme); (2) Is the following word spoken louder than this question? (volume discrimination); (3) Is the following word similar in meaning to————? (association), (4) Is the following word good (bad)? (evaluation); and (5) Is the following word self-descriptive? (self-reference). Finally, as in all of our facial EMG research, subjects in this study knew bioelectrical activity was being recorded, but they were not told that activity over which they had voluntary control was being monitored.

Results revealed that mean recognition confidence ratings were ordered as follows: self-reference, evaluation, association, rhyme, and volume discrimination. Importantly, all means except the last two differed significantly from one another. In addition, (1) the mean amplitude of perioral *(orbicularis oris)* EMG activity was lowest for the nonsemantic tasks of rhyme and volume discrimination, intermediate for the task of association, and equally high for the tasks of evaluation and self-reference; (2) cardiac activity and the mean amplitude of EMG activity over a nonoral muscle region (that is, nonpreferred *superficial forearm flexors* region) did not vary as a function of the type of task performed; and (3) the association between task and perioral EMG activity was temporally specific, with task-discriminating EMG activity observed only while subjects analyzed the aurally presented trait adjectives and formulated their response.

In a follow-up study, we found that evaluative and self-referent tasks have different effects on perioral EMG activity, but that the effect is on the *form* rather than mean amplitude of the task-evoked response (Cacioppo, Petty, and Morris 1985). Subjects performed structural, grammatical, evaluative, and self-referent orienting tasks. EMG activity and response latency were assessed during each trial, either task difficulty (replication 1) or reported cognitive effort (replication 2) was assessed following each trial, and recall was assessed at the conclusion of the study. Analyses of the cognitive measures revealed that recall was poorest when trait words were judged in terms of their structural appearance, moderately poor and moderately good when words were judged in terms of their grammatical and evaluative features, respectively, and best when words were judged in terms of their self-descriptiveness—all this despite the finding that subjects took longest to perform the grammatical task and rated this task the most difficult and most cognitively effortful to perform.

More interestingly here, analyses revealed that the form rather than the mean amplitude of perioral EMG activity differentiated these simple cognitive tasks, with significant differences emerging during semantic and nonsemantic processing and between evaluative and self-referent processing. Perioral EMG activity, for instance, was characterized by more frequent bursts of EMG activity during the self-referent than evaluative tasks. Further analyses revealed that perioral EMG activity covaried more closely with indices of cognitive deliberation (for example, rated cognitive effort) than long-term memory processes (that is, recall). Although EMG activity over the forearm rose more sharply, later in the processing epoch, when subjects performed simple structural instead of semantic tasks, the form of EMG activity over the preferred forearm was similar for evaluative and self-referent processing. Moreover, little evidence was found to support the hypothesis that simply accessing or evaluating the meaning of positive or negative trait words was sufficient to evoke traces of emotional facial displays.

These results, obtained using a within-subjects rather than between-subjects design (compare McCaul and Maki 1984), support Osgood, Suci, and Tannenbaum's notion (1957) that a central dimension along which incoming information is effectively categorized, stored, and retrieved is the evaluative dimension. Contrary to Ferguson, Rule, and Carlson's suggestion (1983), however, these results also suggest that self-referent and evaluative processing are distinguishable quantitatively if not qualitatively. Finally, these data support the notion that long-term memory for incoming information is affected both by short-term memory processes and by the accessibility and structure of existing knowledge domains, but that short-term working memory processes have the more direct effect on perioral EMG activity. To illustrate, consider an individual who has difficulty retrieving information from long-term memory either because there is so little in a particular memorial domain or because there is so much in that domain. The results of our research on perioral EMG activity suggests that in both instances the individual should show an elevation of perioral EMG activity over levels observed during relaxation since it is the short-term cognitive work, not the amount of information in long-term memory, that has the immediate effect on perioral EMG activity.

Effects of Affective Experience on Facial EMG

Although the muscles of the lower face are clearly involved in overt expressions of emotions (Ekman 1982a; Ekman and Friesen 1975, 1978), perioral EMG activity does not appear to be related to the affective tone of an individual's information processing, given the low levels of affect and the visual and auditory stimuli with which we are dealing in these studies. For instance, some of the trait words employed in the Cacioppo and Petty (1981b) study were positive, others were neutral, and still others were negative in meaning. Although we have observed differential hemispheric EEG activity to these stimuli (Cacioppo and Petty 1980), we found no differences in perioral EMG activity as a function of word valence.

In a corroborating experiment, subjects were forewarned of an impending recommendation that differed slightly, moderately, or considerably from their own attitude on an issue (Cacioppo and Petty 1979a). Following each forewarning, subjects were instructed to collect their thoughts on the issue for the next minute, and, at the end of the minute, they were asked to list everything about which they had thought. Analyses of subjects' retrospective verbal reports revealed that the profile of listed thoughts, rather than the total number of thoughts listed, changed as communication discrepancy increased: agreement and the frequency of counterarguments increased whereas the frequency of proarguments decreased. More interestingly here were the findings that (1) localized increases in perioral EMG activity were observed during the collect-thoughts interval; but (2) communication discrepancy had *no* effect on perioral EMG activity. Although the level of perioral EMG activity was related to the total number of listed thoughts, there simply was no evidence that perioral EMG activity changed as the affective tone of issue-relevant thinking changed.

Whereas the extent of cognitive deliberation rather than people's affective reactions has been apparent in perioral EMG activity, EMG activity over muscles that control the movement of facial landmarks in the lower, middle, and upper face *has* been found to vary as a function of the affective tone of attitudinal processing. In the initial studies on facial EMG and emotional imagery, Schwartz and his colleagues (Schwartz et al. 1976a, 1976b) demonstrated that (1) when subjects followed instructions to imagine a *happy* situation, the level of EMG activity increased over the cheek *(zygomatic major)* and lower lateral chin *(depressor anguli oris)* regions and tended to decrease over the brow *(corrugator)* region; (2) when subjects followed instructions to imagine a *sad* situation, EMG activity increased primarily over the brow region; (3) this patterning of facial muscle activity reliably distinguished positive and negative emotional imagery in normals and clinically depressed patients; and (4) the depressed patients showed an attenuated pattern of facial EMG activity during happy imagery and an exaggerated pattern of facial EMG activity to sad imagery. Fridlund and Izard (1983), however, have argued that demand characteristics may have contributed to, or accounted for, the results of facial EMG studies of affective imagery. The crux of their criticism was that the placement of multiple electrodes on a subject's face sensitizes the subject to the importance of his or her face as a response system. They further reasoned that the imagery instructions may artifactually induce subjects to use their face to express the psychological state believed to be the focus of study.

This led us to conduct a study with three specific aims (Cacioppo, Petty, and Marshall-Goodell 1984). First, we sought to conceptually replicate our research showing that perioral EMG activity was greater while people thought about an attitude issue than when they were engaged in a nonlanguage task and that the perioral EMG activity was unrelated to the valence of the attitude processing.

Second, Ekman and Friesen (1975, 1978) have emphasized that emotional expressions are evident in the upper (for example, brows), middle (for example, eyes, nose), and lower (for example, mouth) regions of the face. The unequivocal expression of anger, for instance, requires rapid signals emanating from all three regions (Ekman and Friesen 1975). Another aim of our study, therefore, was to determine whether EMG activity over muscles that control the movement of facial landmarks in the lower (for example, *zygomatic major,* which pulls the corners of the mouth upward and back when forming a smile), middle (for example, *levator labii superioris* and *levator labii superioris alaequa nasi,* which raises the lip and dilates the nostril in the primitive expression of disgust), and upper (for example, *corrugator* and *depressor supercilii,* which draw the brows down and/or together in negative emotions such as anger and sadness) regions of the face varied as a function of the affective tone of attitudinal processing.

Our third aim was to examine whether demand characteristics were necessary for the facial patterning during emotional imagery observed by Schwartz and his colleagues. Subjects were led to believe they were participating in a study on involuntary neural responses during action and imagery. Subjects on any given trial either lifted (action) or imagined lifting (imagery) a *light* or *heavy* weight or either silently read (action) a neutral communication as if they agreed or disagreed with its thesis or imagined reading (imagery) an editorial with which they agreed or disagreed. Based on previous research (for example, see reviews by Ekman and Friesen 1975; Fridlund and Izard 1983) and our own pilot research on overt facial actions during physical exertion, EMG activity was recorded over the brow *(corrugator supercilii),* cheek *(zygomatic major),* nose *(levator labii superioris),* jaw *(masseter,* whose action raises and protracts the mandible), periocular *(orbicularis oris),* and forearm *(superficial forearm flexors)* muscle regions. It was expected that (1) EMG activity over the perioral *(orbicularis oris)* region would be greater for the attitudinal than physical tasks; (2) perioral EMG activity would not vary as a function of the valence of the attitudinal tasks, but instead EMG activity over the regions of the brow, cheek, and nose would differentiate the positive and negative attitudinal tasks; and, of course, (3) EMG activity over the forearm flexors would be greater during the physical than attitudinal tasks and would differentiate the physical tasks.

In addition, we found in preliminary research that expressions of physical exertion (such as when a person lifts a heavy weight) were characterized by a tensing of a variety of facial muscles including the brow, periocular, and jaw. If the simple placement of multiple electrodes on a subject's face cued the subject to the importance of his or her facial actions in this paradigm, then not only might EMG responses over the regions of the brow, cheek, and nose differ as subjects adopted an agreeable vs. disagreeable attitudinal set, but EMG responses over at least selected facial muscles (for example, brow, jaw, periocular) might vary when subjects were instructed to lift or imagine lifting what was described to them as being a heavy in contrast to a light weight. In fact, subjects worked with 16 gram and 35 gram weights in the physical tasks, both of which are fairly light, and subjects were exposed to identical neutral text in the attitudinal tasks when they were asked to silently read the text in an agreeable vs. disagreeable manner. Hence, nothing about the stimuli per se should have evoked facial actions of any kind. Finally, at the end of each session, subjects were interviewed and were asked specifically what they believed to be the experimental hypothesis. Since subjects might reason that they should not disclose how much they knew, we emphasized that it was important that they respond honestly and accurately.

Results provided support for the hypotheses. Perioral EMG activity was higher during the attitudinal than physical tasks, but perioral EMG activity was again essentially unchanged by the affective tone of attitudinal processing. Yet, whether subjects thought about the topic in an agreeable versus disagreeable manner affected EMG activity over the facial regions of the brow, cheek, and nose. These results replicate and extend the research on emotional imagery conducted by Schwartz and his colleagues (compare Brown and Schwartz 1980).

Moreover, a strikingly different pattern of somatic activity was evoked by the physical tasks. As expected, EMG activity over the forearm flexors was higher during the physical than attitudinal tasks, and the EMG activity over the forearm varied across the physical tasks. Facial EMG activity, in contrast, was unaffected by the type of physical task performed. There was simply no hint that subjects were modifying their facial displays when lifting, or imagining lifting, what were described to subjects as heavy and light weights. Furthermore, the postexperimental interviews failed to reveal any evidence for the operation of experimental demands. All subjects appeared convinced of the cover story (that is, the sensors were used to detect involuntary physiological reactions), and no subject articulated anything resembling the experimental hypothesis. Indeed, the postexperimental interviews of subjects indicated that they tended implicitly to organize the experimental trials in terms of whether they imagined or performed some task (for example, lifting a weight or silently reading a text) rather than in terms of whether the task was physical or attitudinal. Finally, what we found to be the most compelling evidence against the operation of experimental demands was that rarely were visible facial actions observed during the tasks and data from those few trials on which actions could be seen were deleted prior to analysis. It seems implausible that subjects chose to support the hypothesis by making only covert facial responses.

In sum, these data support the view that experimental demands are not necessary for the somatic patterning observed during affective processing and imagery, that perioral EMG activity is greater during silent language processing (for example, reading) than during nonlanguage processing (for example, lifting a weight), and that EMG activity over selected facial muscle regions including the brow *(corrugator supercilii)* and the cheek *(zygomatic major)* differentiates positive from negative affects.

There is also evidence for the utility of facial EMG recordings as a continuous and objective probe of the low-level cognitive and affective responses evoked when subjects anticipate and are exposed to a persuasive communication (Cacioppo and Petty 1979a). Students in our study were recruited for what they believed was an experiment on *biosensory processes*. As in the previous research, subjects were told that we were studying the involuntary neural responses evoked by communicative stimuli and were monitored unobtrusively to avoid invoking display rules. After subjects adapted to the laboratory, we obtained recordings of basal EMG activity, forewarned subjects that in 60 seconds they would be hearing an editorial with which they agreed, an editorial with which they disagreed, or an unspecified message, obtained another 60 seconds of physiological recording while subjects sat quietly, and obtained yet another 120 seconds of data while subjects listened to a proattitudinal appeal, counterattitudinal appeal, or what turned out to be a pleasant news story about an archeological expedition.

Consistent with the observations of facial activity during emotion and emotional imagery, results indicated that EMG activity over the cheek *(zygomatic major)* region was higher and the activity over the brow *(corrugator supercilii)* region was slightly lower when subjects anticipated and listened to a proattitudinal instead of a counterattitudinal appeal. Although this patterning was evident during the postwarning–premessage period, it was magnified when subjects were actually confronted by the proattitudinal or counterattitudinal message. We also found perioral increased EMG activity over the basal level when subjects anticipated a counterattitudinal message, and it increased to an equally high level across conditions when an actual message was presented regardless of the valence of the appeal. Together, these data suggest that the presentation of a communication about which subjects think increases perioral EMG activity. The affective attributes of the persuasive appeal was again unrelated to the level of perioral EMG activity; instead, it was reflected in the pattern of facial EMG activity over the brow and cheek regions. Finally, the selective activation of perioral EMG activity during the postwarning–premessage period provided convergent evidence for the view that people engage in anticipatory cognitive activity to buttress their beliefs when they anticipate hearing a personally involving, counterattitudinal appeal (compare Hass and Grady 1975; Petty and Cacioppo 1977).

Although these results are encouraging, Ekman (1982b) has expressed a concern that electromyographic studies of visually imperceptible facial actions may not prove useful in distinguishing among specific emotional states. Brown and Schwartz (1980), for instance, used standardized affective imagery instructions and observed that happy emotional imagery increased the mean amplitude of EMG activity over the cheek *(zygomatic major)* muscle region, whereas sad, anger, and fear imagery all increased the EMG activity over the brow *(corrugator supercilii)* region. Changes in EMG activity over the jaw *(masseter)* and forehead *(lateral frontalis,* whose action raises the outer eyebrows and wrinkles the forehead) muscle regions failed to distinguish these imagery conditions even though these muscles can be involved when forming overt facial expressions of emotions (compare Fridlund, Schwartz, and Fowler 1984).

Although further research is necessary, it is useful to think about the expression of affect in terms of a hierarchy of neuromuscular action. Rudimentary or low-level affective reactions to auditory and visual stimuli may tend to be discriminated in only a few facial muscle actions (for example, *corrugator supercilii, zygomatic major*) that reflect the general valence of the stimuli, whereas more intense emotional reactions may be differentiated within these muscle regions and/or across a greater number of facial muscles (compare Cacioppo, Petty, and Marshall-Goodell 1984). Moreover, both research on the communication of emotion through facial expressions (Osgood 1966) and studies of the conceptual organization of emotion suggest distinguishing between positive and negative affects and between mild and intense affects captures much of people's emotional experience. Russell (1983), for instance, conducted a multidimensional scaling study of the similarity judgments of emotionally descriptive words (for example, happy, annoyed, sad, angry). To study the pancultural aspects of people's conceptualization of emotions, subjects from five distinct cultures were tested. Russell found that within each culture the organization of emotions was described adequately by two dimensions: valence (pleasant–unpleasant) and intensity (calm–excited; see also, McHugo, Smith, and Lanzetta 1982). Similarly, Osgood (1966) investigated what dimensions of emotional experience could reliably be communicated to others using facial expressions. He found pleasantness, intensity, and control to be the most important dimensions. Hence, the difficulty in discriminating among the negative affects using low-level facial EMG responses would be less of a limitation in the study of affect if facial EMG activity—at least when recorded in controlled laboratory settings—could be used to gauge the intensity as well as the valence of affective processing.

In a study bearing on this issue, subjects were exposed to slides of moderately unpleasant, mildly unpleasant, mildly pleasant, and moderately pleasant scenes (Cacioppo et al. in preparation). Subjects viewed each slide for five seconds and rated how much they liked the depicted scene, how familiar the scene appeared, and how aroused it made them feel. Examination of the videorecordings of subjects' facial expressions during the five-second stimulus presentations indicated that the scenes were sufficiently mild to avoid evoking perceptible facial actions. Nevertheless, both analyses of variance and correlational analyses revealed that EMG activity over the brow (*corrugator supercilii*) muscle region differentiated the direction *and* intensity of people's affective reaction to the scenes: the more subjects liked the scene, the lower the level of EMG activity over the brow region. Also, EMG activity over the cheek (*zygomatic major*) region was also greater for liked than disliked scenes. Importantly, neither EMG activity over the brow region nor over the cheek region covaried with reported arousal, nor did EMG activity over the perioral *(orbicularis oris)* region or a peripheral muscle region *(superficial forearm flexors)* vary as a function of stimulus valence. A second study replicated these results and also demonstrated than an independent set of judges could not accurately guess the emotional nature of the stimulus to which subjects were exposed when they viewed the subjects' overt facial actions. These data are clearly more compatible with the view of response specificity in the facial actions accompanying cognition and affect than with the view that somatic activity varies as a function of affective intensity (compare Cacioppo and Petty 1981a; Winton, Putman, and Krauss 1984).

With these bridges between psychological constructs and psychophysiological data specified, we should emphasize the sometimes circuitous route to these bridges. Specifically, this psychophysiological research does not indicate that distinctive and naturally occurring incipient facial actions can be invariantly linked to low-level cognitive or affective states (Cacioppo and Petty 1985). The EMG patterning observed in our research has been subtle and is easily distorted, requiring optimal experimental conditions to obtain. Facial actions are clearly controllable, and facial expressions serve communicative, deceptive, and emotionally expressive functions with admirable facility. It should be borne in mind, therefore, that special conditions have been established in this research to maximize the likelihood of observing task-related somatic responses and to minimize the likelihood that these responses would be masked or altered by display rules. For instance, subjects are given an introductory lecture on bioelectrical recording principles and a tour of the testing rooms prior to volunteering to participate, and they undergo progressive relaxation and practice tasks prior to being exposed to experimental stimuli. These procedures are employed to minimize their overall level of somatic activity and apprehension about participating in the research so that they are responsive to the experimental tasks per se. Subjects have numerous dummy electrodes attached to them, are given a cover story so that they are unaware that somatic (much less facial EMG) activity is being recorded, are placed alone in a testing room, and are observed unobtrusively. As a result, throughout most of this research subjects appear to be sitting quietly and void of emotion. Although this research illustrates the existence of unique relationships between facial EMG and the nature, intensity, and timing of certain classes of cognitive and affective processes, the ecological validity for these relationships is limited (Cacioppo and Petty 1985).

For example, Lauren Bush recently completed a study in our laboratory that examined the features of EMG activity that differentiate spontaneous facial expressions to mildly pleasant or unpleasant visual stimuli from actions designed to mask affective reactions to these stimuli and expressions that were deliberately constructed by subjects to subtly communicate their feelings about these stimuli. Based on the work by Ekman and his colleagues, it was hypothesized that under certain circumstances the timing of the spontaneously produced and deliberately constructed EMG responses would differ, with the latter developing more slowly and over a longer period of time. Facial EMG activity was recorded as subjects viewed slides of mildly pleasant or mildly unpleasant faces and scenes. Each slide was presented for five seconds, and during the first set of slides subjects were simply instructed to examine each when it was presented and to rate how much they liked it following its presentation. Following this initial series of slides, subjects were told to imagine two individuals were seated in front of them—one a close friend, the other a stranger. Subjects were instructed that, as they examined the photographs projected onto the screen, they should either try not to reveal through their facial displays whether the stimulus was pleasant or unpleasant (posed unexpressive facial displays) or through subtle facial displays, they should try to communicate to the friend, but not the stranger, whether the stimulus was pleasant or unpleasant (subtly posed expressive facial displays). Subjects practiced each task before the experimental trials, and the order of these last two instructions was counterbalanced across replications of the study. Data from the few trials on which emotional facial expressions were noticeable were deleted prior to analysis.

Results revealed that facial EMG activity associated with spontaneous affect versus interpersonal masking and communication of affect *were* distinguishable. EMG activity over the brow *(corrugator supercilii)* region was again greater in response to unpleasant than pleasant visual stimuli; deliberately masked facial displays were characterized by a maintenance of EMG activity at prestimulus levels across the facial muscles; and deliberately posed expressive facial displays were characterized by affect-discriminating EMG responses that developed more intensely and were maintained over a longer period of time than were spontaneous emotional expressions. These data illustrate that the connections between facial EMG activity and affect are not invariant. On the other hand, and although it is not known whether the observed differences between spontaneous and deliberately constructed expressions of emotion generalize to conditions in which subjects are told simply to exaggerate or misrepresent displays of their feelings about a stimulus, this study also demonstrates that spontaneous and deliberately constructed expressions of affect can be distinguished quantitatively if not qualitatively within at least some contexts (compare Hager and Ekman 1985).

Conclusion

Difficulties in extracting information regarding affect from ongoing organismic processes are to be expected given the nonpsychological (for example, homeostatic) functions served by the human organism, the paucity of current knowledge about the neurophysiological mechanisms serving affective processes, and the methodological limitations inherent in studying human subjects using noninvasive somatovisceral recording procedures (compare Coles, Donchin, and Porges 1985). Indeed, although somatovisceral measures have been used with some success to index psychological states such as the use of deception (Lykken 1981; Podlesny and Raskin 1977; Waid and Orne 1981) and the intensity or direction of reported attitudes (Cacioppo and Sandman 1981; Petty and Cacioppo 1983; Tursky and Jamner 1983), physiological measures of enduring and accessible psychological states have often proved to be expensive, cumbersome, and less sensitive than traditional methods such as verbal reports (for example, Rogers 1983; Crider 1983; Shapiro and Schwartz 1970) or simple variations on these assessments, such as the bogus pipeline (Jones and Sigall 1971; see review by Petty and Cacioppo 1983).

It is noteworthy, therefore, that a major advantage of somatovisceral measures and manipulations—augmenting our means for studying the role of affective processes and their relationship to language processing—has remained largely unexplored. As noted above, the somatic nervous system is the ultimate mechanism through which humans interact with and modify their environments, and the muscles of facial expression have the further distinction of being linked to connective tissue and fascia rather than to skeletal structures. This endows the facial response system with an interesting (although not unique) functional property: the effects on the environment of the neural activation of the facial muscles of expression are in part indirect—mediated by the construction of facial configurations that communicate information (for example, ideas, inferences), misinformation (for example, deception), and emotion (for example, threat, approval). It is perhaps less than surprising, therefore, that the understanding of people's preferences and actions can be enriched by analyses of the facial response system.

On the other hand, one cannot expect facial EMG responses alone to provide a definitive basis for unequivocally inferring consumer's reactions in applied settings. As indicated in our introduction, affect is viewed as having motivational, perceptual, cognitive, motor expressive, physiological, and subjective manifestations, and no given episode of emotion is likely to result in changes across all these modes of expression. Moreover, the range of construct validity of the facial EMG measures is limited and is unlikely to extend to a broad range of applications without the introduction of additional experimental controls. For instance, facial reactions to gustatory stimuli—for instance, in a market food test—can potentially unmask a consumer's gut reaction to a product, but consumer researchers would first need to be concerned with the facial actions involved in mastication and with the social context in which the assessment was conducted (for example, to avoid experimenter bias, self-presentation). Hence, additional research on the facial response system in applied settings using naturalistic stimuli is clearly needed before procedures such as the facial EMG can be used confidently to address and resolve specific theoretical questions having practical significance to the manager or decision maker in an applied area.

In sum, the present research suggests that specific dimensions of affect have reliable effects on the location, intensity, and timing of EMG activity recorded over facial muscle regions. Studies using verbal reports or visual observations have further revealed that emotions can be highly transient, occur in combinations (blends), and at times go undetected (for example, Haggard and Issacs 1966; Schwartz et al. 1976a; Kunst-Wilson and Zajonc 1980). Although the analyses of the dynamic aspects of overt expressive behaviors using videotapes (in contrast to drawings or photographs) to augment verbal reports have revealed a wealth of information regarding communication and emotion (Ekman and Friesen 1978; Izard 1971, 1977), there is room for yet other convergent, concomitant measures because not all affective processes are accompanied by visually (Ekman 1982b) or socially perceptible (Love 1972; Rajecki 1984) expressive behaviors. Love (1972), for instance, videotaped people's facial expressions while they were exposed to a proattitudinal or counterattitudinal appeal and reported detecting no differences in overt expressions. As noted above, we replicated this result while also demonstrating that the mean amplitude of the EMG activity recorded over facial muscle regions (for example, corrugator, zygomatic) during the communication differentiated between subjects who were exposed to a proattitudinal appeal from those who were exposed to a counterattitudinal appeal (Cacioppo and Petty 1979a). Thus, the research on overt facial action illustrates the utility of convergent operations that allow measurement of affective processes as they unfold over time (for example, Ekman and Friesen 1974, 1975; Ekman, Friesen, and Ancoli 1980; Izard 1977; Zuckerman, DePaulo, and Rosenthal 1981), whereas the research on facial EMG suggests psychological events (for example, positive–negative affect) too fleeting or subtle to evoke an overt expression may nevertheless be examined objectively.

5
Advertising and Emotionality

Rebecca H. Holman
Young & Rubicam, Inc.

T he topic of emotion in human and consumer behavior is as complex and intriguing as the issue of how emotion can be used in advertising. Both topics are being explored with increasing frequency in an environment characterized, perhaps coincidentally, by greater use than ever before of emotional expression in advertising.

To approach an understanding of how emotion can best be used in advertising, this chapter briefly reviews the history of advertising and consumer behavior as well as prevailing perspectives on human emotion, presents a typology of product roles in the emotional lives of consumers, and adapts a perspective on the relationship between advertising and real life. The chapter ends by synthesizing the preceding into a point of view on how advertising effectively portrays emotions. Examples of advertising that illustrate relevant points are presented, and all commercials discussed are summarized in the appendix.

Brief History of Advertising and Consumer Insights

From a perspective of human or consumer behavior, the most unsophisticated form of advertising is the announcement (or some other piece of marketplace news) that a product or service is offered for sale by a particular manufacturer. Such advertising assumes there is considerable unsatisfied demand for the product or service offered and that consumers are eagerly awaiting this announcement. The economic environment characteristic of such a situation (a *seller's* market) does not encourage sellers to understand the underlying dynamics of purchase and use, because whatever is offered is quickly consumed. Hence, the seller's insight into the consumer is minimal.

A slightly more complicated situation occurs when consumer demand has been met by production capabilities, and competition among manufacturers results. In such an environment, a seller must claim a competitive superiority to attract buyers and usually relies on advertising to communicate that claim. Claims frequently result from manufacturing superiority or production of products with the most desirable features. In this situation, certain types of consumer research become necessary to the manufacturer, who assumes that knowing how consumers evaluate attributes of products will help determine an optimal mix of those attributes. This mix should cause the consumer to buy more of the manufacturer's brands. Although such research contains a wealth of information pertaining to consumers' *thoughts* (information processing) about brands, it stops short of insight. Similarly, advertising emerging from such research communicates manufacturing superiority in coolly rational terms without questioning whether such terms reflect consumers' perspectives on the products being advertised.

Another level of complexity occurs when manufacturing parity among competitors is reached. Any manufacturer claiming superiority on the basis of attributes finds competitors responding with identical or even better claims in a short span of time. Effective competition must rest outside of manufacturing (and R&D). Pricing and physical distribution can provide a temporary edge, but these also are easily duplicated. Similarly, advertising that focuses on consumer *benefits,* derivable from the product's attributes, can provide a preemptive position for the brand. However, when consumers recognize that such benefits are derivable from all brands in the category, benefit-based advertising becomes more like category promotion than brand promotion. Consumer research in such an environment edges toward insight in that it explores consumers' values and motivations. It stops short of understanding the consumer as anything more than someone who buys the brand, however.

To compete effectively in an environment in which manufacturing or technological processes cannot provide a competitive edge (a postproducer environment), manufacturers must turn to effective communication that has been preceded by full consumer insight. It is important to understand how consumers think about brands, but it is *crucial* to understand how brands fit into the lives of consumers—how products and brands make it easier for the consumer to live a more rewarding and fulfilling life. One manifestation of such a competitive edge can be found in advertising that shows the consumer (whether directly or covertly) that the manufacturer *really* understands the needs, motivations, feelings, and thoughts associated with use of the brand. The Merrill Lynch advertising, "China Shop," shows the kind of consumer insight discussed here. The bull successfully makes it through the china shop without any mishaps, much as the heavy investor wants to successfully traverse the complicated task of optimally investing his or her money. The bull is a metaphor for both the investor who is unafraid to take risks and the company, Merrill Lynch, which is able to successfully guide the investor.

Another example of such consumer insight is the advertising for *Time* magazine, which recognized that what readers want goes greatly beyond mere information or clever writing. Readers want to understand the world in which they live and use *Time* as a way of enhancing that understanding.

Both commercials illustrate that advertising cannot ignore the emotional components of consumers' lives in a postproducer environment; instead, such aspects become central to advertising executions and advertising research. True consumer insight is a means to survival over time.

A mix of the above scenarios characterizes the current competitive environment. Few brands can compete effectively with only announcement advertising, but not all face postproducer environments. Most indications are, however, that the vast majority of brands using advertising to support sales will eventually face such an environment. The research questions that emerge from such an environment have only begun to be posed. This chapter deals with only a few: the role of emotion in people's lives, the ways in which product use is associated with emotional experiences, and the relationship between advertising expression of emotion and real life. Even though the bulk of the research needed has yet to be formulated, tentative conclusions from practical experience can be drawn and are presented at the end of this chapter.

Emotion in People's Lives

Cognitive psychologists (and their step-siblings in consumer behavior research) discovered human emotions in the 1980s. This discovery was led by Zajonc (1980) and Bower (1981), who documented the critical interrelationships of information processing and emotional states. Before these discoveries, cognitive psychologists had focused (some would say rather myopically) on only one aspect of the human psyche, the intellectual. (See Holbrook and O'Shaughnessy 1984, for a recent review of the research.) It is now generally acknowledged that learning is facilitated or inhibited, *depending* on the emotional mood of the learner.

Anthropologists have long known that two aspects of the human brain, the paleomammalian and the neomammalian, are roughly associated with emotional and intellectual responses, respectively (MacLean 1964, 1967; Esser 1973). Similarly, the research on brain hemispheric differences has revealed right-brain or emotional processes and left-brain or logical processes (Ornstein 1972). What these two physiological approaches to human thoughts have in common with the research of the cognitive psychologists are scientific explanations for what nonscientists have known for years: humans think *and* humans feel. There are, of course, times when emotions are largely dormant and intellectual processes prevail. Conversely, emotions at times so overwhelm us that rational thought is virtually impossible. For the most part, however, both processes are in evidence and both influence human behavior. Perhaps it is because we tend to equate higher-order activities with intellect (and thus reward intellectual activities more than emotional ones) that we have intellectually studied intellect and not emotion. The fact that psychology has begun to look at the relationships between these two aspects of human existence reflects a maturation of the discipline and a growing sophistication in the study of human behavior (compare Ornstein 1972, p. 80, on this point).

Unfortunately, much of the research that has emerged since cognitive psychologists have discovered emotions has not displayed such maturity and sophistication. It has employed a "which is better" paradigm aimed at delineating when it is best to stimulate the right brain and when to evoke the left, or it has conceptualized emotions as little more than special types of cognitions (Olson and Mitchell 1981; Srull 1984). Most of the research on brain hemispheric dominance has taken such an either-or posture (for example, Appel, Weinstein, and Weinstein 1979). The same implicit posture characterized the research that investigated how emotion-laden manipulations of respondents produce better, or at least different, responses from nonemotion-laden manipulations (Batra and Ray n.d.; Isen et al. 1978; Zielske 1982; Golden and Johnson 1983). Such research, although perhaps necessary to convince those who have not accepted the fact that people are as emotional as they are intellectual, perpetuates an older, reductionist approach to the study of human psychology. A framework that allows the exploration of the interrelationships between these two processes without having to *choose* one or the other in any given context is clearly needed.

Research that has as its goal the uncovering of whatever emotional and intellectual ties the consumer has with the product might be one solution. Such research focuses on the consumer as a genuine person who happens to use products in the course of his or her life, not as someone who fills in the periods between consumption experiences by loving, dreaming of the future, having relationships with others, working, and so forth. From this perspective, research attempts to unravel how products are natural adjuncts to people's lives. It does not attempt to make products any more important than they are from the consumer's viewpoint.

Roles of Products in Emotional Lives of Consumers

Within the framework identified above, there are at least five roles that products can play in people's lives, each of which will have different types and intensities of emotions associated with them. They also vary in the centrality of the product to the consumer. (See Bloch and Bruce 1984, on this point.) Importantly, a product can play one role for one person and a different role for another. Table 5–1 summarizes these relationships.

Table 5–1 lists five roles that products play in people's lives. These five roles (background, mediator to interactions, enhancement of social interac-

Table 5–1
Illustrative Product Roles

Role of Product	Definition	Product Involvement	Source of Emotional Associations	Examples
Background	normal part of the environment in which interactions occur	very low	product as part of the scene in which important emotional events occurred	furniture; grooming products; appliances; office furnishings
Mediator to interactions	reason for an interaction to occur; reason for people getting together	moderate–low	quality of the interactions that occur because of these items	collections (stamps, coins, and so forth); communication items (greeting cards, telephones); pets; objects on display; board or card games; souvenirs
Enhancement of social interaction	part of an actor's role performance; needed to facilitate that performance	moderate–high	success or failure at the role performance using products	cosmetics; food and beverages; music as background; kitchen gadgets; perfume
Expression of self	statement about the actor's self image; who he or she would like to be	high	degree of self-esteem; relationship between actual and ideal self; success at gaining ideal	clothing, other apparel; automobiles; house decorations; things made by person (food, arts and crafts)
Object of emotions	products are cathected objects	very high	substitute for human relationships; pleasure at sensory/aesthetic dimensions	automobiles; electronic equipment; art objects; pets; computers; cameras; wine; food; collections

tions, expressions of self, and object of emotions) are arranged in the table from top to bottom in increasing centrality to a person's life. Each role is briefly defined, the hypothetical degree of involvement with the products playing that role specified, the source or basis for an emotional association of the product for a consumer discussed briefly, and examples of products filling each role provided.

The product role least central to the consumer's life is that of *background,* a normal part of the scene in which relationships are played in ordinary day-to-day functioning. Examples include room furnishings, most appliances, and products used in personal grooming. These are not *un*important objects, since their presence is necessary to set the stage on which the important things of life occur. Their importance is more of a negative type: their absence would be missed, but their presence is not always acknowledged or even salient. These products have emotional content to the extent that they are able to make or break a scene that itself is associated with emotion-laden events. "This is the sofa where he proposed to me" might be an example.

For its line of baby products, the Johnson and Johnson commercial clearly illustrates products that play a background role. A new mother is far more interested in her baby than in the products she uses to care for the baby, but those products are still an important part of her overall caring function. If such products successfully aid in keeping the baby clean, comfortable, and smelling good, they become, in a sense, a part of the baby and gain, by reflection, the emotional associations the mother has with her child.

A second role for products is as a *mediator to interactions.* In this case, the product is not only necessary for the interaction to occur but also forms a focal point for the interaction. Products used in communication over long distances (greeting cards, telephones, flowers) are obvious examples, but other products can also play this role, namely, the reason (or excuse) for an interaction.

The Hallmark commercial "Ballerina Everyday" shows how a product can bridge a physical distance between people. Because it so empathically shows the relationship between the young ballerina and her distant boyfriend, the commercial leads the viewer to easily accept the greeting card in this role. A similar role is played by a Coke in the "Mean Joe Green" commercial. In this instance, however, it is the fact that the small boy offers a Coke that establishes his relationship with Mean Joe Green. When the man offers his jersey to the child, he, too, celebrates and symbolizes the bond between them. Other examples of commercials that illustrate how products can often initiate relationships between people include Kodak's "First Day of School" (a first grade teacher overcomes children's reticence by taking their pictures with an instant camera) and Dr Pepper's "Detective" (the detective establishes rapport with his new client by offering her the "out of the ordinary" beverage).

Products involved in leisure activities (board or card games, athletics) certainly bring people together, as do objects on display (in museums, at auctions) and objects that strangers can easily discuss (pets, collections). These products take on emotional associations linked to the interactions that occur because of them. Souvenirs of events also fall into this category because they enable a reconstruction of these events, either to share with others who were or were not present or to indulge oneself in nostalgia.

Products can also, by their use, *enhance the nature of the social interaction*. Here the product becomes part of an actor's role performance and serves to make that performance better or worse. Sharing cherished products with another is one example (food for instance). The General Foods International Coffee "Beach Sisters" commercial shows adult siblings sharing a quiet moment and celebrating it with a special type of coffee. Because the coffee *is* special, it serves as a tangible symbol of the importance of the relationship to the two women. Because the symbol is tangible, the interaction is heightened, as are the emotions of the participants.

The McDonalds commercial, "Stranger in the House," shows what might be thought of as behavior antecedent to that shown in "Beach Sisters." The young boy, initially jealous of his baby sister, learns to look at her from a more mature perspective (someone who will show her the ropes). He makes his intention to perform this role manifest by saving some McDonalds french fries for her.

Products that enhance the physical features of an actor—thereby making that actor more attractive to self and others—also play the mediation role. Cosmetic products, perfumes, and clothing are obvious examples, but so is a facial moisturizer, as depicted in Oil of Olay's "Sea Shells." In this commercial a man is reminded of how beautiful he thought the woman he loves was when he first met her; her use of Oil of Olay helps to keep her skin looking young and thus sets the stage for loving feelings between the two. Diet Rite Cola uses a similar beauty appeal in a commercial featuring Lee Majors. In this case, the man wants to make himself more physically attractive to the woman who, coincidentally, is impressed because the product is also salt-free.

Background music is probably another product that is used to mediate interactions. Playing music is likely a direct attempt at mood manipulation, which presumably makes the participants in an interactional scene more receptive to one another and heightens their expectations of what will ensue.

Products, because of their symbolic value as communication, can also serve as *expressions of self*. Particularly with apparel and other products identified as belonging to an actor, such objects serve to define the self both to oneself and to others (Holman 1981a). Levi Strauss has used such an appeal in the "501 Blues" commercial. The point is made that because the product shrinks to fit the body, what is otherwise a mass-produced product becomes highly personalized. As such, it is, in a sense, a quintessential expression of what one is.

Other products, in expressing the self, function as powerful components or reminders of self-esteem. Such is the case with AT&T's calling card, as depicted in the "Peter Benchley" execution. One only *needs* one of these cards when one is a busy, important person who travels a great deal (and must phone into the office). The card, if one has one, then is a reminder of one's status and reinforces self-esteem.

Another example of a product serving as a powerful reinforcement of self-esteem is the automobile. Datsun's 280ZX commercial, "Some Day," shows how a young boy dreams of owning this beautiful car, knows that he is not ready for it now, but promises himself that some day he will own one. The look of longing on his face lets the viewer know that this boy will realize he has made his mark in life when he is able to claim one of these cars as his own.

Some products help to clarify, or are a component of, role definition within interactional settings. This aspect of products has been researched more than any other (see Holman 1981b, on this point) and is a key component of person–product relationships. Products have emotional values associated with them in this context to the extent that they represent goals that have been obtained or that they represent desired role performances. Automobiles and clothing are products most frequently associated with self-expression, but this category also includes ornamental objects (jewelry, house decorations) and products made by the person him- or herself (home-cooked meals, arts and crafts).

Finally, products can themselves become *objects of the emotions* of consumers (compare Bloch and Bruce 1984). Such a situation is characterized by extremely high product involvement and might be called the *aficionado effect*. Such an effect is often observed among avid collectors (coins, stamps, campaign buttons), pet owners, gourmets, or those who become enchanted with the technological aspects of products (stereo buffs, automobile tinkerers, computer hacks). At times, the cathected object may become a substitute for human relationships, especially with pets (Peck 1978; Holden 1981; Meer 1984).

The Gainesburgers commercial, "Meat Vignettes," illustrates the love and affection dog owners feel for their pets. Indeed, the dog is often seen as an important member of the family who is always cheerful, patient, and faithful. As such the dog deserves special treats just as (or perhaps more than) other family members do. More typically, however, products are appreciated for aesthetic reasons (objets d'art) or for sensory ones (wine connoisseurs). Of course, products may be invested with negative emotional connections, probably as a displacement for disagreeable interactions that have occurred while these products were performing one of the other roles.

Although it is relatively easy to find advertising examples of each of the above, the question of how advertising can most effectively treat these relationships has not yet been answered. In moving toward such an answer, it is appropriate to examine the relationship between life as it actually happens and life as it is portrayed (or should be, for optimal effect) in advertisements.

Advertising and Real Life

One statement of the relationship between advertising and real life was presented by Erving Goffman (1976), a sociologist who turned to advertising as a source of information about male and female gender displays. Although Goffman limited his analysis to print advertising (because he wanted to publish his sources in print), his observations about the relationship between the world as depicted in advertising and the real world as experienced by consumers can be generalized to all advertising media.

Goffman argued that advertisements do not show life as people actually experience it but are rather "illustrations of ritual-like bits of behavior" (1976, p. 84) portraying ideal conceptualizations of the relationships among people. Goffman identified three ways in which scenes of advertisements and scenes from actual life differ.

First, advertisements are characterized by what Goffman called *hyper-ritualizations*. Advertisements standardize, exaggerate, or simplify the rituals of daily life, which are themselves standardizations, exaggerations, and/or simplifications. Advertising makes a ritual out of rituals.

Two commercials for soft drinks illustrate how advertisements contain hyper-ritualizations. These are Coke's "Younger Brother" and Pepsi's "Michael Jackson Street." Both commercials depict a part of the ritual associated with a young boy emerging into adolescence and manhood in the United States. An important part of that ritual entails the identification of a desirable role model (an older boy, in these two cases) and careful emulation—or imitation—of the behavior of the role model. In the case of the Coke commercial, an older brother is the role model, whereas in the Pepsi execution, Michael Jackson is the role model. In both commercials, the idealized consummation of the younger boy's imitation, namely explicit approval expressed by the role model, is dramatized. Although the two commercials deal with young boys from different implied socioeconomic strata, the fundamental ritual is the same in both. Because such a ritual is characteristic of

U.S. culture, these commercials will presumably have wide appeal, which is essential to the marketing plans for both brands.

Second, advertising ritualizes social ideals by eliminating, through careful direction and editing, all aspects of the situation that do not exhibit the ideal. As Goffman pointed out, real life often contains bits of behavior not pertinent to the actual ritual being depicted and often detract from the ideal. Two Jell-O Gelatin commercials illustrate this point.

"Cousins Reunion" shows mealtime at an idealized family reunion. Everyone is friendly and loving, enjoying the food and the interactions that occur involving the food. What has been eliminated from the depiction is the normal aspects of human interaction that do not constitute the ideal: kids fighting, someone harboring jealousies from the past, someone bored with the entire event, spouses resentful that a whole day is wasted on other persons' relatives, cousins resentful at being there out of guilt and not out of genuine affection, and someone hating the food.

Similarly, "Out to Sea" shows a man and woman gently teasing one another—she, because he's been working on his model boat and ignoring her, and he, because of the food she serves him. They are intimate with one another in a way that suggests the spark has not gone out of their relationship. It is clearly a scenario with which individuals who have been married for a number of years can identify. Possible missing pieces are that she has a headache, he is tired, the kids barge in demanding attention, her sister calls, the dog has to go out.

It is necessary to carefully delete the irrelevant parts of the ritual in advertising because, unlike ordinary human interactions, advertising must be highly focused and unambiguous to get its message across in one page or thirty seconds of air time. Advertisers do not have the luxury of *cinema verite* or novelists because readers/viewers have short attention spans when it comes to commercial communication.

The third way advertisements differ from actual life scenes is that they portray only the colorful poses of living, whereas in "real life, we are . . . stuck with a considerable amount of dull footage" (Goffman 1976, p. 84). Advertisements, in order to capture the reader's or viewer's attention, must be dramatic. The Jell-O pudding commercial "First Words" plays on this concept. Bill Cosby, while eating Jell-O pudding with a child, makes an outrageous claim, namely, that the first words out of his mouth as a child were "more Jell-O pudding please." He pretends that the boy's baby sister said those words and she obligingly gurgles something unintelligible, apparently proving his point. That the camera was able to capture the baby's vocalizations makes this commercial highly dramatic and memorable. Similarly, Cadbury's "Typewriter Girl," using both action and sound effects, dramatizes the experience of eating other forms of chocolate candy in contrast to that of eating a thick Cadbury bar. The Cadbury experience is shown as soothing and sensual; the competition as harsh and abrasive. Ordinary life is occasionally as dramatic as life depicted in ads (or even more dramatic) but is mostly quite routine and boring.

In other words, when advertisements display people relating to one another, the behavior shown is not always what actually occurs among people but what the culture believes should occur. The advertiser does not, for example, replicate family behavior exactly, but presents family behavior as family members would like to see it happen. Budweiser did the same with factory workers' relationships. In the commercial entitled "Carl Henderson's Daughter," Budweiser tells the story of how Carl Henderson's colleagues gave up their weekends and worked overtime so that their friend could go to the Olympics to watch his daughter compete in gymnastics. When she performs on television, they all gather in the supervisor's office to watch her from a distance. The affection of the men for one another and the emotion they feel in watching the girl perform are palpable in the commercial.

As Gornick stated in the foreword to Goffman's monograph, "Advertisements depict for us not necessarily how we actually behave as men and women but how we think men and women behave" (Goffman 1976, p. vii). Furthermore, people are not particularly troubled by the discrepancy between life as they know it and life as they see it in ads. In Goffman's terms:

> The magical ability of the advertiser to use a few models and props to evoke a life-like scene of his own choosing . . . is due primarily to those institutionalized arrangements in social life which allow strangers to glimpse the lives of persons they pass, and to the readiness of all of us to switch at any moment from dealing with the real world to participating in make believe ones (1976, p. 23).

Goffman believed that, to a large extent, advertisers are very skillful in their display of ritual. The underlying assumption for Goffman was that in order to be successful, advertisements have to show basic truths about human relationships, even if those truths deal more with what ought to be than with what is. If advertisers depart markedly from reality as either desired or experienced by members of the target audience, they risk alienating that audience, building a resentment against the advertised brand, and such serious marketplace consequences as loss of sales. In deciding what to show, advertisers draw from the same sources of information about the culture, namely ordinary human behavior, as do all other participants in the culture. Goffman flatly rejected the notion that advertisers create the rituals they employ. To do so would risk portrayals out of step with the culture at large, hence risking rejection by potential prospects for the brand being advertised. What advertisers do, however, is "conventionalize our conventions, stylize what is already a stylization, make frivolous use of what is already something considerably cut off from cultural controls" (Goffman 1976, p. 84).

Advertising Portrayals of Emotion

If Goffman's premises can be accepted, then the relationship between advertising and emotionality is clear: in order to be maximally effective, advertising should portray products in the context of the rituals of life of which they are a part; if those rituals contain emotional components, they should also be part of the portrayal of the ritual; the focus of these rituals should be on life as it ought to be (or as we wish it were) with products taking their proper role in life, as perceived by consumers.

Research must necessarily play a very large part in successfully executing the above. The rituals must be determined, the roles of products in those rituals documented, the contrast between ideal life and actual life monitored, proper execution of all the above must be explored, and finally, since the culture is becoming increasingly polarized, all of the above should be contrasted across disparate segments of the population.

Very little published research has addressed these issues. Rook (1984; Rook and Levy 1983) has begun to study rituals in some depth, and Levy's work on food (1981, 1982) addresses some of these same issues. Proprietary research at Young and Rubicam (Y&R) deals in more depth with all the above. That research cannot be shared here, but several rules of thumb have begun to emerge from the work that Y&R and others have done.

First, it is not necessary to use emotional appeals in promoting every brand. If marketing for the brand has not reached the point at which the manufacturing processes are no longer competitive (attribute advantages still exist and are relevant for the consumer), then attribute-based messages, or perhaps even announcements, are appropriate. Such is the case for the drug ibuprofen marketed in over-the-counter strength under the brand name Advil. The introductory advertising for Advil was a simple announcement in which its attributes were contrasted with the characteristics of other anti-inflammatory pain relievers. Because a manufacturing advantage existed for Advil, more sophisticated advertising incorporating consumer insight was not necessary at the introduction of the brand.

Second, it is better to use no emotional appeals at all than to force an emotional association (compare Plummer 1984 on this point). If the product or brand is not a part of the emotion-laden ritual being depicted, then more damage than good can be done, especially when an attribute-based story is still possible. Recent advertising for Tasters Choice decaffeinated coffee is a case in point. At one time Tasters Choice tried to link consumption of its brand to other rituals. For example, the commercial "Party" tried to suggest that drinking Tasters Choice was preliminary to more intimate interaction between a man and woman. Most recently, however, Tasters Choice has returned to an emphasis on brand ingredients (Arabica beans) and the benefit of superior taste.

Third, the level of emotionality expressed in the advertisement should not be more intense than the level of emotion experienced by the consumer (or the level that the consumer believes ought to be experienced). Two commercial executions for different brands of yogurt illustrate this point. Whitney's "Flashdance" shows a young woman dancing and tries to make the analogy between her desire for personal excellence in her performance and Whitney's desire for excellence in its yogurt. By contrast, Friendship pokes fun at a consumer who is unconcerned about all the manufacturing details that precede the act of eating yogurt and who is, instead, concerned that the yogurt tastes good ("Dedication"). In so doing, Friendship gets to the heart of what currently drives the category and in effect ridicules the Whitney's execution. It is better, when expressing emotions, to be subtle than hyperbolic. The Breyers ice cream commercial "Supermarket Square" shows how one phrase, "Locust Beans," stated simply, with accompanying facial expressions and voice intonation, can make a point very effectively.

Fourth, it is very important not to ridicule the consumer's emotional associations with the brand or product. Such ridicule is a great temptation, especially in a fragmented culture, since it is likely to be very funny to those outside the group being ridiculed. The United Airlines commercial "Every Four Years" contains scenes that are potentially offensive although the overall concept is probably sound. The idea is that ordinary people empathize with the Olympic athletes and thus derive a vicarious pleasure from watching the Olympics. The commercial illustrates the concept by showing mature adults—in their fifties and sixties—apparently enacting Olympiclike athletic moves. For example, a large, overweight woman is shown doing a poorly executed dive into a swimming pool. The camera focuses on her bulges and is an unfortunate depiction of actual—not ideal—life. When consumers feel that they have been ridiculed, results can be disastrous for the brand.

Such was the case with advertising several years ago for Excedrin as in the execution "Excedrin Headache Number 1040." The advertising campaign included very funny portrayals of situations in which people got terrible headaches. Although the advertising was widely acclaimed, received many awards, and was greatly enjoyed, sales for Excedrin suffered to the point that the agency was fired and the advertising changed dramatically.

Finally, one should keep in mind that there is a difference between a consumer's emotions associated with the product or brand and a consumer's emotional reaction to the advertisement itself (Schlinger 1979). If possible, these two should be congruent. If using the brand evokes humor, for example, then a humorous execution can be used for effect. Similarly, a brand that evokes warm and fuzzy feelings can benefit from a warm and fuzzy execution.

This situation is exemplified in advertising for three brands: Kentucky Fried Chicken's "America," United Negro College Fund's "Case History," and Jamaica Tourist Board's "Paradise." All three commercials evoke emotions that, although different from one another, are each appropriate to respective brands because it is the emotion the consumer experiences when using the product. However, one must be very careful with humor. Using humor when using the brand does not evoke humor is risky: consumers may remember the advertising but have no motivation to use the brand since the advertiser has not conveyed a compelling reason for doing so. Such might be the case with a New Jersey lottery commercial titled "Michael Winslow." Michael Winslow is a very funny comedian whose forte is funny noises. The noises, however, are so distracting that the fact that Winslow is trying to sell New Jersey lottery tickets gets lost. Buying lottery tickets is not a funny or amusing experience, especially when one is not a winner. Thus, the lack of congruence between the emotion associated with using the product and emotion conveyed in the commercial probably results in consumer confusion, at best. Nevertheless, an advertising execution that elicits an emotional response from consumers and also makes a dramatic statement about the brand being advertised can result in the most powerful advertising of all.

Conclusion

The study of emotionality in advertising is a fascinating topic worthy of considerable research attention. However, much work is still needed before we have a better understanding of human behavior that can lead to better advertising and better competitive opportunities for the brands being advertised.

Appendix 5A

Merrill Lynch "China Shop"

An off-camera announcer says "Picking and choosing investments requires careful handling. Size and strength are valuable; but sensitivity and agility are what makes Merrill Lynch a breed apart." During this viewers see a large bull delicately passing through the aisles of a china shop. The bull finally emerges without breaking a single piece of china or crystal.

Time "Time Flies VI"

The commercial shows different people reading *Time* with clips of past news events interspersed between each scene. All the clips show very emotional, though varied, scenes. The words of the song are: *"Time* flies and you are there, *Time* cries and lets you care, you understand the world we share . . . Read *Time* and understand."

Johnson & Johnson "Newborn Babies"

The first part of the commercial shows a mother with her newborn son. She carefully examines his ten toes, his fingers. Other mothers are shown cuddling their babies in the hospital. Music and words: "Now he's born he's yours to keep safe and keep warm." Then cut to whole product line for babies. Powder, Q-tips, shampoo, and so forth. Announcer continues: "Safest, purest products to help mothers. Johnson & Johnson cares about babies like their mothers."

Hallmark "Ballerina Everyday"

The commercial opens on a girl and her boyfriend sitting on a couch. She has received a dance scholarship but is afraid to go away from home because she thinks her boyfriend will forget her when he goes to college. He persuades her that opportunities like this one do not come along every day, and he will not forget her. The rest of the commercial shows her at school, dancing in a studio and him in his college dorm, writing a message on a Hallmark card. The camera cuts back and forth with the song consisting of his thoughts of her. In the end she is alone in the dance studio when she opens the card from him.

Coke "Mean Joe Green"

The first shot is of Joe Green limping out of a football stadium into a passageway toward the locker room. A little boy holding a Coke asks him if he needs any help; he asks Green if he wants his Coke. Joe Green finally accepts the Coke and guzzles it down. As the boy turns to walk away, Joe Green yells, "Hey kid—catch," and throws him his jersey. The kid says "Wow," with the happiest face to go along with it. ("Have a Coke and a smile.")

Kodak "First Day of School"

At the beginning of the commercial, mothers are practically pushing their respective children into a classroom, sympathizing with their reluctance to start school. The teacher seats everyone and begins taking pictures with a Kodak instant camera. The pictures develop instantly; one child looks at the photograph and breaks into a smile. Then all the children are happy and posing for pictures. One even takes a picture of the teacher. The commercial ends with a collage of many snapshots of the expressions of these little children.

Dr. Pepper "Detective"

The commercial begins in black and white, showing a bored private detective in his messy office on what seems a slow, hot night. The words are his thoughts: "then she walked in." Woman says she has no place to turn. Detective offers her a beverage—his java, then a regular soft drink. Finally it hits him that "this was no ordinary dame." He whips out a Sugar Free Dr Pepper and her face lights up as she takes it. The commercial changes to color; she drinks the soda and commercial ends by showing regular and Sugar Free Dr Pepper cans.

General Food's International Coffees "Beach Sisters"

At first viewers see one woman sitting on a terrace overlooking a beach, the wind gently blowing her hair. Her sister comes out with a tray of international coffees. The first woman says how these cups of coffee will "really make my day complete" and "how nice it is to have a sister who is a friend, too." Music comes in: "Celebrate the moments of your life."

McDonalds "Stranger in the House"

The commercial opens with parents bringing home a newborn girl. Both grandparents and parents are shown fawning over the baby in various scenes, each with an older brother sadly looking on but apart from the commotion. It is clear that he feels unwanted, but then his dad asks him what he's doing for lunch. Next, they are at McDonalds, "talking things over, with a cheese-burger man-to-man." Dad says to son that his sister will need someone to show her the ropes. The son, warming up to the idea, tucks some of his fries into a pocket for his sister.

Diet Rite "Lee Majors"

Majors is working out in a gym, trying to impress a woman who is also working out. She is not impressed by Majors. Music: "Everyone's got to Diet Right, it doesn't matter who you are." Woman keeps on walking by the sweating and straining Majors. Finally, he is sitting in the sauna, and she comes over and is finally impressed because he's avoiding sodium and sugar by drinking Diet Rite.

Oil of Olay "Sea Shells"

The music "First time ever I saw your face" plays as a man and woman walk down the beach. As the woman picks up a shell, the man remembers when he first met her. Viewers see different flashbacks of their younger days, including the woman putting Oil of Olay on her face. Then a scene in which the man is rowing her in a boat fades into the present, with the man looking into the woman's face. Music and song end.

Levi's "501 Blues"

The commercial contains different scenes of people in their jeans while an older, black man plays the guitar in his room as he looks out the window. "Sometimes when I'm blue, I sit awhile and think of you, in your personal fit, Levis 501 blues, how good it seems." Music goes on throughout commercial with the camera occasionally cutting back to the guitar player. Scenes include man washing car, three men being driven away in back of pick-up truck, and a girl roller skating down the street.

AT&T Calling Card "Peter Benchley"

The commercial alternates between Benchley in front of a typewriter and at a public phone because that's all he says he's ever doing, writing or seeing and calling someone concerning his writing. He says how great Calling Card is to have anywhere, anytime except down in the sea. (Picture is of him underwater watching a hungry-looking shark in a cage.)

Datsun 280ZX "Some Day"

A young boy cycles up to a Datsun. He looks it over, saying "some day," looks at the markings, the interior, makes revving noises and repeats "some day" and speeds off on his bicycle.

Gainesburgers "Meat Vignettes"

The commercial shows a variety of scenes in which a dog is looking with apparent longing at beef-based "people food." Gainesburgers is for all the times the dog did not get the beef that he craves.

Coke "Younger Brother"

As a teen-aged boy flies out the front door of his house past his younger brother, who is sitting on the front steps, we hear a woman say, "Take your younger brother with you." The younger brother follows his older brother down the street, jumps over a fire hydrant like his brother did, tries to jump up to touch a Coca-Cola sign like his brother and essentially imitates him all along the way. His older brother approaches a Coke machine. After first stopping in front of a competitor's machine, the younger boy quickly selects a Coke. Finally, his older brother smiles at him, and as he leaves to go off with his friends, he calls his brother to join the older boys.

Pepsi "Michael Jackson"

We first see young boys break dancing, one of whom is dressed to look like a miniature Michael Jackson. As a group of them make their way up the street the Jackson Brothers emerge and begin dancing. The Michael Jackson look-alike backs up as he's dancing and collides with the real Michael Jackson. His eyes get wide with wonder. The camera pans to the Jacksons singing, all of them dancing and drinking Pepsi. Little kids continue dancing as Jacksons back away and disappear.

Jell-O Gelatin "Cousins Reunion"

The scene is a typical family reunion with relatives sitting around picnic tables. One woman says to her cousin (the hostess) that she hopes she made a good dessert. The hostess acts like there is no dessert. Everyone groans and complains. Then she says she made some fun and produces a Jell-O gelatin mold. The music and picture concentrate on the jiggling of Jell-O and how much fun there is in eating it.

Jell-O Gelatin "Out to Sea"

A woman decides to shake up her husband who's been involved with his model ship for too long by serving him a Jell-O fruit parfait. They savor it. The recipe is demonstrated. Big Jell-O letters go across the screen several times throughout commercial. He agrees that he has been out to sea far too long.

Jell-O Pudding "First Words"

Bill Cosby is sitting on a porch with a boy and a baby girl, telling them that his first words were "more Jell-O pudding, please." The boy does not believe it. So Cosby asks the little boy if the girl said something and he turns his head and says "more Jell-O pudding, please," pretending that she is really saying that as her first words. She gurgles something in apparent affirmation of Cosby's claim.

Cadbury "Typewriter Girl"

The commercial first shows a highly proper woman eating a chocolate bar longways with words "before, eating a chocolate bar could be anything but a smooth experience," accompanied by sound effects as if her chewing sounded like a typewriter. The scene changes to introduce Cadbury Thick Bar. A very pretty and sensuous young woman wearing a long dress and floppy white hat is shown gently swinging on a swing. She eats the chocolate bar, obviously savoring every morsel.

Budweiser Light "Carl Henderson's Daughter"

The scene is of men working in a steel factory. An off-camera announcer tells us how a couple of guys have put off their fishing trips, another has worked so many shifts of overtime, how each man helped a fellow worker take time off to go watch his daughter in the Olympics. The commercial ends with all the men crowded around a television set watching the daughter (a gymnast) performing at the Olympics.

Advil "Advil Bottle Rev. 9"

The off-camera announcer says that aspirin was introduced in 1899, Tylenol in 1955, and in 1984 there is Advil, "Advanced medicine for pain." The rest of the commercial shows the announcer holding an Advil bottle explaining the attributes of the product.

Tasters Choice "Party"

The commercial shows a man and a woman dressed very formally and standing in a sophisticated apartment. Each blames the other as being the one who wanted to go to the party. The woman suggests they make some coffee and talk about it. They relax on the couch and share their decaffeinated coffee.

Tasters Choice "Arabica Beans"

The commercial opens with a woman asking longingly whether there is a coffee made with those beans one gets in gourmet coffee shops. The camera pans a coffee store, with the store owner spooning from an Arabica beans drawer. Off-camera announcer explains about Arabica beans and ends saying that the more consumers know about coffee, the more the choice for taste will be Tasters Choice.

Whitney's Yogurt "Flashdance"

An off-camera announcer states: "You have a dream." We see a woman in a dance studio performing as two people note how good she is. The announcer makes the analogy between yogurt and the dancer's quest for perfection and why someone like her eats Whitney's Yogurt. The camera also goes back and forth between dancer and the natural fruit and yogurt flowing out of a basket. It end with the dancer savoring yogurt. "Discover the greatness within."

Friendship Yogurt "Dedication"

Viewers see a self-possessed woman eating yogurt as the off-camera announcer questions whether she knows about its fresh ingredients, and so forth. As she denies every query, the announcer raises his voice telling her about the people that make Friendship, demanding to know if she cares, what she cares about, until finally she declares "taste" and he calls her selfish. Ends with all varieties of Friendship yogurt shown on the screen.

Breyers Ice Cream "Supermarket Square"

The commercial opens with two women at freezer section of supermarket. One of the women reads all of the unnatural ingredients in a nondescript ice cream container. The other woman takes out a Breyers container and announcer recites what's in it. Woman (buyer) is shown sitting down, enjoying her ice cream while the other woman is still in the now dark supermarket reading the ingredients as the janitor is washing the floor around her. She wearily reads "Locust Beans" and they both do a double take, "Locust Beans?"

United Air Lines "Every Four Years"

The commercial contains vignettes of mature adults performing athletic feats while the off-camera announcer, in the style of a sports announcer, describes their behavior as if they were Olympic athletes. The scenes include a balding man in his backyard building a fence from large tree branches, an overweight woman diving into a swimming pool, an elderly couple ice-skating together, and a baggage handler lifting a trunk above his head.

Excedrin "Excedrin Headache #1040"

The camera slowly converges on a man smoking a cigarette, watching an IRS tax agent auditing his return. The tax agent questions many of the man's deductions and ends with a query about his medical expenses. The man says they were for his Excedrin because he has so many Excedrin headaches, like now.

Kentucky Fried Chicken "America"

The commercial shows different scenes of older relatives and children with each child playing a musical instrument (the Kentucky Fried Chicken song, "It's so nice to feel so good about a meal"). The scenes span the United States both geographically and culturally. The commercial ends with all participants singing and playing their instruments while gathered around Colonel Sanders and Kentucky Fried Chicken employees.

United Negro College Fund "Case History"

Viewers see a young black woman sadly packing up her books and her belongings because she can no longer afford college tuition. She has tears in her eyes as she packs a picture of her parents and herself. Picture turns into the young woman in her graduation gown with her parents as the announcer tells how helpful the United Negro College Fund can be. Commercial ends with her as a doctor in her office talking with a little black girl: "A mind is a terrible thing to waste."

Jamaica Tourist Board "Paradise"

The commercial contains various scenes of Jamaica with a number of Jamaican natives saying "Come back to Jamaica" as the music sings a "come back" song.

New Jersey Lottery "Michael Winslow"

The camera focuses on Winslow describing what New Jersey lottery games he plays while making humorous sounds to go along with his narration. At the end of the commercial, he disappears out of the top of the picture, apparently with rockets attached to his shoes.

6
Reflections on the Role of Affect ~ Consumer Behavior

Robert A. Peterson and Wayne D. Hoyer
University of Texas at Austin
William R. Wilson
Rice University

C ollectively, the preceding chapters provide a rich and diverse perspective on the role of affect in consumer behavior and decision making. The authors have, in quite different ways, provided compelling evidence for the need to rethink models of consumer behavior that provide for only a weak or secondary role for affective processes in determining the outcome of purchase and consumption behavior. In this final chapter we attempt to identify some theoretical and research directions that may lead to a better understanding of the influence of affect on consumer behavior. Before doing so, however, some of the basic conclusions that can be drawn from the preceding material are briefly summarized.

On a general level, the authors agree that consumer behavior results from the combination of two forces—affect and cognition. Although there are differences in how affect and cognition are defined, affect is typically treated as a synonym for feelings or emotions that are either physiologically based or at least have a physiological component. In contrast, cognition is portrayed as the neural–mental activity permitting information processing, categorizing, alternative weighing, action planning, and the like.

The notion that consumer behavior depends on two forces (affect and cognition) is not in conflict with most current thinking, nor do the approaches represent a departure from the way these concepts are usually treated. What differs, however, is the perceived relationship(s) between affect and cognition in consumer decision making. Traditional consumer behavior models and theories assume that an orderly set of events or activities occur when consumers process information: cognitive activity is followed by an affective evaluation that ultimately results in behavior. Stated simply, the assumption is that cognition mediates affect and directs it, whereas affect mediates behavior. This is illustrated by the Howard–Sheth (1969), Engel–Blackwell (1982), Bettman (1979), Fishbein–Azjen (1975) and many other multiattribute models.

Since the mid 1970s, however, there has been an increasing awareness that decisions exist wherein affect need not be a consequence of cognition. Rather, in some instances affect may occur simultaneously or in a parallel process with cognition, whereas in other instances it may actually precede or even direct cognitive processes related to a particular activity. The extreme case occurs when the dominant force in decision making is affect. In this instance affect shapes cognition, therefore, cognition is at best a by-product of affective activity. An obvious response from cognitive-oriented consumer behavior researchers might be: "Yes, our models often characterize the consumer as a dispassionate information processor and there indeed are times when feelings appear to override or dominate the decision, but these are rare occasions. After all, cognitive models have long been able to predict consumer buying behavior both in the laboratory and in the field. Therefore, if the general approach were inappropriate, we would not expect our predictions to be successful."

There are several reasons to question this argument and not to become overconfident with respect to research documenting a strong cognitive component in consumer decision making. One source of evidence is human behavior that occurs outside the laboratory. Most researchers would agree that few decisions are not colored by at least some feelings and emotion.

In fact, considerable anecdotal evidence exists that shows that whether a person is selecting a spouse, house, or blouse emotions not only are present but often dominate the decision process. For example, when the staid, completely rational professor in the movie *Blue Angel* threw away his career and finally his life for the woman he loved, audiences were sad but not surprised. Passion has a way of dominating even the most finely tuned, well-established decision processes. Any good real estate agent knows home sales typically do not result from finding homes that match buyers' copious descriptions of the attribute-value content of their preference structure. Rather, sales are produced by showing buyers a home they "just love" and then getting a purchase offer before they have the opportunity to calmly and rationally review the purchase decision. Likewise, it is difficult to imagine a secondary role for emotion in the decision of a consumer to buy a $200 designer blouse. Or, merely consider the role of affect in the brouhaha culminating in the decision of the Coca-Cola Company to bring back Classic Coke.

If such examples are generalizable, the question arises as to why consumer behavior researchers have been able to derive numerous sources of support for a cognitively based decision process in the laboratory. The answer is straightforward. The importance of affective influences on the decision-making process has been significantly underestimated in laboratory studies because researchers have consciously designed research that is void of affective information. The obvious corollary is that different decision or preference outcomes would result if affective information, normally found in real-life decision making, were explicitly included in these studies. In the second part of this chapter two examples of preliminary research in this area are described. This research suggests affect can enter into decision processes very early on and/or play a major role in the decision process.

Historical Digression

Before discussing this research, though, several points merit brief mention. First, a brief digression is warranted to place the treatment of affect in perspective. Shortly after consumer behavior became recognized as a worthwhile subject of inquiry, the notion that cognition was the dominant force in consumer decision making led to it becoming the basis of most consumer behavior research paradigms. As the emphasis on cognition increased, researchers believed that affect became less and less of an influence in guiding consumer behavior. At a certain point, affect was almost considered an epiphenomenon or even an artifact of the decision-making process.

The authors of this book all agree affect deserves, if not a greater role than cognition in the consumer decision-making process, at least a role equal to that of cognition. Morris Holbrook made an interesting comment about the sort of treatment evolution affect has gone through. One possible explanation for it, he noted, is that study of consumer behavior lags behind psychology by ten to fifteen years. This is why the role of affect in consumer behavior is only beginning to be seriously considered, and why it may be another five years before it is fully integrated into consumer behavior research paradigms. Such a conclusion obviously is not flattering to consumer behavior research; however, it is also important to point out that the discipline of psychology is also lacking in this regard.

In fact, if one takes a longer historical perspective, the differential emphasis accorded affect is seen much more vividly. Beginning with Freud, then Bruner, Postman, and the "New Look," the favored approach to understanding human behavior consisted of focusing on feelings and emotions. For Freud, the key to understanding neurotic behavior was to examine the extent to which people consciously or unconsciously attempt to block their feelings or to somehow control levels of feelings that are inconsistent with the way they think or want to behave. Research conducted during the "New Look," which occurred in the 1940s and 1950s, focused on demonstrating that affect can distort, bias, or influence the basic processes of learning, perception, and information handling. For instance, in the area of perception, even the formation of a percept (which is thought of as a relatively straightforward effect) was seen to be subject to tremendous distortion or bias. Research examining people's judgment of coin size found that feelings about money and economic background dramatically affected perceptions of size. Other researchers found that the ability to form a percept word slowly brought up from memory through longer periods of duration was influenced by the emotional context of the word. Specifically, emotion interfered with the ability to form a percept.

The idea that emotions and feelings play an important role in human behavior has a long tradition in psychology. Also, the notion that affect may precede or parallel cognitive activity or even, in certain instances, direct that activity is not new. Thus, although ideas espoused in this book may appear radical in the current context of consumer behavior, when the longer psychological tradition is considered, it is surprising that the perceived role of emotion and affect in human behavior could have declined so quickly from being central and dominant at the turn of the century through the 1950s to approaching the status of an artifact. However, given the general recognition of the importance of affect, the fact that the relatively brief period when researchers concentrated on the cognitive domain to the exclusion of affect is now coming to an end should have been anticipated.

Difficulties in Studying Affect

If one attempts to determine why affect was deemphasized in modern psychology, contributory reasons are immediately apparent. First, there are problems simply in grappling with the role of affect in decision-making processes. Most importantly, affect tends to be a messy construct to investigate either theoretically or empirically. Indeed, as noted previously, there is no consensus on how to define it. Consequently, it is not surprising that affect is a very difficult construct to measure or operationalize. Paradoxically, direct measurement from a psychological perspective requires the invocation of cognition. This is a partial explanation for the emerging emphasis on its physiological measurement (recall chapter 4 by Cacioppo et al.) Furthermore, research that was conducted often produced unpredictable results similar to how emotion actually impacts day-to-day decision making. In other words, affect may lead people to behave in ways that appear irrational and are therefore hard to explain. Although affect research has the potential to produce productive and interesting findings, the path is difficult and the rewards problematic, especially when an alternative path—cognitive research—is considered. Hence, when the hurdles involved in publishing research on affect are taken into account, it is not surprising that research into the role of affect in consumer decision making declined.

Why Study Affect?

The recurring theme of this book is that affect must be explicitly and unequivocally incorporated into current consumer behavior theory and research.

More generally, affect should not be ignored because it most often gives us the meaning of things. In Osgood's work (Osgood, Suci, and Tannenbaum 1957), affect is represented as an evaluative dimension that surfaces as the strongest of three *meaning* dimensions. Affect also guides our lives and helps us make the right decisions. In other words, knowing what is good or bad or liked or disliked is a useful decision rule. It is a simple heuristic, one whose successful application makes us feel good.

When we make consumption decisions on the basis of things that we like or that are good, our affective system helps protect us by filtering information subsequent to the decision and by assisting in organizing future information, recurring information, or thought to make our world seem consistent and predictable. This activity is critical in helping us function in a complex environment.

Affect also protects us in a social context. Often in social situations we believe we need to be rational. When others ask why we behave in a certain fashion, we like to be able to respond with an explanation that, at least to us, appears logical and consistent. Affect, on the other hand, operates in a slightly different manner. Once people are aware of their preferences (that is, what they think is good or bad or liked or disliked, especially if these preferences are very strong), these affective feelings guide their behavior and determine how they relate to other people and situations. In particular, frequently our cognitions attempt to justify our affective feelings.

An example of this phenomenon involves an acquaintance named Linda who was shopping for a suit. She was in the process of evaluating her alternatives and turned to her friend Ann for advice. The suit she clearly preferred cost about $400, which was double her monthly disposable income. It was very clear to Ann after the discussion that Linda wanted this particular suit over the others. Ann thus realized "My job was not to be there to help her make the right decision or to weigh alternatives. My job was to help her find a way to rationally purchase that suit because it was the one she wanted." This type of phenomenon probably occurs often. When people have feelings and are aware of them, they frequently alter their behavior to justify these feelings. Again, this phenomenon emphasizes the important role affect plays in guiding behavior.

In summary, in terms of consumer behavior there is virtual consensus regarding the existence of a sort of hedonic component. There is also a utility, practical, or normative (cognitive) component whose influence varies as a function of the nature of the decision. In certain, typically trivial situations, the hedonic component may dominate the decision process. The hedonic component may also dominate in some important situations, but it will be in conflict with cognitive forces that would tend to tell us we have limits or constraints. The theoretical focus in consumer behavior should *not* be whether affect precedes cognition but rather on determining what decisions are likely to be primarily affective, what is likely to be the strength of the affect, and what happens when affect and cognition are in conflict. From an applied perspective, the focus should be on how affect can be manipulated or enhanced through available marketing activities such as advertising and sales promotion.

The next section contains a discussion of preliminary research on affect we conducted. It needs to be emphasized that this research is exploratory and not meant to be conclusive. Rather, the research efforts represent initial attempts to test some of the concepts set forth above. In particular, this research illustrates that when certain kinds of affect are present expected information processing may be significantly altered.

Research on Affective Influences in Decision Making

As mentioned in previous chapters, although the role of affect in consumer decision making has long been recognized conceptually, it has generally been addressed or modeled in the context of the C–A–B (cognition–affect–behavior) paradigm (for example, Howard and Sheth 1969). Empirically, affect typically has been investigated as the value component in Fishbein-type (Fishbein and Ajzen 1975) multiattribute attitude models. As such, it has largely been considered the result of a cognitive process. This, though, is too narrow a conceptualization.

Affect is a complex construct that includes emotions and feelings as well as evaluative impressions. Whereas it may be the result of a cognitive process, it may also develop independently of cognition (Zajonc 1980). Theoretically, affect can play a variety of roles in consumer decision making ranging from influencing how information is processed (for example, Petty, Cacioppo, and Goldman 1981) or stored in memory (for example, Srull 1984; Moore and Hutchinson 1983) to determining product or brand choice (for example, Gorn 1982; Zajonc and Markus 1982).

The exploratory research first reported here focuses on one specific type of affect—the extensive domain of feelings linked to the consumption experience per se. As such, it includes both motivational feelings that initiate a consumer decision-making process as well as anticipatory feelings or expectations regarding what the consumption experience would be like if a given choice were made. Paralleling Batra (chapter 3), the type of affect traditionally studied is termed *decision value affect*, whereas that addressed here is termed *general hedonic affect*.

As Hirschman and Holbrook (1982) noted, it is not clear why general hedonic affect, which intuitively would appear important in influencing and/ or determining consumer choices, has been effectively ignored in the consumer behavior literature while decision value affect has been accorded a central role. One possible explanation is that consumer researchers have implicitly assumed that measures of decision value affect are reliable surrogate indices of general hedonic affect. If true, there is no need to treat general hedonic affect as a separate, independent influence. Recently, however, Kahneman and Tversky (1984) have specifically addressed the reasonableness of this assumption for general decision-making models.

> It is tacitly assumed that decision values and experience [general hedonic] values coincide. This assumption is part of the conception of an idealized decision maker who is able to predict future experiences with perfect accuracy and evaluate options accordingly. For ordinary decision makers, however, the correspondence of decision values between experience values is far from perfect (Kahneman and Tversky 1984, p. 349).

Thus, to the extent the above assumption is incorrect, empirical research needs to be conducted that explicitly addresses the nature and influence of general hedonic affect in consumer decision making.

Decision Framing and Affect

The primary purpose of the study presented here was to investigate the extent to which the explicit introduction of general hedonic affect into a choice situation influenced the choice outcomes. Although many different research approaches could have been employed, the general framing paradigm proposed by Tversky and Kahneman (1981) was selected to guide the research.

According to Tversky and Kahneman, "a decision problem is defined by the acts or options among which one must choose, the possible outcomes or consequences of these acts, and the contingencies or conditional probabilities that relate outcomes to acts" (1981, p. 453). The manner in which a decision maker conceives the acts, outcomes, and contingencies associated with a particular choice is referred to as the *decision frame*. Tversky and Kahneman have repeatedly demonstrated that altering the decision frame produces systematic changes and even reversals of judgments or choices despite the fact that such effects would not be predicted by rational choice models.

Analogous to the research of Tversky and Kahneman, our investigation addressed decision-framing issues by manipulating variations in the framing of acts, outcomes, and contingencies associated with a particular choice. More importantly, though, our investigation sought to influence how consumers frame particular decision problems by explicitly cuing them to general hedonic affect relating to feelings that would be expected to *precede* a decision situation. Hence, unlike the decision scenarios of Tversky and

Kahneman, which were essentially devoid of affective considerations, the decision scenarios used in our research explicitly incorporated affect as a framing element.

The decision scenario was drawn directly from Kahneman and Tversky's research (1984) investigating the concept of mental or psychological accounting. They hypothesized that an individual sets up a mental account that specifies the advantages and disadvantages associated with a particular decision option compared to some multiattribute reference state. These advantages and disadvantages are then balanced relative to the reference state, and the decision option is evaluated. If the advantages of the decision option exceed its disadvantages, the option is acceptable.

Kahneman and Tversky tested their notion of psychological accounting by means of a simple two-group research design. Using undergraduate students as subjects, they asked individuals in one group (lost ticket group) to:

> imagine that you have decided to see a play and paid the admission price of $10 per ticket. As you enter the theater, you discover that you have lost the ticket. The seat was not marked, and the ticket cannot be recovered.

Subjects were then asked if they would pay $10 for another ticket.

Subjects in the second group (lost $10 bill group) were asked to:

> imagine that you have decided to see a play where admission is $10 per ticket. As you enter the theater, you discover that you have lost a $10 bill.

They were then asked whether they would still pay $10 for a ticket to see the play.

The above manipulation (ticket–$10 bill) constituted one factor in our investigation. The second manipulation involved explicitly cuing subjects to general hedonic affect that typically underlies one's initial motivation to attend a play—expected satisfaction or enjoyment. It seems unlikely that people would attend a play if they did not have prior feelings that they would like it. Hence, it is at least intuitively logical that attendance at a play would be motivated by general hedonic affect, regardless of whether affect was explicitly incorporated in the decision scenario. The second manipulation tested this notion by inserting the following statement after the first sentence in the Kahneman and Tversky treatment conditions: "Several of your friends have strongly recommended that you see the play, and you have wanted to see it for several weeks."

In brief, the four treatments in our decision scenario consisted of (1) lost ticket with affective cue; (2) lost ticket with no affective cue; (3) lost $10 bill with affective cue; and (4) lost $10 bill with no affective cue. Thus, although the study had as its primary purpose investigation of the possible influence of general hedonic affect on the choice outcome, it also served to replicate earlier work by Kahneman and Tversky. Moreover, although the construct of affect was construed broadly, its portrayal was consistent with what would be expected in real-world decision making.

Data were collected by means of a questionnaire mailed to a sample of 1,600 adults who were members of a national consumer panel. Responses were obtained from 909 individuals, representing a response rate of 57 percent.

Table 6–1 contains the results for the decision scenario study. It is interesting to note the correspondence between the results of Kahneman and Tversky (1984) and those of our investigation. Kahneman and Tversky found that 46 percent of their subjects who lost the theater ticket would purchase another one, and 88 percent who lost a $10 bill would purchase a ticket. In our study (no cue condition), corresponding percentages of 42 percent and 76 percent were obtained. Hence, it appears the results of Kahneman and Tversky are quite robust even under circumstances where different subjects and data collection methods are used. Indeed, the general concept of psychological accounting was strongly supported by the data; 16 percent of the variance in choice behavior was accounted for by the ticket–$10 bill main effect.

More importantly, however, table 6–1 also reveals that cuing general

Table 6–1
Decision Scenario Results

Source of Variation	Sum of Squares	ANOVA Results Degrees of Freedom	F-statistic	p	ω^2
Lost ticket/$10 bill	16.97	1	83.98	.001	.161
Cue	3.33	1	16.42	.001	.057
Interaction	.89	1	4.38	.040	.008
Residual	178.00	881			
Total	199.19	884			

Percentage of Subjects Purchasing Ticket[a]

		Cue		
		Present	Absent	
Lost	Ticket (46%)	61% (n = 218)	42% (n = 213)	52%
	$10 bill (88%)	82% (n = 241)	76% (n = 213)	79%
		72%	59%	

[a]Percentages in parenthesis are those obtained by Kahneman and Tversky 1984.

hedonic affect significantly influenced choice behavior. The presence of the affective cue increased the overall likelihood that subjects would be willing to buy a ticket regardless of the nature of the prior loss (ticket or $10 bill). When affect was explicitly cued, subjects stating they would purchase a ticket increased an average of 13 percent compared to the noncued scenario. Furthermore, as can be seen from the interaction effect, the influence of affect is stronger in the lost-ticket condition (19 percent increase) than the lost-$10-bill condition (6 percent increase).

It is important to emphasize that the purpose of this research was not to invalidate or criticize previous work in consumer decision making. Rather, the purpose was to suggest that the direct inclusion or integration of general hedonic affect into existing cognitive models of the decision process may result in a significant improvement in our knowledge of decision making.

This study illustrates the importance of general hedonic affect in influencing one specific information processing bias—decision framing. Hence, it corroborates the general conclusion that affect not only influences various specific judgments but also has an impact on cognitive processes in general. Moreover, the study reinforces Isen's view (1984) of the powerful role of affect in consumer behavior. Indeed, the effect of affect in the decision scenario persuasively demonstrates the need for further research on both its nature and influence.

General hedonic affect can be viewed as a powerful type of information that supplements and/or complements cognitive attribute information. As such, it may play an important role in determining when perceptual biases such as frequency or availability (Tversky and Kahneman 1973) will occur. Consequently, research is needed to examine how affect impacts on these and other judgmental biases. Eventually, research on general hedonic affect may culminate in the elimination of perceptual biases based largely on affective processes.

Alternatively, general hedonic affect may serve as the basis of a heuristic used to reduce cognitive effort. This notion has been previously recognized by Wright (1975), who believed consumers sometimes make decisions simply on the basis of liking or disliking. He referred to this as an *affect referral* strategy. More specifically, Hoyer (1984) postulated that consumers employ simplifying heuristics or tactics when making choice decisions, one of which could be affective (buy the most pleasing brand). Analogous to the use of judgmental (cognitive) heuristics, affective heuristics may be used by consumers to lessen the effort or cognitive strain required when making purchase decisions. In fact, affective heuristics may even require less effort than many of the judgmental or cognitive heuristics suggested in the consumer behavior literature (for example, Bettman 1979). Consequently, affective heuristics may enhance or complement the influence of judgmental heuristics or, at times, even override or replace judgmental heuristics.

It could be argued that the results obtained in our study are ambiguous since general hedonic affect was not directly manipulated. The only manipulation was explicitly cuing subjects to its presence. However, even under such minimal cuing conditions with relatively innocuous information, the effects were found to be quite substantial. Nevertheless, there is a need for further research that more directly manipulates the presence, degree, and directionality of general hedonic affect.

In brief, general hedonic affect is a construct whose implications are endemic to virtually all consumer choice behavior. Despite the practical difficulty of studying general hedonic affect experimentally (due to measurement problems and the like), it requires thorough creative and empirical investigation if a comprehensive understanding of consumer behavior is ever to ensue.

Familiarity and Affect

Another preliminary study investigated the role of affect in consumer decision making (Hoyer and Gates 1985). The purpose of this study was to investigate the role of familiarity (see Zajonc 1980) as an influence in consumer decision making. Traditionally, liking or disliking has been viewed as a postcognitive event. Zajonc and Markus (1982, p. 125) have nicely summed up this traditional belief as: "Before you can like something, you must know what it is." However, studies of the mere-exposure effect have established that positive affect toward an object can be generated simply as a result of repeated exposure to it (Zajonc 1980; Zajonc and Markus 1982). The explanation is that repeated exposure to a stimulus builds familiarity. Then, since individuals tend to prefer familiar objects to unfamiliar objects, familiarity builds liking.

These findings can be linked to consumer behavior by noting, as Zajonc and Markus (1982) have, that the advertising industry appears to have an intuitive understanding of the importance of affect and familiarity. Brand names are ingrained in people's memories as they are repeatedly exposed to advertisements, and brand images are created as products are coupled with scenes of good times and beautiful surroundings. Other research has supported the notion that repeated exposure to a stimulus leads to the creation of conditioned affect toward that stimulus if certain conditions are present (Harrison 1977; Sawyer 1977, 1981). In addition, Ray and Batra (1983) have discussed the possible effects of affective ad executions and have linked these effects to theoretical phenomena such as the mere-exposure effect and hemispheral lateralization.

Although the importance of affect in the processing of advertisements has been clearly recognized on a general level, research is needed to link this key construct to specific decision processes. Hoyer and Gates (1985) attempted to expand on the authors' study by examining the impact of affect on actual consumer choice. In particular, interest focused on two major questions: (1) Given that affect is present in a choice context, to what extent is it used as a basis for making a choice? and (2) If affect is introduced prior to cognitive processing, will it have a biasing effect on subsequent ability to accurately judge product quality?

To examine the issues raised in these questions, Hoyer and Gates designed an experimental study that specifically assessed consumer decision strategies. Subjects were 173 freshmen and sophomore college students. None of the subjects was experienced in purchasing the product of inquiry, peanut butter. A majority of the subjects had never purchased peanut butter for themselves, whereas the remainder had purchased peanut butter for themselves only a few times.

Subjects were asked to engage in a simulated peanut butter choice task. Half of the subjects ($n = 83$) evaluated a familiar brand and two unfamiliar brands (the familiarity condition); the remaining subjects ($n = 90$) evaluated three unknown brands (the no-familiarity condition). Various dependent variables, such as the evaluative criteria employed when selecting a brand of peanut butter and the accuracy of choice, were then assessed.

In the familiarity condition, subjects were presented with three brands of peanut butter. The first was a well known, heavily advertised national brand that in a pretest was found to possess a high degree of recognition. Only subjects who recognized this brand were included in the familiarity condition. The two unknown brands consisted of store brands from other regions of the country. To be included in the familiarity condition subjects could not recognize either of these two brands or the stores from which they were derived.

In the no-familiarity condition, subjects were asked to evaluate three totally unfamiliar brands. Two of these brands were identical to the unfamiliar brands included in the familiarity condition. The third was another store brand from a different region of the country. Only subjects who exhibited no recognition of these brands were included in the no-familiarity condition. The primary purpose of this condition was to serve as a control group against which to compare the impact of familiarity.

The first question addressed the impact of affect on the criteria used to select a brand. Initially, subjects were exposed to one of two peanut butter displays. They were asked to select one of the three brands displayed, spread a sample of the selected brand on a cracker, and taste-test it. After this taste test, subjects were asked why they selected the particular brand they did and were allowed four additional trials so the other two brands could be sampled. (Details of the procedures are given in Hoyer and Gates 1985.) After the fifth trial, subjects were asked to indicate which brand they now preferred and why they selected this brand.

Table 6–2 presents the results of an open-ended choice criterion question asked subjects at both points in time. The criterion subjects used to make their first selection was initially used to examine the effect of affect on their choices. As shown in table 6–2, affect had a considerable impact on the first selection. A large segment of the familiarity condition subjects (60 percent) made their selection based on the most familiar brand. Another 22 percent based their decision on a combination of familiarity and some other attribute. The remaining 18 percent of the sample employed a variety of evaluative criteria.

This pattern can be contrasted sharply with the criteria employed by the no-familiarity condition subjects. The largest percent of subjects in this condition (45 percent) stated that they based their choice on the package (also an affect-related strategy), whereas the second largest group employed a combination of price and some other attribute (14 percent) to arrive at a choice. Eleven percent of the subjects based their decision on product ingredients.

One inference (perhaps more appropriately a hypothesis) from these percentages is that first-time buyers are likely to base a purchase decision on familiarity if brands differ on this attribute. However, when all brands are unfamiliar, other attributes, including packaging, ingredients, and price (in combination with other factors), are more likely to be employed.

A second finding is that in the no-familiarity condition subjects were more likely to base their final choice on the taste of the product than were

Table 6–2
Peanut Butter Study Results

	First Selection			Final Selection		
Criterion	No Familiarity[a]	Familiarity[a]	Z-Value[b]	No Familiarity[a]	Familiarity[a]	Z-Value[b]
Familiar brand	0.0	60.0	11.11*	5.4	17.8	2.76
Taste/texture	4.3	0.0	n.s.	62.4	41.1	3.04
Best price	2.2	0.0	n.s.	3.2	1.1	n.s.
Ingredients	10.8	3.3	2.16*	0.0	1.1	n.s.
Package	45.2	4.4	6.95*	0.0	3.3	n.s.
Try new brand	1.1	0.0	n.s.	4.3	7.8	n.s.
Familiar and taste	0.0	3.3	n.s.	6.5	13.3	n.s.
Familiar and other	0.0	18.9	4.41*	0.0	2.2	n.s.
Price and taste	1.0	0.0	n.s.	5.4	3.3	n.s.
Price and other	14.0	4.4	2.63*	1.1	3.3	n.s.
Other	21.4	5.7	—	11.7	5.7	—
	n = 90	n = 83		n = 90	n = 83	

[a]Values are percentages.
[b]For test of differences in response proportions (* indicates the difference was statistically significant at $p < .05$).

subjects in the familiarity condition (62 percent vs. 41 percent). Without brand familiarity to rely on, these no-familiarity condition subjects apparently relied more heavily on information acquired from tasting the product than did those familiar with a brand. In the presence of a familiar brand, however, although taste perceptions were cited most frequently, they were less important in determining final choice than when no familiar brand was present. This implies that consumers trust well-known brands; therefore taste perceptions are not as important choice determinants as in the case of unfamiliar brands.

Finally, it is instructive to compare differences between first and final selections. For the no-familiarity condition sample, a striking change is the switch from packaging and ingredients attribute responses to taste (45 percent and 11 percent to 62 percent). In this instance, when no brands were initially familiar, subjects relied on their taste perceptions when making a final choice.

A similar pattern exists for familiarity condition subjects. However, the magnitude of switching is not as great. For the first selection, 82 percent of the subjects based their decision at least partially on familiarity-related attributes, while 33 percent continued to do so when making their final selection. This finding is taken as evidence that familiarity had a significant impact on subjects' choice processes even after they physically tasted a number of brands.

The second issue investigated was the extent to which subjects could accurately choose the highest quality brand. To study this issue, brand quality was manipulated. An advantage of this manipulation is that a behavioral indicant of affect is provided. This is important because, given the noncognitive aspects of the affect construct, the effects of such a manipulation may be difficult to verbalize (Zajonc 1980).

To identify high and low quality brands of peanut butter, eight different brands were evaluated by a group of pretest subjects in a blind taste test. On the basis of this pretest, two brands were selected. These consisted of the brand with the highest quality rating (that is, a well-known national brand) and the brand with the second lowest rating (a generic brand).[a] These two brands were then employed to create two conditions in order to assess accuracy of choice. In the first condition (quality difference), subjects were presented with the high quality brand and two low quality brands. An accurate choice occurred when the subject was able to correctly select the high quality brand.

In the no-quality-difference condition, all three jars contained the low

---

[a]The brand with the lowest quality rating was not employed because it was too disliked. Use of this brand would have made the manipulation transparent. See Hoyer and Gates (1985) for details.

quality peanut butter. This group served as a control against which to compare the results of the quality-difference condition and to assess the impact of affect on quality judgments in a situation where no quality differences actually existed. Thus, this manipulation permitted an examination of the extent to which subjects could select the highest quality brand both when affect was present and when it was absent.

Several different analyses were performed. First, choice was examined for no-familiarity condition subjects. This group served as a benchmark of discrimination ability in the absence of familiarity. Of the subjects in the no-familiarity condition, 56 percent were successful in selecting the best quality brand. This percentage is significantly better than chance (33 percent).

More interesting are the results for familiarity condition subjects. Figure 6–1 summarizes these findings. The rows of the figure display the brand containing the highest quality peanut butter, and the columns indicate the brand chosen. The diagonal of this matrix reflects accurate choices.

Several key findings are worth noting. First, when quality differences occurred among the brands, only 41 percent of the subjects were able to correctly choose the highest quality brand. A large percentage of these correct guesses (67 percent) was attributable to the selection of the familiar brand (that is, the well-known brand was selected as the one with the highest quality). Seventy-seven percent of the subjects believed the familiar brand possessed the highest quality regardless of which brand actually did. When an unfamiliar brand possessed the highest quality (that is, in two-thirds of the cases), only 20 percent of the subjects made an accurate choice; 73 percent selected the familiar brand even though it was not the highest quality brand. The former percentage is substantially lower than the 56 percent evidenced in the no-familiarity condition. Thus, it appears familiarity had a dramatic effect on the ability of subjects to accurately choose the highest quality brand. Second, when subjects were familiar with a brand and there were no quality differences between brands, 69 percent of the subjects selected the well-known brand. These differences again illustrate the apparent ability of familiarity to alter perceptions during the decision-making process.

In summary, the purpose of this study was to demonstrate the influence of affect formed through brand familiarity on the consumer choice process. Considered collectively, the findings suggest familiarity (and, by extension, affect) has a major role in influencing brand choices for inexperienced consumers. A familiar brand is preferred over unfamiliar brands and the ability to accurately choose the highest quality brand is significantly hampered in the presence of familiarity.

More specifically, when confronting a purchase choice where little prior knowledge is available, consumers may be drawn toward the brand with which they are most familiar. Thus, the mere-exposure effect, demonstrated by Zajonc (1980) in other contexts, may also prove to be a useful expla-

Quality Differences	Brand Chosen: Familiar	Unfamiliar A	Unfamiliar B	Total
Familiar	12 [1]	1 [2]	1 [3]	14
Unfamiliar A	9 [4]	4 [5]	1 [6]	14
Unfamiliar B	13 [7]	1 [8]	2 [9]	16
	34 (77.3%)	6 (13.6%)	4 (9.1%)	44

Highest Quality Brand:

No Quality Difference	Brand Chosen: Familiar	Unfamiliar A	Unfamiliar B	
All Same Quality	27 (69.2%)	9 (23.1%)	3 (7.7%)	39

Figure 6–1. Selection of Highest Quality Brand (Subject in Familiarity Condition Only)

nation of choice in certain purchase-related contexts. Further, even after brands have been formally evaluated, familiarity may have the lasting effect of reducing the importance of other brand attributes, such as taste, in the selection process.

The study also suggests another form of affect may play a role in the choice process in the absence of brand familiarity. A large percentage of subjects (45 percent) made their initial choice on the basis of liking the package. Consequently, the attractiveness of a package may also create a general liking for a brand and itself determine the choice for inexperienced consumers.

Finally, the finding that brand familiarity had a dramatic impact on decision accuracy merits scrutiny. A large percentage of subjects stated that the well-known brand possessed the highest quality even when it did not. Further, when all three brands were of equal quality, a majority of the subjects believed the well-known brand possesed the highest quality. It is possible that familiarity has an impact on the evaluation process through the formation of consumer expectations (Olson and Dover 1978). Consumers may possess an expectation that well-known brands are of higher quality than lesser-known brands. This belief then serves to bias the nature of the evaluation process with the end result being consumers believe the well-known brand is superior in quality even when it is not. This suggests advertising may also have an indirect influence on choice by altering the nature of the postpurchase evaluation process.

To conclude this section, it is necessary to reiterate certain caveats. Both of the above studies were designed to serve as demonstrations or illustrations, not to provide substantive conclusions. Consequently, there may be some ambiguities as to how the data can best be interpreted. Even so, the purpose in discussing them is to reinforce the notion that the presence of even relatively innocuous affective information can dramatically alter decision processes.

Epilogue

The symposium and this resulting book were purposefully designed to be provocative and stimulate thought rather than to pose direct questions and to provide answers to these questions. Independently of how the respective contributions to the symposium and book are judged, one has to consider seriously how affect is defined, used, and incorporated into models of consumer behavior. In future consumer behavior research, it will be necessary to reexamine the findings of previous research that generated results and conclusions derived from relatively affect-free contexts to determine whether different results and conclusions would be produced if affect were explicitly considered.

Numerous issues can be studied with respect to the role of affect in information processing and consumer behavior. One important issue, which surfaces in previous chapters and has been a major source of discussion in the affect literature (for example, Zajonc 1984; Lazarus 1984), centers on whether affect precedes cognition or cognition precedes affect. Much of this discussion focused on the physiological bases of information processing. This topic is especially interesting when considering minimal conditions for the formation of preference.

However, issues such as these are often not of central importance in consumer behavior. For a variety of reasons, it is probably not in the best interest of consumer behavior researchers to focus their efforts on answering the question of whether affect always precedes cognition or cognition always precedes affect. From a practical perspective this distinction is probably arbitrary and partially depends on how affect and cognition are defined. At any rate, the distinction has little impact on the importance of affect and the fact that it should be studied.

Another aspect of the primacy discussion is that there are a number of transformations that occur when information is processed in any consumer decision. Incoming information immediately begins to be altered and reformed, reduced and so forth, and this occurs in a very short time period. However, this initial activity is probably not the most important activity going on in consumer decision making. There are few consumption decisions that are made within three milliseconds and, consequently, consumer behavior researchers probably should not be overly concerned about what happens in the first ten milliseconds or hundred milliseconds of information processing by the brain. It is a major concern if one is studying the minimal condition for the formation of a preference, but it should not be a target of emphasis in consumer behavior research.

Finally, in discussions of the primacy issue the parties seem to be dealing implicitly with a very static state. The question "Did the person think first or feel first?" is not very meaningful. Individuals are always in a stream of thinking and feeling; therefore, it is irrelevant to say, "Are there any thoughts preceding an affect" or "is there affect preceding cognition?" Both of these activities are continually occurring. People do not exist in a state of no thought or no feeling only to be occasionally presented with a stimulus. Mental activities are dynamic, not static. The important issue to be addressed is how affect and cognition interact to influence behavior.

There *has* to be a cognitive component in consumer behavior. As one example, cognitions related to price are likely to be present in virtually all purchase situations. However, at times affect may be so strong that what the individual is trying to do is to somehow overcome it through cognition. Nevertheless, the point to be made is that both cognition and affect will be present in most consumer decision making. Thus, one goal of future research in consumer behavior should be to understand under what conditions cognition or affect dominates decision making (and why). A subsequent goal would then be to discover ways in which affect and cognition, individually as well as collectively, can be influenced so as to produce particular affective or cognitive responses.

In closing, it should be noted that a literature on affective processing in consumer behavior is rapidly developing. Since the symposium, research has appeared on the mere-exposure effect (Obermiller 1985a, 1985b), affective responses to advertising and the influence of affect in risk preferences (see

Proceedings of the Division of Consumer Psychology, American Psychological Association 1985, for examples). It is hoped that this book will stimulate even more research on the role of affect in consumer behavior.

References

Abbott, Bruce B.; Schoen, Lawrence S.; and Badia, Pietro. 1984. "Predictable and Unpredictable Shock: Behavioral Measures of Aversion and Physiological Measures of Stress." *Psychological Bulletin* 96:45–71.

Abelson, Robert P.; Kinder, Donald R.; Peters, Mark D.; and Fiske, Susan T. 1982. "Affective and Semantic Components in Political Person Perception." *Journal of Personality and Social Psychology* 42:619–630.

Abelson, Robert P., and Levi A. 1985. "Decision Making and Decision Theory." In *Handbook of Social Psychology,* Vol. 1, eds. G. Lindzey and E. Aronson. New York: Random House, pp. 231–310.

Ahtola, Olli T. 1985. "Hedonic and Utilitarian Aspects of Consumer Behavior: An Attitudinal Perspective." In *Advances in Consumer Research,* Vol. 12, eds., E. C. Hirschman and M. B. Holbrook. Ann Arbor, Mich.: Association for Consumer Research, pp. 7–10.

Alderson, Wroe. 1957. *Marketing Behavior and Executive Action.* Homewood, Ill.: Richard D. Irwin.

Anderson, D. R. 1983. "Online Cognitive Processing of Television." Paper presented at the Second Annual Conference on Advertising and Consumer Psychology, Chicago, Ill.

Anderson, Norman H. 1968. "Likableness Ratings of 555 Personality-trait Words." *Journal of Personality and Social Psychology* 9:272–279.

Andreasen, Alan R. 1965. "Attitudes and Customer Behavior: A Decision Model." In *New Research in Marketing,* ed. L. E. Preston, Berkeley. Calif.: Institute of Business and Economic Research.

Andrews, Frank M., and Withey, Stephen B. 1976. *Social Indicators of Well-Being: Americans' Perceptions of Life Quality.* New York: Plenum Press.

Anisfeld, Moshe. 1984. *Language Development From Birth to Three.* Hillsdale, N. J.: Erlbaum.

Appel, Valentine; Weinstein, Sidney; and Weinstein, Curt. 1979. "Brain Activity and Recall of TV Advertising." *Journal of Advertising Research* 19:7–16.

Arnold, Magda B. 1960. *Emotion and Personality.* New York: Columbia University Press.

———. 1970. "Perennial Problems in the Field of Emotion." In *Feelings and Emotions,* ed. M. B. Arnold. New York: Academic Press, pp. 169–185.

Aronson, Elliott. 1966. "The Psychology of Insufficient Justification: An Analysis of Some Conflicting Data." In *Cognitive Consistency: Motivational Antecedents and Behavioral Consequences,* ed. S. Feldman. New York: Academic Press, pp. 115–133.

Assael, Henry. 1981. *Consumer Behavior and Marketing Action.* Boston: Kent.

Averill, James R. 1980. "A Constructivist View of Emotion." In *Emotion: Theory, Research, and Experience,* Vol. 1, eds. R. Plutchik and H. Kellerman. New York: Academic Press.

Ax, Albert F. 1953. "The Physiological Differentiation between Fear and Anger in Humans." *Psychosomatic Medicine* 15:433–442.

Baddeley, A. D. 1978. "The Trouble with Levels: A Reexamination of Craik and Lockhart's Framework for Memory Research." *Psychological Review* 85:139–152.

Bagozzi, Richard P. 1978. "The Construct Validity of the Affective, Behavioral, and Cognitive Components of Attitudes by the Analysis of Covariance Structures." *Multivariate Behavioral Research* 13:9–31.

———. 1981, "An Examination of the Validity of Two Models of Attitude." *Multivariate Behavioral Research* 16:323–359.

Bagozzi, Richard P., and Burnkrant, Robert E. 1979. "Attitude Organization and the Attitude-Behavior Relationship." *Journal of Personality and Social Psychology* 37:913–929.

Bagozzi, Richard P., and Silk, Alvin J. 1982. "Recall, Recognition, and the Measurement of Memory for Print Advertisements." *Marketing Science* 2:95–134.

Bagozzi, Richard P.; Tybout, Alice M.; Craig, C. Samuel; and Sternthal, Brian. 1979. "The Construct Validity of the Tripartite Classification of Attitudes." *Journal of Marketing Research* 16:88–95.

Batra, Rajeev. 1984a. *"Low Involvement" Message Reception—Processes and Advertising Implications.* Ph.D. Diss., Stanford University.

———. 1984b. "One More Time: How Do We Measure Attitudes?" Working paper, Graduate School of Business, Columbia University.

———. 1985. "Understanding the Likability/Involvement Interaction: The 'Override' Model." In *Advances in Consumer Research,* Vol. 12, eds. E. C. Hirschman and M. B. Holbrook. Ann Arbor, Mich.: Association for Consumer Research, pp. 362–367.

Batra, Rajeev, and Ray, Michael L. n.d. "Advertising Repetition 'Build': The Moderation Effects of Message Response Involvement." Graduate School of Business, Columbia University. Mimeo.

———. 1983a. "Advertising Situations: The Implications of Differential Involvement and Accompanying Affect Responses." In *Information Processing Research in Advertising,* ed. R. J. Harris. Hillsdale, N. J.: Erlbaum, pp. 127–151.

———. 1983b. "Operationalizing Involvement as Depth and Quality of Cognitive Response." In *Advances in Consumer Research,* Vol. 10, eds. R. P. Bagozzi and A. M. Tybout. Ann Arbor, Mich.: Association for Consumer Research, pp. 309–313.

———. 1984a. "How Advertising Works at Contact." In *Psychological Processes and Advertising Effects: Theory, Research, and Application,* eds. L. Alwitt and A. A. Mitchell. Hillsdale, N. J.: Erlbaum, pp. 13–43.

———. 1984b. "Affective Responses Mediating Acceptance of Advertising." Working paper, Graduate School of Business, Columbia University. Mimeo.

———. 1984c. "Identifying Opportunities for Repetition Minimization." Working paper, Marketing Science Institute, Cambridge, Mass. Typeset.

Batra, Rajeev, and Silk, Alvin. 1983. "Recall, Recognition and the Measurement of Memory for Print Advertisements." *Marketing Science* 2:95–134.

Batra, Rajeev; Tybout, Alice M.; Craig, C. Samuel; and Sternthal, Brian. 1979. "The Construct Validity of the Tripartite Classification of Attitudes." *Journal of Marketing Research* 16:88–95.

Beaber, Rex J. 1975. *The General Characteristics of Covert Resistance Mechanisms and Their Relationship to Attitude Change and Speaker Perception.* Ph.D. Diss., University of Southern California.

Beattie, A., and Mitchell, Andrew A. 1984. "Advertising Recall and Persuasion." In *Psychological Processes and Advertising Effects: Theory, Research and Application,* eds. L. Alwitt and A. A. Mitchell. Hillsdale, N.J.: Erlbaum.

Beckwith, Neil E., and Lehmann, Donald R. 1975. "The Importance of Halo Effects in Multi-Attribute Attitude Models." *Journal of Marketing Research* 12:265–275.

Belch, George E. 1982. "The Effects of Television Commercial Repetition on Cognitive Response and Message Acceptance." *Journal of Consumer Research* 9:56–65.

Belch, George E., and Lutz, Richard J. 1982. "A Multiple Exposure Study of the Effects of Comparative and Noncomparative Television Commercials on Cognitive Response, Recall, and Message Acceptance." Working paper, Marketing Science Institute, Cambridge, Mass. Typeset.

Beldoch, Michael. 1964. "Sensitivity to Expression of Emotional Meaning in Three Modes of Communication." In *The Communication of Emotional Meaning,* ed. J. L. Davitz. New York: McGraw-Hill, pp. 31–42.

Beloff, John. 1973. *Psychological Sciences.* London: Crosby, Lockwood, and Staples.

Bem, Daryl J. 1965. "Self-Perception Theory." In *Advances in Experimental Social Psychology,* Vol. 6, ed. L. Berkowitz. New York: Springer-Verlag, pp. 352–389.

Berger, David. 1981. "A Retrospective: RCB Recall Study." *Advertising Age* (October 26):S-36–37.

Bernard, Claude. 1927. *An Introduction to the Study of Experimental Medicine,* Trans. H. C. Green. New York: Macmillan.

Bettman, James R. 1979. *An Information Processing Theory of Consumer Choice.* Reading, Mass.: Addison-Wesley.

———. 1982. "A Functional Analysis of the Role of Overall Evaluation of Alternatives in Choice Processes." In *Advances in Consumer Research,* Vol. 9, ed. A. A. Mitchell. Ann Arbor, Mich.: Association for Consumer Research, pp. 87–93.

Birdwhistell, Ray L. 1970. *Kinesics and Context: Essays on Body Motion Communication.* Philadelphia: University of Pennsylvania Press.

Bloch, Peter H., and Bruce, Grady D. 1984. "Product Involvement as Leisure Behavior." In *Advances in Consumer Research,* Vol. 11, ed. T. C. Kinnear. Ann Arbor, Mich.: Association for Consumer Research, pp. 197–202.

Block, Jack. 1957. "Studies in the Phenomenology of Emotions." *Journal of Abnormal and Social Psychology* 54:358–363.

Bower, Gordon H. 1981. "Mood and Memory." *American Psychologist* 36:129–148.

Bower, Gordon H., and Gilligan, Stephan G. 1979. "Remembering Information Related to One's Self." *Journal of Research in Personality* 13:420–432.

Boyd, Harper W., Jr., and Levy, Sidney J. 1963. "New Dimensions in Consumer Analysis." *Harvard Business Review* 41:129–140.

Brehm, Sharon S., and Brehm, Jack W. 1981. *Psychological Reactance: A Theory of Freedom and Control.* New York: Academic Press.

Brenner, Charles. 1974. "On the Nature and Development of Affects: A Unified Theory." *Psychoanalytic Quarterly* 43:532–556.

Broadbent, Donald E. 1958. *Perception and Communication.* London: Pergamon Press.

Brown, Serena-Lynn, and Schwartz, Gary E. 1980. "Relationships between Facial Electromyography and Subjective Experience during Affective Imagery." *Biological Psychology* 11:49–62.

Burnkrant, Robert E., and Page, Thomas J., Jr. 1982. "An Examination of the Convergent, Discriminant, and Predictive Validity of Fishbein's Behavior Intention Model." *Journal of Marketing Research* 19:550–561.

Cacioppo, John T.; Harkins, S. G.; and Petty, Richard E. 1981. "The Nature of Attitudes and Cognitive Responses and Their Relationships to Behavior." In *Cognitive Responses in Persuasion,* eds. R. E. Petty, T. M. Ostrom, and T. C. Brock. Hillsdale, N.J.: Erlbaum, pp. 31–54.

Cacioppo, John T.; Marshall-Goodell, Beverly; and Dorfman, Donald D. 1983. "Skeletomuscular Patterning: Topographic Analysis of the Integrated Electromyogram." *Psychophysiology* 20:269–283.

Cacioppo, John T., and Petty, Richard E. 1979a. "Attitudes and Cognitive Response: An Electrophysiological Approach." *Journal of Personality and Social Psychology* 37:2181–2199.

———. 1979b. "Effects of Message Repetition and Position on Cognitive Response, Recall and Persuasion." *Journal of Personality and Social Psychology* 37:97–109.

———. 1979c. "Lip and Nonpreferred Forearm EMG Activity As a Function of Orienting Task." *Journal of Biological Psychology* 9:103–113.

———. 1980. "The Effects of Orienting Task on Differential Hemispheric EEG Activation." *Neuropsychologia* 18:675–683.

———. 1981a. "Electromyograms As Measures of Extent Affectivity of Information Processing." *American Psychologist* 36:441–456.

———. 1981b. "Electromyographic Specificity during Covert Information Processing." *Psychophysiology* 18:518–523.

———. 1981c. "Social Psychological Procedures for Cognitive Response Assessment: The Thought-Listing Technique." In *Cognitive Assessment,* eds. T. V. Merluzzi, C. R. Glass, and M. Genest. New York: Guilford Press, pp. 309–342.

———. 1982. "A Biosocial Model of Attitude Change: Signs, Symptoms, and Undetected Physiological Responses." In *Perspectives in Cardiovascular Psychophysiology,* eds. J. T. Cacioppo and R. E. Petty. New York: Guilford Press, pp. 151–188.

———. 1985. "Social Processes." In *Handbook of Psychophysiology,* eds. M. G. H. Coles, E. Donchin, and S. Forges. New York: Guilford Press.

Cacioppo, John T.; Petty, Richard E.; Losch, Mary E.; and Kim, H. S. In preparation. "Electromyographic Activity over Facial Muscle Regions Can Differentiate the Valence and Intensity of Affective Reactions."

Cacioppo, John T.; Petty, Richard E.; and Marshall-Goodell, Beverly. 1984. "Electromyographic Specificity during Simple Physical and Attitudinal Tasks: Location and Topographical Features of Integrated EMG Responses." *Biological Psychology* 18:85–121.

Cacioppo, John T.; Petty, Richard E.; and Morris, Katherine J. 1985. "Semantic, Evaluative, and Self-Referent Processing: Memory, Cognitive Effort, and Somatovisceral Activity." *Psychophysiology* 22:371–384.

Cacioppo, John T., and Sandman, Curt A. 1981. "Psychophysiological Functioning, Cognitive Responding, and Attitudes." In *Cognitive Responses to Persuasion,* eds. R. E. Petty, T. M. Ostrom, and T. C. Brock. Hillsdale, N.J.: Erlbaum, pp. 81–104.

Calder, Bobby J.; Insko, Chester A.; and Yandell, Ben. 1974. "The Relation of Cognitive and Memorial Processes to Persuasion in a Simulated Jury Trial." *Journal of Applied Social Psychology* 4:62–93.

Calder, Bobby J., and Sternthal, Brian 1980. "Television Commercial Wearout: An Information Processing View." *Journal of Marketing Research* 17:173–186.

Campbell, Donald T., and Fiske, Donald W. 1959. "Convergent and Discriminant Validation by the Multitrait-Multimethod Matrix." *Psychological Bulletin* 56:81–105.

Campos, Joseph J., and Barrett, K. C. 1984. "Toward a New Understanding of Emotions and Their Development." In *Emotions, Cognition, and Behavior,* eds. C. E. Izard, J. Kagan, and R. B. Zajonc. Cambridge: Cambridge University Press, pp. 17–37.

Cartwright-Smith, J. 1979. *The Grimace: Facilitating Forearm Strength by Exaggerating the Nonverbal Facial Display of Effort.* Paper presented at the annual meeting of the Eastern Psychological Association, Philadelphia, Pa.

Cermak, Laird S., and Craik, Fergus I. M., eds. 1979. *Levels of Processing in Human Memory.* Hillsdale, N.J.: Erlbaum.

Chaiken, Shelley. 1980. "Heuristic Versus Systematic Information Processing and the Use of Source Versus Message Cues in Persuasion." *Journal of Personality and Social Psychology* 39:752–766.

Cialdini, Robert B.; Petty, Richard E.; and Cacioppo, John T. 1981. "Attitude and Attitude Change." *Annual Review of Psychology* 32:357–404.

Clark, Margaret S., and Fiske, Susan T., eds. 1982. *Affect and Cognition: The 17th Annual Carnegie Symposium.* Hillsdale, N.J.: Erlbaum.

Clore, Gerald, and Ortony, Andrew. 1983. "The Cognitive Causes of Emotion." Paper presented at the Nags Head Conference on Emotion, Stress, and Conflict, Nags Head, N.C.

Clynes, Manfred. 1980. "The Communication of Emotion: Theory of Sentics." In *Emotion: Theory, Research, and Experience,* eds. R. Plutchik and H. Kellerman. New York: Academic Press.

Cohen, Joel B.; Fishbein, Martin; and Ahtola, Olli T. 1972. "The Nature and Uses of Expectancy-Value Models in Consumer Attitude Research." *Journal of Marketing Research* 9:456–460.

Coles, Michael G. H.; Donchin, Emanuel; and Porges, Stephen, eds. 1985. *Handbook of Psychophysiology*. New York: Guilford Press.

Colley, Russell. 1961. *Defining Advertising Goals for Measured Advertising Results*. New York: Association of National Advertisers.

Cook, Thomas D. 1969. "Competence, Counterarguing and Attitude Change." *Journal of Personality* 37:342–358.

Craik, Fergus I. M. 1979. "Human Memory." *Annual Review of Psychology* 30:62–103.

Craik, Fergus I. M., and Lockhart, R. S. 1972. "Levels of Processing: A Framework for Memory Research." *Journal of Verbal Learning and Verbal Behavior* 11:156–163.

Craik, Fergus I. M., and Tulving, Endel 1975. "Depth of Processing and the Retention of Words in Episodic Memory." *Journal of Experimental Psychology: General* 104:268–294.

Crider, Andrew. 1983. "The Promise of Social Psychophysiology." In *Social Psychophysiology: A Sourcebook,* eds. J. T. Cacioppo and R. E. Petty. New York: Guilford Press, pp. 37–47.

Cross, Henry A.; Halcomb, Charles G.; and Matter, William W. 1967. "Imprinting or Exposure Learning in Rats Given Early Auditory Stimulation." *Psychonomic Science* 7:233–234.

Daly, Eleanor M.; Lancee, William J.; and Polivy, Janet. 1983. "A Conical Model for the Taxonomy of Emotional Experience." *Journal of Personality and Social Psychology* 45:443–457.

Darwin, Charles. 1872. *The Expression of the Emotions in Man and Animals*. Chicago: The University of Chicago Press, 1965.

Davitz, Joel R. 1969. *The Language of Emotion*. New York: Academic Press.

———. 1970. "A Dictionary and Grammar of Emotion." In *Feelings and Emotions,* ed. M. B. Arnold. New York: Academic Press, pp. 251–258.

Delgado, J. M. R. 1966. *Emotions*. Dubuque, Iowa: William C. Brown.

Denzin, Norman K. 1984. *On Understanding Emotion*. San Francisco: Jossey-Bass.

de Rivera, Joseph. 1977. *A Structural Theory of the Emotions*. New York: International Universities Press.

Dichter, Ernest. 1964. *Handbook of Consumer Motivations*. New York: McGraw-Hill.

Dienstbier, Richard A. 1979. "Emotion-Attribution Theory: Establishing Roots and Exploring Future Perspectives." In *Nebraska Symposium on Motivation,* Vol. 26, ed. R. A. Dienstbier. Lincoln: University of Nebraska Press.

Dimberg, Ulf. 1982. "Facial Reactions to Facial Expression." *Psychophysiology* 19:643–647.

Dubner, Ronald; Sessle, B. J.; and Storey, A. T. 1978. *The Neural Basis of Oral and Facial Function*. New York: Plenum Press.

Eagly, Alice H., and Himmelfarb, Samuel. 1978. "Attitudes and Opinions." *Annual Review of Psychology* 29:517–554.

Edfeldt, Aake W. 1960. *Silent Speech and Silent Reading*. Chicago: University of Chicago Press.

Eibl-Eibesfeldt, I. 1972. "Similarities and Differences between Cultures in Expressive

Movements." In *Nonverbal Communications*, ed. R. A. Hinde. Cambridge: Cambridge University Press.

Ekman, Paul. 1972. *"Universal and Cultural Differences in Facial Expressions of Emotion."* In *Nebraska Symposium on Motivation*, Vol. 19, ed. J. Cole. Lincoln: University of Nebraska Press, pp. 207–283.

———. 1973. *Darwin and Facial Expression: A Century of Research in Review*. New York: Academic Press.

———. 1982a. *Emotion in the Human Face*. 2nd ed. Cambridge: Cambridge University Press.

———. 1982b. "Methods for Measuring Facial Action." In *Handbook of Methods in Nonverbal Behavior Research*, eds. K. R. Scherer and P. Ekman, Cambridge: Cambridge University Press, pp. 45–90.

Ekman, Paul, and Friesen, Wallace V. 1971. "Constants across Cultures in the Face and Emotion." *Journal of Personality and Social Psychology* 17:124–129.

———. 1974. "Detecting Deception from the Body of Face." *Journal of Personality and Social Psychology* 29:288–298.

———. 1975. *Unmasking the Face*. Englewood Cliffs, N.J.: Prentice-Hall.

———. 1976. "Measuring Facial Movement." *Environmental Psychological and Nonverbal Behavior* 1:56–75.

———. 1978. *Facial Coding Action System (FACS): A Technique for the Measurement of Facial Actions*. Palo Alto, Calif.: Consulting Psychologists Press.

Ekman, Paul; Friesen, Wallace V.; and Ancoli, S. 1980. "Facial Signs of Emotional Experience." *Journal of Personality and Social Psychology* 39:1125–1134.

Ekman, Paul; Levenson, Robert W.; and Friesen, Wallace V. 1983. "Autonomic Nervous System Activity Distinguishes among Emotions." *Science* 221:1208–1210.

Ekman, Paul, and Oster, Harriet. 1979. "Facial Expressions of Emotion." *Annual Review of Psychology* 30:527–554.

Ellsworth, Phoebe C. 1977. "From Abstract Ideas to Concrete Instances: Some Guidelines for Choosing Natural Research Settings." *American Psychologist* 32:604–615.

Engel, James F., and Blackwell, Roger D. 1982. *Consumer Behavior*. Chicago: Dryden Press.

Engel, James F.; Kollat, David T.; and Blackwell, Roger D. 1973. *Consumer Behavior*. Hinsdale, Ill.: Dryden Press.

Englis, Basil G.; Vaughan, Katherine B.; and Lanzetta, John T. 1982. "Conditioning of Counter-Empathic Emotional Responses." *Journal of Experimental Social Psychology* 18:375–391.

Esser, Artistide H. 1973. "Experiences of Crowding: Illustration of a Paradigm for Man–Environment Relations." *Representative Research in Social Psychology* 4:207–218.

Faaborg-Anderson, K., and Edfeldt, Aake W. 1958. "Electromyography of Intrinsic and Extrinsic Laryngeal Muscles during Silent Speech: Correlation with Reading Activity." *Acta Otolaryngologica* 49:478–482.

Ferguson, Tamara J.; Rule, Brenda G.; and Carlson, Dona. 1983. "Memory for Personally Relevant Information." *Journal of Personality and Social Psychology* 44:251–261.

Festinger, Leon. 1957. *A Theory of Cognitive Dissonance.* Stanford, Calif.: Stanford University Press.

Fishbein, Martin, and Ajzen, Icek. 1975. *Belief, Attitude, Intention, and Behavior: An Introduction to Theory and Research.* Reading, Mass.: Addison-Wesley.

Fridlund, A. J.; Ekman, Paul; and Oster, Harriet. In press. "Facial Expressions of Emotion: Review of Literature, 1970–1983." In *Nonverbal Communication,* ed. A. Siegman. Hillsdale, N.J.: Erlbaum.

Fridlund, A. J., and Izard, Carroll E. 1983. "Electromyographic Studies of Facial Expressions of Emotions and Patterns of Emotion." In *Social Psychophysiology: A Sourcebook,* eds. J. T. Cacioppo and R. E. Petty. New York: Guilford Press, pp. 243–286.

Fridlund, A. J.; Schwartz, Gary E.; and Fowler, Stephen C. 1984. "Facial Electromyography and Emotion: Implementation of Multivariate Pattern-Classification Strategies." *Psychophysiology* 21:622–637.

Friesen, Wallace V. 1972. *Cultural Differences in Facial Expression in a Social Situation: An Experimental Test of the Concept of Display Rules.* Ph.D. diss., University of California.

Gallistel, C. R. 1980. "From Muscles to Motivation." *American Scientist* 68:398–408.

Gandiglio, G., and Fra, L. 1967. "Further Observations on Facial Reflexes." *Journal of Neuorological Science* 5:273–285.

Gans, C., and Gorniak, G. C. 1980. "Electromyograms are Repeatable: Precautions and Limitations." *Science* 210:795–797.

Garrity, Linda I. 1977. "Electromyography: A Review of the Current Status of Subvocal Speech Research." *Memory and Cognition* 5:615–622.

Gaylin, Willard. 1979. *Feelings: Our Vital Signs.* New York: Ballantine Books.

Gilligan, Stephen G., and Bower, Gordon H. 1984. "Cognitive Consequences of Emotional Arousal." In *Emotions, Cognition, and Behavior,* eds. C. E. Izard, J. Kagan, and R. B. Zajonc. Cambridge: Cambridge University Press, pp. 547–588.

Giorgi, Amedeo. 1970. *Psychology As a Human Science: A Phenomenologically Based Approach.* New York: Harper and Row.

Glencross, D. J. 1977. "Control of Skilled Movements." *Psychological Bulletin* 84:14–29.

Goffman, Erving. 1976. *Gender Advertisements.* New York: Harper and Row.

Goldberger, Paul. 1980. "Building on the Emotions: The New Trend in Architecture Reflects a Shift Away from Purely Cerebral Design." *The New York Times Magazine* (September 28):39–78.

Golden, Linda L., and Johnson, Keren A. 1983. "The Impact of Sensory Preference and Thinking Versus Feeling Appeals on Advertising Effectiveness." In *Advances in Consumer Research,* Vol. 10, eds. R. P. Bagozzi and A. M. Tybout. Ann Arbor, Mich.: Association for Consumer Research, pp. 203–208.

Goldstein, I. B. 1972. "Electromyography: A Measure of Skeletal Muscle Response." In *Handbook of Psychophysiology,* eds. N. S. Greenfield and R. A. Sternbach. New York: Holt, Rinehart and Winston, pp. 329–366.

Gorn, Gerald J. 1982. "The Effects of Music in Advertising on Choice Behavior: A Classical Conditioning Approach." *Journal of Marketing* 46:94–101.

Greenwald, Anthony G. 1968. "Cognitive Learning, Cognitive Response to Persuasion, and Attitude Change." In *Psychological Foundations of Attitudes,* eds. A. Greenwald, T. Brock, and T. Ostrom, New York: Academic Press, pp. 147–170.

Greenwald, Anthony G., and Leavitt, Clark. 1984. "Audience Involvement in Advertising: Four Levels." *Journal of Consumer Research* 11:581–592.

Grings, William W., and Dawson, Michael E. 1978. *Emotions and Bodily Responses: A Psychophysiological Approach.* New York: Academic Press.

Hager, Joseph, and Ekman, Paul. 1985. "Different Asymmetries of Facial Muscular Actions." *Psychophysiology* 22:317–318.

Haggard, E. A., and Issacs, F. S. 1966. "Micromomentary Facial Expressions as Indicators of Ego Mechanisms in Psychotherapy." In *Methods of Research in Psychotherapy,* eds. C. A. Gottschalk and A. Averback. New York: Appleton-Century-Crofts.

Hansen, Flemming. 1981. "Hemispheral Lateralization: Implications for Understanding Consumer Behavior." *Journal of Consumer Research* 8:23–36.

Harrison, Albert A. 1977. "Mere Exposure." In *Advances in Experimental Social Psychology,* Vol. 10, ed. L. Berkowitz. New York: Academic Press.

Hass, R. Glen, and Grady, Kathleen. 1975. "Temporal Delay, Type of Forewarning, and Resistance to Influence." *Journal of Experimental Social Psychology* 11: 459–469.

Hassett, James. 1978. *A Primer of Psychophysiology.* San Francisco: W. H. Freeman.

Haugeland, John. 1978. "The Nature and Plausibility of Cognitivism." *Behavioral and Brain Sciences* 2:215–260.

Havlena, William J., and Holbrook, Morris B. 1985. "The Varieties of Consumption Experience." Working paper, Graduate School of Business, Columbia University. Mimeo.

Henneman, E. 1980. Organization of the Motor Systems: A Preview." In *Medical Physiology,* ed. B. Bountcastel. Vol. 1, 14th ed. St. Louis: C. V. Mosby.

Hilgard, Ernest R. 1980. "Consciousness in Contemporary Psychology." *Annual Review of Psychology* 31:1–26.

Hirschman, Elizabeth C., and Holbrook, Morris B. 1982. "Hedonic Consumption: Emerging Concepts, Methods and Propositions." *Journal of Marketing* 46:92–101.

Hochschild, Arlie Russell. 1983. *The Managed Heart: Commercialization of Human Feeling.* Berkeley, Calif.: University of California Press.

Holbrook, Morris B. 1978. "Beyond Attitude Structure: Toward the Informational Determinants of Attitude." *Journal of Marketing Research* 15:545–556.

———. 1981. "Integrating Compositional and Decompositional Analyses to Represent the Intervening Role of Perceptions in Evaluative Judgments." *Journal of Marketing Research* 18:13–28.

———. 1983a. "Product Imagery and the Illusion of Reality: Some Insights from Consumer Esthetics." In *Advances in Consumer Research,* Vol. 10, eds. R. P. Bagozzi and A. M. Tybout. Ann Arbor, Mich.: Association for Consumer Research, pp. 65–71.

———. 1983b. "Using a Structural Model of Halo Effect to Assess Perceptual Distortion Due to Affective Overtones." *Journal of Consumer Research* 10:247–252.

————. 1984a. "Axiology in Consumer Research: The Nature of Value in the Consumption Experience." Working paper, Graduate School of Business, Columbia University. Mimeo.

————. 1984b. "Theory Development Is a Jazz Solo: Bird Lives." In *Proceedings, Winter Educators' Conference,* eds. Paul F. Anderson and Michael J. Ryan. Chicago: American Marketing Association, pp. 48–52.

————. 1985. "Why Business Is Bad for Consumer Research: The Three Bears Revisited." In *Advances in Consumer Research,* Vol. 12, eds. E. C. Hirschman and M. B. Holbrook. Ann Arbor, Mich.: Association for Consumer Research, pp. 145–156.

Holbrook, Morris B.; Chestnut, Robert W.; Oliva, Terence A.; and Greenleaf, Eric A. 1984. "Play As a Consumption Experience: The Roles of Emotions, Performance, and Personality in the Enjoyment of Games." *Journal of Consumer Research* 11:728–739.

Holbrook, Morris B., and Corfman, Kim P. 1984. "Quality and Value in the Consumption Experience: Phaedrus Rides Again." In *Consumer Perception of Merchandise and Store Quality,* eds. J. Jacoby and J. C. Olson. Lexington, Mass.: Lexington Books, pp. 31–57.

Holbrook, Morris B., and Hirschman, Elizabeth C. 1982. "The Experiential Aspects of Consumption: Consumer Fantasies, Feelings, and Fun." *Journal of Consumer Research* 9:132–140.

Holbrook, Morris B., and Huber, Joel. 1979. "Separating Perceptual Dimensions from Affective Overtones: An Application to Consumer Aesthetics." *Journal of Consumer Research* 5:272–283.

Holbrook, Morris B.; Huber, Joel; and Stinerock, Robert. 1985. "Types of Value in Consumption Experiences." Working paper, Graduate School of Business, Columbia University. Mimeo.

Holbrook, Morris B., and Lehmann, Donald R. 1980. "Form Versus Content in Predicting Starch Scores." *Journal of Advertising Research* 20:53–62.

Holbrook, Morris B.; Lehmann, Donald R.; and O'Shaughnessy, John. 1983. "Using Versus Choosing: The Relationship of the Consumption Experience to Reasons for Purchasing." Working paper, Graduate School of Business, Columbia University. Mimeo.

Holbrook, Morris B., and Moore, William L. 1982. "Using Canonical Correlation to Construct Product Spaces for Objects with Known Feature Structures." *Journal of Marketing Research* 19:87–98.

Holbrook, Morris B., and O'Shaughnessy, John. 1984. "The Role of Emotion in Advertising." *Psychology and Marketing* 1:45–64.

Holbrook, Morris B., and Westwood, Richard A. 1983. "The Structure of Emotional Responses to Advertising." Working paper, Graduate School of Business, Columbia University. Mimeo.

Holden, Constance. 1981. "Human–Animal Relationship Under Scrutiny." *Science* 214:419–420.

Holman, Rebecca H. 1981a. "Apparel as Communication." In *Symbolic Consumer Behavior,* eds. E. C. Hirschman and M. B. Holbrook. Ann Arbor, Mich.: Association for Consumer Research, pp. 7–15.

————. 1981b. "Product Use As Communication: A Fresh Appraisal of a Venerable

Topic." In *Review of Marketing 1981,* eds. B. M. Enis and K. J. Roering. Chicago: American Marketing Association, pp. 106–119.

Houston, Michael J., and Rothschild, Michael L. 1977. "A Paradigm for Research on Consumer Involvement." Graduate School of Business, University of Wisconsin. Mimeo.

Hovland, Carl I.; Janis, Irving L.; and Kelley, Harold H. 1953. *Communications and Persuasion.* New Haven, Conn.: Yale University Press.

Howard, John A. 1963. *Marketing Management.* Homewood, Ill.: Richard D. Irwin.

———. 1977. *Consumer Behavior: Application of Theory.* New York: McGraw-Hill.

———. 1983. "Marketing Theory of the Firm." *Journal of Marketing* 47:90–100.

Howard, John A., and Sheth, Jagdish N. 1969. *The Theory of Buyer Behavior.* New York: John Wiley.

Hoyer, Wayne D. 1984. "An Examination of Consumer Decision Making for a Common Repeat Purchase Product." *Journal of Consumer Research* 11:822–829.

Hoyer, Wayne D., and Gates, Fliece R. 1985. "The Impact of Familiarity on the Common Repeat Purchase Decision Process." Working paper, The University of Texas at Austin. Photocopy.

Huber, Joel. 1975. "Predicting Preferences on Experimental Bundles of Attributes: A Comparison of Models." *Journal of Marketing Research* 12:290–297.

Hyde, Lewis. 1983. *The Gift: Imagination and the Erotic Life of Property.* New York: Vintage Books.

Isen, Alice M. 1984. "The Influence of Positive Affect on Decision Making and Cognitive Organization." In *Advances in Consumer Research,* Vol 11, eds. E. C. Hirschman and M. B. Holbrook. Ann Arbor, Mich.: Association for Consumer Research, pp. 534–537.

Isen, Alice M.; Shalker, Thomas E.; Clark, Margaret; and Karp, Lynn. 1978. "Affect, Accessibility of Material in Memory, and Behavior: A Cognitive Loop?" *Journal of Personality and Social Psychology* 36:1–12.

Izard, Carroll E. 1971. *The Face of Emotion.* New York: Appleton-Century-Crofts.

———. 1977. *Human Emotions.* New York: Plenum Press.

Izard, Carroll E., and Buechler, Sandra. 1980. "Aspects of Consciousness and Personality in Terms of Differential Emotions Theory." In *Emotion: Theory, Research, and Experience,* eds. R. Plutchik and H. Kellerman. New York: Academic Press.

Izard, Carroll E.; Kagan, Jerome; and Zajonc, Robert B., eds. 1984. *Emotions, Cognition, and Behavior.* Cambridge: Cambridge University Press.

Jackson, John H. 1958. *Selected Writings of John Hulings Jackson,* Vol. 1, ed. J. Tarjan. New York: Basic Books.

James, William. 1890. *The Principles of Psychology.* New York: Holt, Rinehart and Winston.

Janis, Irving Lester, ed. 1982. *Counseling on Personal Decisions: Theory and Research on Short-term Helping Relationships.* New Haven, Conn.: Yale University Press.

Jaynes, Julian. 1976. *The Origin of Consciousness in the Breakdown of the Bicameral Mind.* Boston: Houghton Mifflin.

Johnston, J. 1972. *Econometric Methods.* New York: McGraw-Hill.

Jones, Edward E., and Sigall, Harold. 1971. "The Bogus Pipeline: A New Paradigm for Measuring Affect and Attitude." *Psychological Bulletin* 76:349–364.

Jöreskog, Karl C., and Sörbom, Dag G. 1981. *LISREL V: Analysis of Linear Structural Relationships by Maximum Likelihood and Least Squares Methods.* Chicago: National Educational Resources.

Kahn, William A. 1984. "The Structure of Exaltation." *American Behavioral Scientist* 27:705–722.

Kahneman, Daniel, and Tversky, Amos. 1984. "Choices, Values, and Frames." *American Psychologist* 39:341–350.

Katz, Daniel. 1960. "The Functional Approach to the Study of Attitudes." *Public Opinion Quarterly* 24:163–204.

Katz, Daniel, and Stotland, E. 1959. "A Preliminary Statement to a Theory of Attitude Structure and Change." In *Psychology: A Study of Science,* ed. S. Koch. Vol. 3. New York: McGraw-Hill, pp. 423–475.

Keenan, J. M., and Baillet, S. D. 1980. "Memory for Personally and Socially Significant Events." In *Attention and Performance VIII,* ed. R. S. Nickerson. Hillsdale, N.J.: Erlbaum, pp. 651–667.

Kelley, Harold H. 1967. "Attribution Theory in Social Psychology." In *Nebraska Symposium on Motivation,* ed. D. Levine, Lincoln: University of Nebraska Press, pp. 192–240.

———. 1973. "The Process of Causal Attribution." *American Psychologist* 28:107–128.

Kleinginna, Paul R., and Kleinginna, Anne M. 1981. "A Categorized List of Emotion Definitions, with Suggestions for a Consensual Definition." *Motivation and Emotion* 5:345–379.

Knapp, P. H. 1983. "Emotions and Bodily Changes: A Reassessment." In *Emotions in Health and Illness: Theoretical and Research Foundations,* eds. L. Temoshok, C. Van Dyke, and L. S. Zegans. New York: Grune and Stratton, pp. 15–27.

Komorita, Samuel S., and Bass, A. R. 1967. "Attitude Differentiation and Evaluative Scales of the Semantic Differential." *Journal of Personality and Social Psychology* 6:241–244.

Kothandapani, Virupaksha. 1971. "Valuation of Feeling, Belief and Intention of Act as Three Components of Attitude and Their Contributions to Prediction of Contraceptive Behavior." *Journal of Personality and Social Psychology* 19:321–333.

Kroeber-Reil, Werner. 1979. "Activation Research: Psychobiological Approaches in Consumer Research." *Journal of Consumer Research* 5:240–250.

———. 1982. "Analysis of 'Non-Cognitive' Behavior Especially by Non-Verbal Measurement." Working paper, Institute for Consumer and Behavioral Research, University of the Saarland, Saarbrucken, West Germany. Photocopy.

Krugman, Herbert E. 1965. "The Impact of Television Advertising: Learning without Involvement." *Public Opinion Quarterly* 29:349–356.

———. 1968. "The Learning of Consumer Likes, Preferences and Choices." In *Applications of the Sciences in Marketing Management,* eds. F. M. Bass, C. W. King, and E. A. Pessemier. New York: John Wiley, pp. 207–225.

———. 1980. "Point of View: Sustained Viewing of Television." *Journal of Advertising Research* 20:65–68.

Kunst-Wilson, William R., and Zajonc, Robert B. 1980. "Affective Discrimination of Stimuli That Cannot be Recognized." *Science* 207:557–558.

Lang, Peter J.; Rice, David G.; and Sternbach, Richard A. 1972. "The Psychophysiology of Emotion." In *Handbook of Psychophysiology,* eds. N. S. Greenfield and R. A. Sternbach. New York: Holt, Rinehart and Winston.

Lange, Carl G., and James, William. 1922. *The Emotions.* Baltimore: Williams and Wilkins.

Langer, Susanne K. 1942. *Philosophy in a New Key.* Cambridge, Mass.: Harvard University Press.

Lanzetta, John T., and Orr, Scott P. 1980. "Influence of Facial Expressions in the Classical Conditioning of Fear." *Journal of Personality and Social Psychology* 39:1081–1087.

———. 1981. "Stimulus Properties of Facial Expressions and Their Influence on the Classical Conditioning of Fear." *Motivation and Emotion* 5:225–234.

Lavidge, Robert J., and Steiner, Gary A. 1961. "A Model for Predictive Measurements of Advertising Effectiveness." *Journal of Marketing* 25:59–62.

Lazarus, Richard S. 1982. "Thoughts on the Relations between Emotion and Cognition." *American Psychologist* 37:1019–1024.

———. 1984. "On the Primacy of Cognition." *American Psychologist* 39:124–129.

Lazarus, Richard S.; Averill, James R.; and Opton, Edward M., Jr. 1970. "Towards a Cognitive Theory of Emotion." In *Feelings and Emotions,* ed. M. B. Arnold. New York: Academic Press, pp. 207–232.

Lazarus, Richard S.; Kanner, Allen D.; and Folkman, Susan. 1980. "Emotions: A Cognitive-Phenomenological Analysis." In *Emotion: Theory, Research, and Experience,* eds. R. Plutchik, and H. Kellerman. New York: Academic Press.

Lenneberg, Eric H. 1967. *Biological Foundations of Language.* New York: John Wiley.

Leventhal, Howard. 1980. "Toward A Comprehensive Theory of Emotion." In *Advances in Experimental Social Psychology,* Vol. 13, ed. L. Berkowitz. New York: Academic Press, pp. 139–207.

———. 1984. "A Perceptual Motor Theory of Emotion." In *Approaches to Emotion,* eds. K. R. Scherer and P. Ekman. Hillsdale, N.J.: Erlbaum, pp. 271–292.

Levy, Sidney J. 1981. "Interpreting Consumer Mythology: A Structural Approach to Consumer Behavior." *Journal of Marketing* 45:49–61.

———. 1982. "Symbols, Selves, and Others." In *Advances in Consumer Research,* Vol. 9, ed. A. A. Mitchell. Ann Arbor, Mich.: Association for Consumer Research, pp. 542–543.

Levy, Sidney J.; Czepiel, John A.; and Rook, Dennis W. 1981. "Social Division and Aesthetic Specialization: The Middle Class and Musical Events." In *Symbolic Consumer Behavior,* eds. E. C. Hirschman and M. B. Holbrook. Ann Arbor, Mich.: Association for Consumer Research, pp. 38–44.

Lippold, O. C. J. 1967. "Electromyography." In *Manual of Psychophysiological Methods,* eds. P. H. Venables and I. Martin. New York: John Wiley, pp. 245–298.

Loudon, David L., and Della Bitta, Albert J. 1979. *Consumer Behavior: Concepts and Applications.* New York: McGraw-Hill.

Love, R. E. 1972. "Unobtrusive Measurement of Cognitive Reactions to Persuasive Communications." Ph.D. diss. Ohio State University, Columbus, Ohio.

Luria, Aleksandr R. 1973. *The Working Brain.* New York: Basic Books.

Lutz, Richard J.; MacKenzie, Scott B.; and Belch, George E. 1983. "Attitude toward the Ad As a Mediator of Advertising Effectiveness: Determinants and Consequences." In *Advances in Consumer Research,* Vol. 10, eds. R. P. Bagozzi and A. M. Tybout. Ann Arbor, Mich.: Association for Consumer Research, pp. 532–539.

Lykken, David T. 1981. *A Tremor in the Blood: Uses and Abuses of the Lie Detector.* New York: McGraw-Hill.

Lyons, William. 1980. *Emotion.* Cambridge: Cambridge University Press.

McCaul, Kevin D., and Maki, Roth H. 1984. "Self-Reference Effects on Memory: A Reply to Ferguson, Rule, and Carlson." *Journal of Personality and Social Psychology* 47:953–955.

McCullough, J. Lee, and Ostrom, Thomas M. 1974. "Repetition of Highly Similar Messages." *Journal of Applied Psychology* 59:395–397.

McGuigan, F. J. 1970. "Covert Oral Behavior during the Silent Performance of Language Tasks." *Psychological Bulletin* 74:309–326.

———. 1978. *Cognitive Psychophysiology: Principles of Covert Behavior.* Englewood Cliffs, N.J.: Prentice-Hall.

———. 1979. *Psychophysiological Measurement of Covert Behavior: A Guide for the Laboratory.* Hillsdale, N.J.: Erlbaum.

McGuigan, F. J., and Bailey, Susan C. 1969. "Covert Response Patterns during the Processing of Language Stimuli." *Intra-American Journal of Psychology* 3:289–299.

McGuigan, F. J.; Dollins, A.; Pierce, W.; Lusebrink, B.; and Corus, C. 1982. "Fourier Analysis of Covert Speech Behavior." *Pavlovian Journal of Biological Science* 17:49–52.

McGuigan, F. J., and Tanner, R. G. 1971. "Covert Oral Behavior during Conversational and Visual Dreams." *Psychonomic Science* 23:263–264.

McGuigan, F. J., and Winstead, C. L., Jr. 1974. "Discriminative Relationship between Covert Oral Behavior and the Phonemic System in Internal Information Processing." *Journal of Experimental Psychology* 103:885–890.

McGuire, William J. 1969. "The Nature of Attitudes and Attitude Change." In *The Handbook of Social Psychology,* Vol. 3, eds. G. Lindzey and E. Aronson. Reading, Mass.: Addison-Wesley, pp. 136–314.

———. 1978. "An Information Processing Model of Advertising Effectiveness." In *Behavioral and Management Science in Marketing,* eds. H. L. Davis and A. J. Silk. New York: Ronald Press, pp. 156–180.

———. 1985. "Attitudes and Attitude Change." In *Handbook of Social Psychology,* Vol. 2, eds. G. Lindzey and E. Aronson. New York: Random House, pp. 233–346.

McHugo, Gregory J.; Smith, Craig A.; and Lanzetta, John T. 1982. "The Structure of Self-Reports of Emotional Responses to Film Segments." *Motivation and Emotion* 6:365–385.

MacKenzie, Scott B., and Lutz, Richard J. 1983. "Testing Competing Theories of Advertising Effectiveness Via Structural Equation Models." In *Research Meth-*

ods and Causal Modeling in Marketing, eds. W. R. Darden, K. B. Monroe, and W. R. Dillon, Chicago: American Marketing Association, pp. 70–75.

MacLean, Paul D. 1964. "Man and His Animal Brains." *Modern Medicine* 32:95–106.

———. 1967. "The Brain in Relation to Empathy and Medical Education." *Journal of Nervous and Mental Disease* 144:374–382.

Maloney, John C. 1963. "Copy Testing: What Course Is It Taking?" In *Proceedings, Ninth Annual Conference.* New York: Advertising Research Foundation. Reprinted in *Advertising Management,* eds. H. W. Boyd, Jr. and J. W. Newman. Homewood, Ill.: Richard D. Irwin, 1965.

Mandler, George. 1975. *Mind and Emotion.* New York: John Wiley.

Mason, John W. 1975. "A Historical View of the Stress Field, Part I." *Journal of Human Stress* 1:6–12.

Matlin, Margaret W. 1971. "Response Competition, Recognition, and Affect." *Journal of Personality and Social Psychology* 19:295–300.

Mazis, Michael E.; Ahtola, Olli T.; and Klippel, R. Eugene. 1975. "A Comparison of Four Multiattribute Models in the Prediction of Consumer Attitudes." *Journal of Consumer Research* 2:38–52.

Meer, Jeff. 1984. "Pet Theories." *Psychology Today* 18:60–67.

Mehrabian, Albert. 1980. *Basic Dimensions for a General Psychological Theory.* Cambridge, Mass.: Oelgeschlager, Gunn & Hain.

Mehrabian, Albert, and Russell, James A. 1974. *An Approach to Environmental Psychology.* Cambridge, Mass.: MIT Press.

Mehrabian, Albert, and Wixen, Warren. 1983. "Lights Out at the Arcade: Restricted Emotional Appeal Limits Video-Game Popularity." *Psychology Today* 17:72–73.

Meltzoff, Andrew N., and Moore, M. Keith. 1977. "Imitation of Facial and Manual Gestures by Human Neonates." *Science* 198:75–78.

Melzack, R., and Wall, P. D. 1965. "Pain Mechanisms: A New Theory." *Science* 150:971–979.

Meyer, Max F. 1933. "That Whale among the Fishes—The Theory of Emotions." *Psychological Review* 40:292–300.

Meyer-Hentschel, G. 1983. "An Activation Profile for Printed Ads." Working paper, Institute for Consumer and Behavioral Research, University of the Saarland, Saarbrucken, West Germany. Photocopy.

Millenson, John R. 1967. *Principles of Behavioral Analysis.* New York: Macmillan.

Miller, H., and Baron, R. S. 1973. "On Measuring Counterarguing." *Journal for the Theory of Social Behavior* 3:101–118.

Mills, Judson, and Harvey, John. 1972. "Opinion Change as a Function of When Information about the Communicator is Received and Whether He Is Attractive or Expert." *Journal of Personality and Social Psychology* 21:52–55.

Mitchell, Andrew A., and Olson, Jerry C. 1981. "Are Product Attribute Beliefs the Only Mediator of Advertising Effects on Brand Attitude?" *Journal of Marketing Research* 18:318–322.

Moore, Danny L., and Hutchinson, J. Wesley. 1983. "The Effects of Ad Affect on Advertising Effectiveness." In *Advances in Consumer Research,* Vol. 10, eds. R. P. Bagozzi and A. M. Tybout. Ann Arbor, Mich.: Association for Consumer Research, pp. 526–531.

Morris, Charles. 1946. *Signs, Language, and Behavior.* New York: George Braziller.

Morris, C. D.; Bransford, J. D.; and Franks, J. J. 1977. "Levels of Processing Versus Transfer Appropriate Processing." *Journal of Verbal Learning and Verbal Behavior* 16:519–533.

Myers, James H., and Shocker, Alan D. 1981. "The Nature of Product-Related Attributes." In *Research in Marketing,* Vol. 5, ed. J. N. Sheth. Greenwich, Conn.: JAI Press, pp. 211–236.

Neisser, Ulrich. 1963. "The Imitation of Man by Machine." *Science* 139:193–197.

Nelson, Phillip. 1974. "Information and Consumer Behavior." *Journal of Political Economy* 82:729–754.

Neslin, Scott A. 1979. "Estimating the Relationship between Perception and Preference As Part of a Features–Perceptions–Preference Loop." Working paper, Amos Tuck School of Business Administration, Dartmouth College. Mimeo.

Nicosia, Franco M. 1966. *Consumer Decision Processes.* Englewood Cliffs, N.J.: Prentice-Hall.

Nisbett, Richard E., and Ross, Lee. 1980. *Human Inference: Strategies and Shortcomings of Social Judgment.* Englewood Cliffs, N.J.: Prentice-Hall.

Norman, Ross. 1976. "When What Is Said Is Important: A Comparison of Expert and Attractive Sources." *Journal of Experimental Social Psychology* 12:294–300.

Nowlis, Vincent. 1965. "Research with the Mood Adjective Check List." In *Affect, Cognition and Personality: Empirical Studies,* eds. S. S. Tomkins and C. E. Izard, New York: Springer-Verlag, pp. 352–389.

———. 1970. "Mood: Behavior and Experience." In *Feelings and Emotions,* ed. M. B. Arnold. New York: Academic Press, pp. 261–277.

Nowlis, Vincent, and Nowlis, H. H. 1956. "The Description and Analysis of Mood." *Annals of the New York Academy of Science* 65:345–353.

Obermiller, Carl. 1985a. "Varieties of Mere Exposure: The Effects of Processing Style and Repetition on Affective Response." *Journal of Consumer Research* 12:17–30.

———. 1985b. "Meaningfulness and the Repetition-Affect Relationship." In *Proceedings of the Division of Consumer Psychology,* ed. D. W. Stewart. Nashville, Tenn.: American Psychological Association, pp. 23–24.

Ogden, C. K., and Richards, I. A. 1923. *The Meaning of Meaning.* New York: Harcourt, Brace and World.

Ohman, A., and Dimberg, Ulf. 1984. "An Evolutionary Perspective on Human Social Behavior." In *Sociophysiology,* ed. W. Waid. New York: Springer-Verlag, pp. 47–86.

Oliver, Richard L. 1980. "A Cognitive Model of the Antecedents and Consequences of Satisfaction Decisions." *Journal of Marketing Research* 17:460–469.

Olshavsky, Richard W., and Granbois, Donald H. 1979. "Consumer Decision Making—Fact or Fiction?" *Journal of Consumer Research* 6:93–100.

Olson, Jerry C., and Dover, Phillip A. 1978. "Cognitive Effects of Deceptive Advertising." *Journal of Marketing Research* 15:29–38.

Olson, Jerry C., and Mitchell, Andrew A. 1981. "Advertising Effects at the Individual Consumer Level." Paper presented at Marketing Science Institute Miniconference, Cambridge, Mass.

Olson, Jerry C., and Ray, William J. 1983. "Using Brain-Wave Measures to Assess Advertising Effects." Working paper, Marketing Science Institute, Cambridge, Mass. Typeset.

Ornstein, Robert. 1972. *The Psychology of Consciousness.* New York: Penguin Books.

Orr, Scott P., and Lanzetta, John T. 1980. "Facial Expression of Emotion as Conditioned Stimuli for Human Autonomic Responses." *Journal of Personality and Social Psychology* 38:278–282.

Osgood, Charles E. 1966. "Dimensionality of the Semantic Space for Communication Via Facial Expressions." *Scandinavian Journal of Psychology* 7:1–30.

Osgood, Charles E.; Suci, George J.; and Tannenbaum, Percy H. 1957. *The Measurement of Meaning.* Urbana, Ill.: University of Illinois Press.

Oster, Harriet, and Ekman, Paul. 1978. "Facial Behavior in Child Development." *Minnesota Symposium on Child Psychology* 11:231–276.

Ostrom, Thomas M. 1969. "The Relationship between the Affective, Behavioral and Cognitive Components of Attitude." *Journal of Experimental Social Psychology* 5:12–30.

———. 1981. "Theoretical Perspectives in the Analysis of Cognitive Responses." In *Cognitive Responses in Persuasion,* eds. R. E. Petty, T. M. Ostrom, and T. C. Brock, Hillsdale, N.J.: Erlbaum, pp. 283–290.

Palda, Kristian S. 1966. "The Hypothesis of a Hierarchy of Effects: A Partial Evaluation." *Journal of Marketing Research* 3:13–24.

Peck, M. Scott. 1978. *The Road Less Traveled.* New York: Simon and Schuster.

Petty, Richard E. 1981. "The Role of Cognitive Responses in Attitude Change Processes." In *Cognitive Responses in Persuasion,* eds. R. E. Petty, T. M. Ostrom, and T. C. Brock. Hillsdale, N.J.: Erlbaum.

Petty, Richard E., and Cacioppo, John T. 1977. "Forewarning, Cognitive Responding and Resistance to Persuasion." *Journal of Personality and Social Psychology* 35:645–655.

———. 1979. "Issue Involvement Can Increase or Decrease Persuasion by Enhancing Message-Relevant Cognitive Responses." *Journal of Personality and Social Psychology* 36:1915–1926.

———. 1981. *Attitudes and Persuasion: Classic and Contemporary Approaches.* Dubuque, Iowa: William C. Brown.

———. 1983. "The Role of Bodily Responses in Attitude Measurement and Change." In *Social Psychophysiology: A Sourcebook,* eds. J. T. Cacioppo and R. E. Petty. New York: Guilford Press, pp. 51–101.

———. 1984. "Motivational Factors in Consumer Response to Advertisements." In *Human Motivation: Physiological, Behavioral, and Social Approaches,* eds. R. Geen, W. Beatty, and R. Arkin. Boston: Allyn and Bacon, pp. 418–454.

———. In press. "Central and Peripheral Routes to Attitude Change." In *Advances in Experimental Social Psychology,* Vol. 19, ed. L. Berkowitz. New York: Academic Press.

Petty, Richard E.; Cacioppi, John T.; and Goldman, R. 1981. "Personal Involvement As a Determinant of Argument-based Persuasion." *Journal of Personality and Social Psychology* 40:847–855.

Petty, Richard E.; Cacioppi, John T.; and Schumann, David. 1983. "Central and

Peripheral Routes to Advertising Effectiveness: The Moderating Role of Involvement." *Journal of Consumer Research* 10:135–146.

Petty, Richard E.; Ostrom, Thomas M.; and Brock, Timothy C., eds. 1981. *Cognitive Responses to Persuasion*. Hillsdale, N.J.: Erlbaum.

Petty, Richard E.; Wells, Gary L.; and Brock, Timothy C. 1976. "Distraction Can Enhance or Reduce Yielding to Propaganda: Thought Disruption Versus Effort Justification." *Journal of Personality and Social Psychology* 34:874–884.

Plummer, Joseph T. 1984. "Consumer Empathy and Advertising." Paper presented at the American Psychological Association Conference, Toronto, Canada.

Plutchik, Robert. 1962. *The Emotions: Facts, Theories and a New Model*. New York: Random House.

———. 1980. *Emotion: A Psychoevolutionary Synthesis*. New York: Harper and Row.

Podlesny, John A., and Raskin, David C. 1977. "Physiological Measures and the Detection of Deception." *Psychological Bulletin* 84:782–799.

Pribram, Karl H. 1978. "Modes of Central Processing in Human Learning and Remembering." In *Brain and Learning*, ed. J. Tayler. Stamford, Conn.: Greylock Press.

———. 1980. "The Biology of Emotions and Other Feelings." In *Emotion: Theory, Research and Experience*, Vol. 1, eds. R. Plutchik and H. Kellerman. New York: Academic Press, pp. 245–269.

Puto, Christopher P., and Wells, William D. 1984. "Informational and Transformational Advertising: The Differential Effects of Time." In *Advances in Consumer Research*, Vol. 11, ed. T. C. Kinnear. Ann Arbor, Mich.: Association for Consumer Research, pp. 638–643.

Pylyshyn, Zenon W. 1980. "Computation and Cognition: Issues in the Foundations of Cognitive Science." *Behavioral and Brain Sciences* 3:169.

Rajecki, D. W. 1984. "Human Aggression in the Laboratory: How You See It, How You Don't," Paper presented at the meeting of the Midwestern Psychological Association, Chicago, Ill.

Ray, Michael L., and Batra, Rajeev. 1983. "Emotion and Persuasion in Advertising: What We Know and Don't Know About Affect." In *Advances in Consumer Research*, Vol. 10, eds. R. P. Bagozzi and A. M. Tybout. Ann Arbor, Mich.: Association for Consumer Research, pp. 543–548.

Ray, Michael L.; with Sawyer, A. G.; Rothschild, M. L.; Heeler, R. M.; Strong, E. C.; and Reed, J. R. 1973. "Marketing Communication and the Hierarchy-of-Effects." In *New Models for Communication Research*, ed. P. Clarke. Beverly Hills, Calif.: Sage Publications, pp. 147–176.

Reibstein, David J.; Lovelock, Christopher H.; and Dobson, Ricardo de P. 1980. "The Direction of Causality between Perceptions, Affect, and Behavior: An Application to Travel Behavior." *Journal of Consumer Research* 6:370–376.

Reisenzein, Rainer. 1983. "The Schachter Theory of Emotion: Two Decades Later." *Psychological Bulletin* 94:239–264.

Rey, Georges. 1980. "Functionalism and the Emotions." In *Explaining Emotions*, ed. A. Oksenberg Rorty. Berkeley, Calif.: University of California Press.

Riney, Hal. 1981. "Emotion in Advertising." In *Viewpoint*, Vol. 1, New York: Ogilvy and Mather. Typeset.

Rinn, William E. 1984. "The Neuropsychology of Facial Expression: A Review of the Neurological and Psychological Mechanisms for Producing Facial Expression." *Psychological Bulletin* 95:52–77.

Roberts, Donald F., and Maccoby, Nathan. 1973. "Information Processing and Persuasion: Counterarguing Behavior." In *New Models for Communication Research,* ed. P. Clarke. Beverly Hills, Calif.: Sage Publications, pp. 269–307.

Rogers, Ronald W. 1983. "Cognitive and Physiological Processes in Fear Appeals and Attitude Change: A Revised Theory of Protection Motivation." In *Social Psychophysiology: A Sourcebook,* eds. J. T. Cacioppo and R. E. Petty. New York: Guilford Press, pp. 153–176.

Rogers, T. B.; Kuiper, N. A.; and Kirker, W. S. 1977. "Self-Reference and the Encoding of Personal Information." *Journal of Personality and Social Psychology* 35:677–688.

Rook, Dennis W. 1984. "Ritual Behavior and Consumer Symbolism." In *Advances in Consumer Research,* Vol. 11, ed. T. C. Kinnear. Ann Arbor, Mich.: Association for Consumer Research, pp. 279–284.

Rook, Dennis W., and Levy, Sidney J. 1983. "Psychosocial Themes in Consumer Grooming Rituals." In *Advances in Consumer Research,* Vol. 10, eds. R. P. Bagozzi and A. M. Tybout. Ann Arbor, Mich.: Association for Consumer Research, pp. 329–333.

Rook, J. C. 1984. "Pain." In *Encyclopedia of Psychology,* Vol. 2, ed. R. J. Corsini. New York: John Wiley.

Rorty, Amelie Oksenberg, ed. 1980. *Explaining Emotions.* Berkeley, Calif.: University of California Press.

Rosenberg, Milton J., and Hovland, Carl I. 1960. "Cognitive, Affective, and Behavioral Components of Attitudes." In *Attitude Organization and Change,* eds. C. I. Hovland and M. J. Rosenberg. New Haven, Conn.: Yale University Press.

Rosenstein, D., and Oster, Harriet. 1981. "Facial Expression as a Means of Exploring Infants' Taste Responses." Paper presented at the annual meeting of the Society for Research in Child Development, Boston, Mass.

Ross, Lee; Lepper, Mark R.; and Hubbard, Michael. 1975. "Perseverance in Self-Perception and Social Perception: Biased Attributional Processes in the Debriefing Paradigm." *Journal of Personality and Social Psychology* 32:880–892.

Russell, James A. 1980. "A Circumplex Model of Affect." *Journal of Personality and Social Psychology* 39:1161–1178.

———. 1983. "Pancultural Aspects of the Human Conceptual Organization of Emotions." *Journal of Personality and Social Psychology* 45:1281–1288.

Sackeim, Harold A., and Gur, Ruben C. 1978. "Lateral Asymmetry in Intensity of Emotional Expression." *Neuropsychologia* 16:473–481.

Sawyer, Alan G. 1977. "Repetition and Affect: Recent Empirical and Theoretical Developments." In *Consumer and Industrial Buying Behavior,* eds. A. G. Woodside, J. N. Sheth, and P. D. Bennett. New York: North Holland, pp. 229–242.

———. 1981. "Repetition, Cognitive Responses, and Persuasion." In *Cognitive Responses to Persuasion,* eds. R. E. Petty, T. M. Ostrom, and T. C. Brock. Hillsdale, N.J.: Erlbaum, pp. 237–262.

Schachter, Stanley. 1971. *Emotion, Obesity, and Crime.* New York: Academic Press.

Schachter, Stanley, and Singer, Jerome E. 1962. "Cognitive, Social, and Physiological Determinants of Emotional State." *Psychological Review* 69:379–399.

Scherer, Klaus R., and Ekman, Paul, eds. 1984. *Approaches to Emotion*. Hillsdale, N.J.: Erlbaum.

Schlinger, Mary J. 1979. "A Profile of Responses to Commercials." *Journal of Advertising Research* 19:37–46.

Schwartz, Gary E. 1975. "Biofeedback, Self-Regulation, and the Patterning of Physiological Processes." *American Scientist* 63:314–324.

Schwartz, Gary E.; Fair, Paul L.; Salt, Patricia; Mandel, Michael R.; and Klerman, Gerald L. 1976a. "Facial Expressions and Imagery in Depression: An Electromyographic Study." *Psychosomatic Medicine* 38:337–347.

———. 1976b. "Facial Muscle Patterning to Affective Imagery in Depressed and Nondepressed Subjects." *Science* 192:489–491.

Scitovsky, Tibor. 1976. *The Joyless Economy*. Oxford: Oxford University Press.

Seamon, David. 1984. "Emotional Experience." *American Behavioral Scientist* 27:757–770.

Seamon, John J.; Brody, Nathan; and Kauff, David M. 1983a. "Affective Discrimination of Stimuli That Are Not Recognized Effects of Shadowing, Masking, and Cerebral Laterality." *Journal of Experimental Psychology: Learning, Memory, and Cognition*. 9:544–555.

———. 1983b. "Affective Discrimination of Stimuli That Are Not Recognized: Part II, Effect of Delay between Study and Test." *Bulletin of the Psychonomic Society* 21:187–189.

Shapiro, David, and Schwartz, Gary E. 1970. "Psychophysiological Contributions to Social Psychology." *Annual Review of Psychology* 21:87–112.

Shimp, Terence A. 1981. "Attitude toward the Ad As a Mediator of Consumer Brand Choice." *Journal of Advertising* 10:9–15.

Simon, Herbert A. 1967. "Motivational and Emotional Controls of Cognition." *Psychological Review* 74:29–39.

Smith, M. Brewster; Bruner, Jerome S.; and White, Robert N. 1956. *Opinions and Personality*. New York: John Wiley.

Snider, James G., and Osgood, Charles E., eds. 1969. *Semantic Differential Technique: A Sourcebook*. Chicago: Aldine.

Sokolov, Aleksandr N. 1972. *Inner Speech and Thought*. New York: Plenum Press.

Solomon, Richard L. 1980. "The Opponent Process Theory of Acquired Motivation: The Costs of Pleasure and the Benefits of Pain." *American Psychologist* 35:691–712.

Solomon, Robert C. 1976. *The Passions: The Myth and Nature of Human Emotion*. Garden City, N.Y.: Anchor Press.

Sorce, J.; Emde, R.; Campos, J.; and Klinnert, M. 1981. "Maternal Emotional Signaling: Its Effects on the Visual Cliff of One-Year Olds." Paper presented at the meeting of the Society for Research in Child Development, Boston, Mass.

Srinivasan, V. 1979. "Network Models for Estimating Brand-Specific Effects in Multi-Attribute Marketing Models." *Management Science* 25:11–21.

Srull, Thomas K. 1984. "The Effects of Subjective Affective States on Memory and Judgment." In *Advances in Consumer Research*, Vol. 11, ed. T. C. Kinnear. Ann Arbor, Mich.: Association for Consumer Research, pp. 530–533.

Steiner, J. E. 1979. "Human Facial Expression in Response to Taste and Smell Stimulation." *Advances in Child Development and Behavior* 13:257–295.

Sternthal, Brian; Dholakia, R.; and Leavitt, Clark. 1978. "The Persuasive Effect of Source Credibility: Tests of Cognitive Response." *Journal of Consumer Research* 4:252–260.

Stewart, David W., and Furse, David H. 1982. "Applying Psychophysiological Measures to Marketing and Advertising Research Problems." In *Current Issues and Research in Advertising,* eds. J. H. Leigh and C. R. Martin. Ann Arbor, Mich.: Division of Research, Graduate School of Business Administration, University of Michigan, pp. 1–38.

Stewart, Douglas K., and Love, William A. 1968. "A General Canonical Correlation Index." *Psychological Bulletin.* 70:160–163.

Stout, Patricia, and Leckenby, John D. 1984. "Dimensions of Emotional Response to Advertising." Department of Advertising, University of Illinois. Photocopy.

Strongman, K. T. 1978. *The Psychology of Emotion.* New York: John Wiley.

Sudnow, David. 1979. *Talk's Body.* New York: Alfred Knopf.

Taylor, Shelley E., and Fiske, Susan T. 1978. "Salience, Attention, and Attribution: Top of the Head Phenomena." In *Advances in Experimental Social Psychology,* Vol. 11, ed. L. Berkowitz. New York: Academic Press, pp. 249–288.

Thorndike, Edward L., and Lorge, Irving. 1944. *The Teacher's Word Book of 30,000 Words.* New York: Teachers College, Columbia University.

Titchener, Edward B. 1910. *A Text-book of Psychology.* New York: Macmillan.

Tomkins, Silvan S. 1962. *Affect, Imagery, Consciousness: The Positive Affects.* New York: Springer-Verlag.

———. 1963. *Affect, Imagery, Consciousness: The Negative Affects.* New York: Springer-Verlag.

———. 1970. "Affect as the Primary Motivational System." In *Feelings and Emotions,* ed. M. B. Arnold. New York: Academic Press, pp. 101–110.

———. 1980. "Affect As Amplification: Some Modifications in Theory." In *Emotion: Theory, Research, and Experience,* eds. R. Plutchik and H. Kellerman. New York: Academic Press.

———. 1981. "The Quest for Primary Motives: Biography and Autobiography of an Idea." *Journal of Personality and Social Psychology* 41:306–329.

———. 1982. *Affect, Imagery, and Consciousness: Cognition and Affect.* New York: Springer-Verlag.

———. 1984. "Affect Theory." In *Approaches to Emotion,* eds. K. R. Scherer and P. Ekman. Hillsdale, N.J.: Erlbaum, pp. 163–196.

Tomkins, Silvan S., and Izard, Carroll E. 1965. *Affect, Cognition and Personality: Empirical Studies.* New York: Springer-Verlag.

Toy, Daniel R. 1982. "Monitoring Communication Effects: A Cognitive Structure/Cognitive Response Approach." *Journal of Consumer Research* 9:66–76.

Treisman, Anne M. 1969. "Strategies and Models of Selective Attention." *Psychological Review* 76:282–299.

Triandis, Harry C. 1971. *Attitude and Attitude Change.* New York: John Wiley.

———. 1977. *Interpersonal Behavior.* Monterey, Calif.: Brooks/Cole.

Tucker, L. R. 1964. "The Extension of Factor Analysis to Three-Dimensional Matrices." In *Contributions to Mathematical Psychology,* eds. N. Frederiksen and H. Gullikson. New York: Holt, Rinehart and Winston, pp. 109–127.

———. 1966. "Some Mathematical Notes on Three-Mode Factor Analysis." *Psychometrika* 31:279–311.

Tulving, E. 1978. "Relation between Encoding Specificity and Levels of Processing." In *Levels of Processing in Human Memory,* eds. L. S. Cermak and F. I. M. Craik. Hillsdale, N.J.: Erlbaum, pp. 19–92.

Tursky, Bernard, and Jamner, Larry D. 1983. "Evaluation of Social and Political Beliefs: A Psychophysiological Approach." In *Social Psychophysiology: A Sourcebook,* eds. J. T. Cacioppo and R. E. Petty. New York: Guilford Press, pp. 102–121.

Tversky, Amos. 1972. "Elimination by Aspects: A Theory of Choice." *Psychological Review* 79:281–299.

Tversky, Amos, and Kahneman, D. 1973. "Availability: A Heuristic for Judging Frequency and Probability." *Cognitive Psychology* 5:207–232.

———. 1981. "The Framing of Decisions and the Psychology of Choice." *Science* 211:453–458.

Tybout, Alice M., and Hauser, John R. 1981. "A Marketing Audit Using a Conceptual Model of Consumer Behavior: Application and Evaluation." *Journal of Marketing* 45:82–101.

Valins, Stuart. 1966. "Cognitive Effects of False Heart-Rate Feedback." *Journal of Personality and Social Psychology* 4:400–408.

Van Boxtel, A.; Goudswaard, P.; Van der Molen, G. M.; and Van den Bosch, W. E. J. 1983. "Changes in Electromyogram Power Spectra of Facial and Jaw-Elevator Muscles during Fatigue." *Journal of Applied Physiology* 54:51–58.

Vaughn, Katherine B., and Lanzetta, John T. 1980. "Vicarious Instigation and Conditioning of Facial Expression in Autonomic Responses to a Model's Display of Pain." *Journal of Personality and Social Psychology* 38:909–923.

Vaughn, Richard. 1980. "How Advertising Works: A Planning Model." *Journal of Advertising Research* 20:27–33.

Waid, William M., and Orne, Martin T. 1981. "Cognitive, Social, and Personality Processes in the Physiological Detection of Deception." In *Advances in Experimental Social Psychology,* Vol. 14, ed. L. Berkowitz. New York: Academic Press, pp. 61–106.

Watson, Paul J., and Gatchel, Robert J. 1979. "Autonomic Measures of Advertising." *Journal of Advertising Research* 19:15–26.

Watts, F. N. 1983. "Affective Cognition: A Sequel to Zajonc and Rachman." *Behavior Research and Therapy* 21:89–90.

Waynbaum, I. 1907. *La Physionomie Humane: Son Mecanisme et son Role Social.* Paris: Alcan.

Weinrich, James D. 1980. "Toward a Sociobiological Theory of the Emotions." In *Emotion: Theory, Research, and Experience,* eds. R. Plutchik and H. Kellerman. New York: Academic Press.

Weinstein, Sidney. 1982. "A Review of Brain Hemisphere Research." *Journal of Advertising Research* 22:59–63.

Weiss, P. A. 1950. "Experimental Analysis of Coordination by the Disarrangement of Central-Peripheral Relations." *Physiological Mechanisms in Animal Behavior* 4:92–111.

Welford, A. T. 1974. "On the Sequencing of Action." *Brain Research* 71:381–392.

Wells, William D. 1964. "EQ, Son of EQ, and the Reaction Profile." *Journal of Marketing* 28:45–52.

———. 1980. "Liking and Sales Effectiveness: A Hypothesis." In *Topline,* New York, MacCollum/Spielman. Typeset.

Wells, William D.; Leavitt, Clark; and McConville, Maureen. 1971. "A Reaction Profile for TV Commercials." *Journal of Advertising Research* 11:11–17.

Willis, W. D., Jr., and Grossman, R. G. 1977. *Medical Neurobiology.* 2nd ed. St. Louis: C. V. Mosby.

Wilson, William R. 1979. "Feeling More Than We Can Know: Exposure Effects without Learning." *Journal of Personality and Social Psychology* 37:811–821.

Winton, W. M.; Putman, L. E.; and Krauss, R. M. 1984. "Facial and Autonomic Manifestations of the Dimensional Structure of Emotion." *Journal of Experimental Social Psychology* 20:195–216.

Wolff, P. H. 1963. "Observations on the Early Development of Smiling." In *Determinants of Infant Behavior II,* ed. B. M. Foss. New York: John Wiley.

Woods, Walter A. 1981. *Consumer Behavior.* New York: North Holland.

Wright, Peter. 1973. "The Cognitive Processes Mediating Acceptance of Advertising." *Journal of Marketing Research* 10:53–62.

———. 1974. "Analyzing Media Effects on Advertising Responses." *Public Opinion Quarterly* 38:192–204.

———. 1975. "Factors Affecting Cognitive Resistance to Advertising." *Journal of Consumer Research* 2:1–9.

———. 1980. "Message-Evoked Thoughts: Persuasion Research Using Thought Verbalizations." *Journal of Consumer Research* 7:151–175.

———. 1981. "Cognitive Responses to Mass Media Advocacy." In *Cognitive Responses to Persuasion,* eds. R. E. Petty, T. M. Ostrom, and T. C. Brock. Hillsdale, N.J.: Erlbaum, pp. 263–282.

Zajonc, Robert B. 1968. "Attitudinal Effects of Mere Exposure." *Journal of Personality and Social Psychology Monograph* 9:1–27.

———. 1980. "Feeling and Thinking: Preferences Need No Inferences." *American Psychologist* 35:151–175.

———. 1984. "On the Primacy of Affect." *American Psychologist* 39:117–123.

———. 1985. "Emotional and Facial Efference." *Science* 228:15–21.

Zajonc, Robert B., and Markus, Hazel. 1982. "Affective and Cognitive Factors in Preferences." *Journal of Consumer Research* 9:123–131.

Zaltman, Gerald, and Wallendorf, Melanie. 1979. *Consumer Behavior: Basic Findings and Management Implications.* New York: John Wiley.

Zanna, Mark P.; Kiesler, Charles A.; and Pilkonis, Paul A. 1970. "Positive and Negative Attitudinal Affect Established by Classical Conditioning." *Journal of Personality and Social Psychology* 14:321–328.

Zielske, Hubert. 1982. "Does Day-after Recall Penalize 'Feeling' Ads?" *Journal of Advertising Research* 22:19–22.

Zillmann, D. 1978. "Attribution and the Misattribution of Excitatory Reaction." In *New Directions in Attribution Research,* Vol. 2, eds. J. H. Harvey, W. J. Ickes, and R. F. Kidd. Hillsdale, N.J.: Erlbaum, pp. 335–368.

Zimbardo, P. G.; Cohen, A. R.; Weisenberg, M.; Dworkin, L.; and Firestone, I.

1969. "The Control of Experimental Pain." In *The Cognitive Control of Motivation,* ed. P. G. Zimbardo. Glenview, Ill.: Scott, Foresman, pp.

Zinkham, George M.; Gelb, Betsy D.; and Martin, Claude R. 1983. "The Cloze Procedure." *Journal of Advertising Research* 23:15–20.

Zuckerman, Miron; DePaulo, Bella M.; and Rosenthal, Robert. 1981. "Verbal and Nonverbal Communication of Deception." In *Advances in Experimental Social Psychology,* Vol. 14, ed. L. Berkowitz. New York: Academic Press, pp. 1–59.

Index

About the Contributors

Rajeev Batra is assistant professor of business at Columbia University. He holds an MS (in advertising) from the University of Illinois and a doctorate (in marketing) from Stanford University. Professor Batra has published a number of articles and book chapters on affective processes in advertising.

John T. Cacioppo is professor of psychology at the University of Iowa. He received his BS from the University of Missouri and his PhD in psychology from Ohio State University. His current research interests concern the cognitive and physiological determinants of social influence.

Morris B. Holbrook is associate professor of marketing at Columbia University. After receiving an undergraduate degree in English from Harvard, he obtained MBA and PhD degrees in marketing from Columbia University. He has authored numerous journal articles as well as book chapters. Professor Holbrook's present research interests lie in the realms of hedonic and esthetic consumption.

Rebecca H. Holman is Director of Consumer Research, Young & Rubicam. Formerly on the faculty of Pennsylvania State University, she has published several articles and book chapters on values, lifestyles, product use and clothing-as-communication. Her doctorate is from the University of Texas at Austin.

Mary E. Losch is presently a doctoral candidate in the Department of Psychology at the University of Iowa. She received her BS at Murray State University and MA in Psychology from the University of Iowa. Her dissertation is concerned with the somatic and autonomic effects of attitude-discrepant behavior.

Richard E. Petty is professor of psychology at the University of Missouri. He did his undergraduate work at the University of Virginia and received his PhD in psychology from Ohio State University. His current research is focused on physiological and psychological processes leading to persuasion and attitude change. He and Dr. Cacioppo have collaborated on numerous journal and book projects.

Louis G. Tassinary is currently assistant research associate in the Department of Psychology at the University of Iowa. He did his undergraduate work at Eckerd College and recently received his PhD in psychology from Dartmouth College. His current research interests focus on affect-laden information processing and the electromyographic measurement of emotional expressions.

Robert B. Zajonc is professor of psychology and director of the Research Center for Group Dynamics at the University of Michigan. He is widely recognized as one of the leading authorities on affective processes. He has published over 90 articles and has received a number of awards and fellowships for his scholarly activities.

About the Editors

Robert A. Peterson holds the John T. Stuart Chair in Business Administration and the Charles Hurwitz Fellowship in the IC² Institute at the University of Texas (Austin). He received his doctorate in marketing from the University of Minnesota. His research interests are wide-ranging and have resulted in more than 100 publications, including *Marketing Research* and *Models for Innovation Diffusion* (with V. Mahajan). Currently he is editor, *Journal of Marketing Research*.

Wayne D. Hoyer is associate professor of marketing and Zale Fellow at the University of Texas (Austin). He holds MA and PhD degrees in consumer psychology from Purdue University. Recently his research has focused on the influence of affect in low involvement decision making. His publications have appeared in the *Journal of Marketing*, the *Journal of Consumer Research*, and the *Journal of Advertising*.

William R. Wilson is assistant professor of business at Rice University. A psychologist by training (his PhD is from the University of Michigan, where he served on the faculty for several years), he recently received an MBA from the University of Texas (Austin). His research on the mere exposure effect, published in such forums as *Science* and the *Journal of Personality and Social Psychology*, has been widely cited in the affect literature.

About the IC² Institute

The IC² Institute at the University of Texas at Austin is a national center for the study of innovation, creativity, and capital. IC² studies are designed to develop alternatives for private sector action aimed at regional and national goals.

Some of the specific areas of research and study at IC² include the management of technology; creative and innovative management; the state of society; dynamic business development and entrepreneurship; new methods of economic analysis; and the determination of attitudes, concerns, and opinions on key issues.

The Institute also maintains a strong interaction between scholarly developments and real-world issues by conducting a variety of conferences. IC² research is published in a series of monographs, policy papers, research articles, and books.

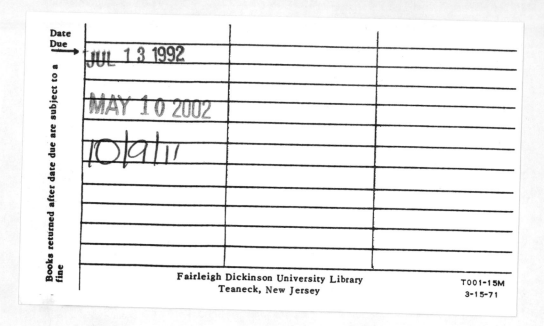